Finding the Voice of the Church

# Finding the Voice of the Church

# of the Church

## GEORGE DENNIS O'BRIEN

University of Notre Dame Press

Notre Dame, Indiana

*Library of Congress Cataloging-in-Publication Data*

O'Brien, Dennis, 1931–
     Finding the voice of the church / George Dennis O'Brien.
         p.    cm.
     Includes bibliographical references and index.
     ISBN-13: 978-0-268-03727-7 (cloth : alk. paper)
     ISBN-10: 0-268-03727-2 (cloth : alk. paper)
     1. Catholic Church—History—21st century.    I. Title.
     BX1390.O27    2007
     262'.02—dc22

                                                    2007019493

Dedicated to all those silenced, suppressed, excommunicated, imprisoned, or executed by Church officials for speaking with *other voices*. A mere sample of those later rehabilitated as heroes, prophets, and saints:

Hildegard of Bingen, Joan of Arc, John of the Cross,

Matteo Ricci, Henri Lacordaire, George Tyrrell, Yves Congar,

John Courtney Murray

*If he really meant what he was shouting, he wouldn't be speaking in that tone of voice.*

Wittgenstein's comment when passing a
street evangelist in Cambridge.

# Contents

## PART 2. THE VOICE OF THE CHURCH

# Preface

I do not believe that the version of Christianity and the Church put forth in this book is heretical, but I should not mind greatly if it is. Cardinal Newman allowed that he was particularly fond of heretics because as voices at or beyond the margins of orthodoxy they sharpened the sense of what was, after all, essential. One of the reasons why a reader may regard the following as unorthodox is that I have tried as much as possible to stay away from traditional theological language and pious tone. Traditional terms and reverent attitude may deceive the reader—and the writer—into thinking that something sensible is being said. Given a sufficient assemblage of special words like "transubstantiation" and "eschatological" and we know that the writer's head is in the right place. Given enough urges to reverential affect and one can believe that his heart is in the right place as well. Unfortunately simply ringing the changes on theological language may fail to connect with either reality or the reader or both. Piety in prose may show reverence but not necessarily for the Christian object. My aim is to rephrase Christian doctrine in nonstandard ways with the hope that these variants will either hit the target or, if wayward, illuminate how traditional language really works and why it is most appropriate.

One of the reasons why I am not overly concerned with the possibility that I have wandered into heresy is that I have spent a lifetime listening to heresy from the Catholic pulpit. In my experience, it is rare to find a priest who in his sermon "opens the Scriptures." On the contrary, the tendency is to "close the Scripture" either in sheer banality or in formal heresy, usually both together. An Ash Wednesday sermon in the magnificent Cathedral of the Assumption in San Francisco epitomized the problem. Being as it was the spring of the year, we were told that we should all look to our spiritual garden and pluck out the weeds (sins). Would that sin could be dug up like dandelions. Sin is not the dandelion in the garden of our goodness, it is a blight on the whole field. It is a bland form of the Pelagian heresy to think that with a bit of effort and holy Weed-B-Gon we can clear up our blighted soul.

Banal heresy can turn tragic. Years ago my wife and I were in conference with a young priest two years out of the seminary. He complained as follows: "The first year out of the seminary, you try to save your congregation. You find out you can't do that, so the second year you try to save yourself. But you can't do that. What do you do the third year?" What do you do? Well, the poor man dropped dead. I think he died of terminal despair. Whatever he may have studied in the seminary, he seems to have gotten the Christian story all wrong. The priest is not there to save the congregation or himself—that has *already* been done by someone else. The message of Christianity is not "Save yourself before it is too late!" it is "Rejoice, you have already been saved. Now live up to this good news."

It is clear that the churches that have carried the message of Christianity over the centuries are in deep trouble. Faith is in a time of crisis that, if it does not lead to extinction similar to the death of the cult of Zeus, will certainly reduce Christianity to being perceived as one of those marginal crank sects that have infested human history. There are those on both the left and right of Christian opinion who would, in fact, welcome a remnant church. Christianity can find its true self by returning to the cultural catacombs: an underground movement rejecting a militaristic-capitalistic society (the left remnant) or the fashionable moral relativism of academic liberalism (the right remnant). In one sense, true Christianity may always be a remnant: the wild early Franciscans, the soup kitchens of the Catholic Worker. If sin is more a blight than bother, one would expect that only a few shining exemplars will get Christianity right in word and deed. But a remnant church has its own temptation, the temptation to look inward, ignoring the clear command to preach the good word to all nations.

If, of course, one preaches an heretical word to all nations, they are well advised to reject the message. I prefer the world's rejection of heresy as an explanation of the crisis of Christianity. Tell the world that all it has to do is weed the garden and the world will recognize, deep in its soul, that the message is useless. The world knows that, under the glitz of consumerism, the thrill of tribalism, or the strange attractions of victimhood, something is *fundamentally* wrong. After great idealisms of the twentieth century failed horrifically—communism in the disasters of the gulag, the tribalism of various facisms in racial annihilation—who could believe that with a tad more moral effort we would all live happily ever after? The Christian message is as deep as the abyss of Auschwitz. It is not a fairy tale message about ghosts and gods, it is a message of the starkest reality about the anguish of the world. It is also a message of salvation in the midst of that anguish.

## Pretensions of Authorship

It should be obvious to any Catholic that the Church is currently in a state of profound crisis. Much the same could be said about mainline Protestantism, but, though its problems are not unrelated to the Catholic malaise, that is a story for another author. At the root of the Catholic crisis is significant confusion about the meaning of faith. Is it the pronouncements of the pope or the practices of the People of God? Public opinion polls show great rifts between papal proclamations against contraception and homosexuality and the Catholic left, and equally great divides between papal declarations about the death penalty and war and the Catholic right. Where is *the* Church? Left, right, or in Rome? Each bases its sense of correctness on the proper nature of the Church as the guardian and dispenser of Christian truth—but they obviously disagree on who speaks as the Church.

This book is an attempt to construct a theology of the Church, to locate the central life and reality of Christianity as Catholics would have it. I confess my own serious misgivings at taking up such a task. The topic is formidable, and there are centuries of comment and controversy on faith and Church. Not only is there vast and intricate scholarship, my training and scholarly discipline are not that of a theologian or Church historian. I have read eclectically in the field of theology, but my basic discipline is philosophy. The theologians who most interest me have often been Protestants like Søren Kierkegaard and Karl Barth, or Jewish philosophers like Franz Rosenzweig and Emmanuel Levinas. As for strictly Catholic sources, I have only the most superficial acquaintance with the monument of Catholic philosophy and theology, Thomas Aquinas. I was greatly taken even as a college student with the so-called Catholic existentialist, Gabriel Marcel. Finally, I have read extensively in several of the "big names" of recent Catholic theology: Karl Rahner, Hans Urs von Balthasar, and

Joseph Ratzinger, now Pope Benedict XVI. All these thinkers write at formidable length and are theologically and historically sophisticated. In contrast to their learned expositions, the tale told in this book is a mere sketch.
It will certainly seem simplistic to many. But sketches have their value. As
any art critic can tell you, a charcoal sketch may reveal more than an elaborated and overworked final canvas.

Having claimed some status as a philosopher, I want to offer serious
qualification even of that. Jack Miles, the author of *The Biography of God,*
wrote an essay contrasting the intellectual with the academic.[1] He marked
the difference between them as that between the hunter and the farmer.
The latter, the academic scholar, spends her time cultivating her field. She
comes to know her patch of ground and its produce with depth and nuance. The intellectual ranges over many fields looking for all sorts of different prey. Because she does not stay in one place nor engage in intensive
farming, the intellectual may be regarded as superficial from the standpoint of the scholar. And that may be true. On the other hand, the intellectual should be a consumer of academic scholarship and a transmitter of
the fruits of that endeavor to the nonscholar. I would hesitate to claim title
as either a learned academic or a certified "intellectual." My own professional career has certainly made me a hunter rather than a farmer. Partly
by circumstance — some thirty years in high-level college and university
administration — and partly by temper, I have never been able or inclined
to have some small piece of an academic field that would be forever mine.
One of the reasons I have enjoyed philosophy is that it seemed to permit
one to hunt in all sorts of places from modern art to the structure of scientific revolutions to revealed religion. Not everyone sees philosophy in that
manner and I honor the academic philosopher — it is just not me.

Beyond personal taste, I would defend intellectual hunting as a proper
approach to religion. Religion should not be viewed as some restricted field
over *here* as contrasted to some other area over *there*. Religion is all pervasive in life. As Iris Murdoch says, "[Religion] has got to be the magnetic
center of everything." To come to some sense of religion I want to break
out of theological technicalities and Church-talk to create conversation
with modern art, psychoanalysis, the nature of scientific proof, or family
life. Intellectual hunting fits the range of religion.

A wide-ranging approach in contrast to academic depth will, I hope,
connect better with the everyday sense of the reader. There are, as noted,

many profound theological treatises, but on the whole they are expressed in insider's language. When I am in the midst of reading some elegant account of, say, the Trinity, I am minded to ask just what one of my highly intelligent non-Christian academic colleagues would make of all the passes back and forth that distinguish true doctrine from modalism, Sabellianism, or tritheism. To be sure, the skillful theologian has the various terms of the discussion arranged in order and marshaled them to their proper task, but the basic game being played may be as obscure to the reader as cricket is to almost all American spectators—even after it is "explained." While I hope that this book will be comprehensible to the nonspecialist, I also hope that professional theologians will be challenged by the presentation. Karl Rahner writing on the Trinity says "the mystery of the Trinity is the last mystery of our own reality, and . . . is experienced in that reality."[2] Really? It hardly seems so from the delicate dialectics of the professional theologians—including Rahner! I often feel in dealing with theologians unraveling the "mystery" of the Trinity like the commentator who said about Stirling's old book, *The Secret of Hegel*: if Stirling had found the secret of Hegel, he certainly had kept it!

What I am aiming for is an account of what philosophers call "the *logic* of faith," "the *grammar* of faith," or, in Wittgenstein's terms, "the *language game* of faith." The grammar of faith or the language game of faith refer to underlying structure. There are relatively few rules of grammar or chess if we contrast them with the infinity of sentences that can be formed or the myriad games that can be played. But none of the sentences or games will make sense unless they follow the rules. Playing checkers with chess pieces is not bad chess, it is not chess at all. Religious concepts only work in the context of the religious language game, and thus it is vitally important to isolate and understand that context.

I seek to characterize the Christian language game as the "voice" of Christian belief. As the initial quotation from Wittgenstein in the frontispiece of this book suggests, the message of Christianity can only be carried in a special voice, the tone that carries the essential message. If we come upon two people talking to one another, we may well ask: What is going on? Suppose I say that they are courting. Courting language is part of the language game of love. The use of the notion of "game" emphasizes that there are "rules" for *how* one speaks in this game. In the courting game one says "I love you," but not with the flat accent of fact or the pomposity of command. Use the wrong voice and the loving message is not conveyed. Voice rules apply both in genuine courting and when courting is *only a game,* such as in a romantic stage play. If the actor speaks in the wrong voice as lover, villain, hero, or clown, the play is ruined. So with the Christian voice: no matter what the dogma uttered or the moral injunction set forward, spoken in the wrong voice—dictatorial, didactic, distant, or demeaning—the message fails. This is a point that will be argued at length in the body of the text.

## The Voice of the Author

Since this is a book about "voice," I need to speak about my voice as author. Kierkegaard thought—correctly, I believe—that religious insight cannot be conveyed objectively in the manner in which one delivers scientific facts. The voice of belief is not the voice of factual statement. Kierkegaard held that religious communication was necessarily passionate, a voice that speaks to human inwardness, to the heart. Correct, but the task of this text is not that sort of direct communication. It is more modest: a preface to the possibility of the communication of inwardness. The text is not a love poem, but a duller text that suggests what a love poem is supposed to accomplish.

This is not to say that this book is wholly dispassionate. I don't believe that frustration quite makes it as a passion, but it is a grumbling emotion that has had a role in generating my effort. The frustration in question relates to my life story—a fact that would please Kierkegaard. My public life has been as a professional academic and a professed Catholic believer. The academic side was carried forward in a series of perfectly splendid secular colleges and universities. The fact that I spent the weekdays in the arena of secularity and scholarship often made Sunday at Catholic worship highly suspicious both to my colleagues and myself. Did one leave the demand for scholarly objectivity at the Church vestibule? Didn't faith contradict science and sound scholarship? Early on I concluded that the sort of objectivity demanded by the scientific and secular model was too restrictive. There was a truth to faith that needed recognition on the quad. That I may have come to such a conclusion did not by any means alleviate the lived tension between academy and Church. As some sort of believer, I have been propelled to offer an *argumentum ab frustratio* against the restrictions of the secular academy.[3]

But if I have been disgruntled by the objectivist restrictions of the academy, I have been downright angry at the objectivist assumptions of all too much official Catholic preaching, proclamation, and dogma. Rather than the passionate inwardness of faith that Kierkegaard demands, one hears citation of dogma, distant proclamation, and dictates from authority. The real interchange of faith vanishes under routine and repetition of stock phrases and tired arguments. As I argue at length in the subsequent text, it was as if the Church, spooked by the power of secular objectivity, had decided to beat science at its own game. Doctrine is "super science" that goes beyond the Big Bang to a Creator God. But super science in ecclesiastic guise is a sure failure: it does not reach inwardness, the living person — it plays the wrong game and leaves *me* outside as a spectator when I wanted to be a participant.

It is easy enough to endure the objectivity of the academy because that objectivity game has great value: the development of modern science, medicine, and technology. A false objectivity in the Church is, however, intolerable because nothing at all is accomplished. The realm of the spirit is bypassed and left empty. An "objective" faith is not only wrongheaded, it is dangerous and perverse. By pretending to live in the realm of the Spirit but actually ignoring it, objective religion damages deep human needs. Later I will try to unravel "objective," "subjective," and "inward" as these terms can be linked to the truth of religion. In rejecting academic objectivity and opting for attention to what is inward in religion, I do not wish by any means to consign religion to the merely subjective, to emotion or whim. One must talk about the truth of Christianity, but that truth can only be understood within the religious language game.

Kierkegaard wrote a treatise that has been translated *An Attack Upon Christendom*. If this text is also seen as an attack against certain dominant understandings of Catholicism, I hope that it is written with at least a shadow of the passion for inwardness. I write to make sense of the language of Christianity but make no effort to persuade a nonbeliever that the claims of Christianity are true and provable on "neutral" ground. I am deeply suspicious of anything that passes as a "proof" of Christianity. Proof is the stuff of science, and science is definitely not what religion can or should strive for. I hope to establish the sense in which there is Truth in Christianity, though that truth is radically other than the truth of good science. Having avoided proof, I do hope nevertheless to set forth a coherent picture of Christian claims. Too often Christianity seems a strange grab bag of morals and miracle stories in which we rummage about for some inspiration, direction, or consolation. I think, on the contrary, that the Christian story is very simple. It is simple because it is absolutely central and fundamental to the mood and manners of everyday life. While I think that there are no proofs of Christianity or any other religion, deep exploration of the human condition points toward the ways of the great religions.

## Acknowledgments and Excuses

I have had the benefit of preliminary reading and comment on various parts of the finished work from a variety of friends and colleagues: Anthony Bartlett, George Dardess, Stanley Hauerwas, Paul Lakeland, Joseph Nolan, and David Tracy. I was encouraged by their positive remarks and much illumined by their criticisms and disagreements. The distinguished feminist theologian Elizabeth Johnson was a reader of the final drafts of the manuscript. Her comments helped me correct certain facts and she properly noted a lack of direct discussion of the Holy Spirit. Her most salient comment, however, was a "fundamental opposition to attempted reconstruction of patriarchy"—something that I attempt in chapters 6 and 7. I must leave it to the reader to judge the adequacy of my "reconstruction" and her opposition.

Strangely enough, Elizabeth Johnson's comment offers an opportunity to thank my copy editor Matthew Dowd for his always helpful corrections and suggestions. There was, however, one issue between us that was difficult to resolve. He thought that I overused quotation marks around certain key terms. I finally accepted his view. My temptation to use quotation marks came from the fact that while I wanted to use standard ecclesiastical terms, I sought to deepen their analysis to arrive at understandings that were not at all standard. Thus, I wanted to examine the traditional notion of the Pope as patriarch but to discover a use of "patriarch" quite removed from the negative, sexist interpretation of the term. Evidently Elizabeth Johnson is not persuaded that the term can be rescued—or that I have performed such a rescue.

Since some of the material in this presentation has already appeared in journals or book form, I have benefitted from comments and reviews of that material. (Specific citations of earlier publications are noted in the relevant sections of the book.) As much as possible, I have tried to meet the criticisms but am very conscious that I have not always succeeded. There are more than a few arguments in the book that trouble me and where I would hope that critics can point to better lines of development or offer definitive refutation. I would, however, offer a preliminary "excuse" for some of the critical points raised in the interchanges with the early readers.

In an earlier version the title of the book was *The Catholic Church Losing its Voice*. The title was changed because the editorial readers thought the book had a more positive message to deliver. I hope they are correct. There was, however, an early reader who raised a different objection. "What do you mean '*Its* voice'? Should it not be 'her voice'? What happened to Holy *Mother* Church?" What indeed! The fundamental constructive argument of the book is that the voice of the Church is parental, and so by all rights I should use "his" or "her" voice. Then why was I tempted by "its"? Because the Church with a capital "C" seems to present itself as "it"—as the depersonalized voice of objectivity, not the passionate pleading of a parent. The depersonalized voice seems embedded in the common expression "the Church teaches." The notion that something called "the Church" teaches implies a sort of aloof didactic stance which fails as the proper voice of faith. In order to avoid the depersonalized tone of "the Church teaches" I was tempted to put "Church" in lower case throughout the text, but the idea of Church is finally too important to admit of even stylistic demotion. Karl Barth was correct to call his magnum opus on faith *Church Dogmatics*. The Church is the inevitable and appropriate outcome of the story of Jesus, and what the Church *teaches* is not some set of truths but, as I quote Cardinal Ratzinger later in the text, the Church teaches Jesus, "the truth in person."

As indicated above, this book is written from what I have learned as a teacher of philosophy. A critic of an earlier book of mine pointed out that philosophers have a penchant for sharp distinctions—sharper than the fuzziness of fact would allow. I am certain that this "fault" is present in the book at hand. Despite the inevitable distortion of distinctions, I think dissections and dichotomies have value. Because religion is so important to people, they are quite prepared to accept any warm haze of argument as acceptable. All well and good in a moment of worship. It is probably just as well in love and marriage to be a bit hazy in appraisal. On the other hand, a fog of sentiment can lead to disaster in marriage and passion for the wrong god. I may have the wrong god in focus in this book, but I hope that at least He (or She) is in focus.


## The Course of the Argument

I have divided the book into two parts with a "philosophical intermission" between the two. The first part, *"Lex orandi, lex credendi"* applies the ancient idea that the law of prayer is the law of belief. After stating what I take to be the problem of "voice" in the Church, I sketch out a Christology as it might be derived from the meaning of liturgy. In the second part, "The Voice of the Church," I look directly at the official voice of the Church, in particular the papal office, as it asserts the claim to infallibility in "faith and morals."

Chapter 1 outlines the problem of voice in the Church as that word has been captured by "liberals" and "conservatives." The Voice of the Faithful (VOTF) is a modest reforming movement precipitated by the sex scandals of the recent past. It's motto: Keep the Faith, Change the Church. Even though VOTF has confined its attention to management issues, its agenda has been strenuously opposed by an alternate group: Faithful Voice. Faithful Voice argues that changing the Church changes the faith. The governance of the Church in a vested hierarchy culminating in the Roman *magisterium* and the Pope is integral to the message of faith. While I wholeheartedly approve of VOTF, Faithful Voice is correct: faith and Church are correlatives so that change in one crucially effects the other. The problem is the Faithful Voice misunderstands the Christian *voice*. It is the burden of the book to locate the proper voice of faith and thus the proper voice of the Church.

The epigraph at the beginning of the book from Wittgenstein suggests that *what* is said should determine *how* it is said. The Christian message is the *what* in the right voice. Wrong voice = wrong message. The observation is correct and crucial, but it poses a dilemma. Can I locate the *how* (proper voice) without some idea about *what* I mean to communicate? Thus, despite the essential role of voice, the *how* of faith, in chapters 2 through 4 I offer a sketch of the *what* of faith. I offer a Christology: the *what* of Jesus.

While Christology is the *what* of the faith, marching up to that topic directly runs a great danger of succumbing to theological abstraction. There are, of course, biblical and theological ways to present the *what* of Christ. But these means have their own temptations toward distortion. *How* one reads the Bible will affect the *what* of its message. One can read the Bible as a moral code. The Jesus who emerges may be a moral teacher or exemplar, but that characterization falls short of "savior" and quite fails for establishing a "Church." The cautious distancing of learned theology may fail to catch the demands that the Crucified makes upon my life. Balthasar says that theology should be practiced on our knees. I have taken his injunction to heart and propose to begin my account of the *what* of faith by examining in chapter 2 the primary voice of Christianity: the *worshiping voice* of the liturgy—baptism, Gospel, and Eucharist. Looking at worship is important because I am concerned throughout to differentiate what Christians do from general morality. Christians and atheists may both seek an end to war and alleviation of the plight of the poor. Atheists do not, however, baptize and celebrate Eucharist. As the primary voice of faith, these strange Christian liturgical *doings* reveal *what* Christians believe. The liturgy links behavior and belief such that we can see the meaning of the Christ story. In the ancient formula of the Church: *lex orandi, lex credendi,* the law of prayer is the law of belief.

The Christology in chapters 3 and 4, developed from a consideration of worship, is necessarily a high Christology in the sense that the Jesus of the Gospels is identified in some substantial way with God. Worship and God are correlatives because it is improper to worship anything less than a god—and not all "gods" are worthy of worship. One might revere and propitiate the Olympian gods of ancient Greece, but with their internal squabbles and patent favoritism for specific mortals they hardly seem worthy of worship. The paradox of a high Christology, however, is that it only works through a low Christology: Jesus must be "very man" without qualification to earn the title "very God." To develop this thesis, I have attempted to recast traditional accounts of creation and salvation as a great drama. God is projected not as "first cause" but as divine Author of the World-Play. Because of the existence of Jesus in the World-Play, history can be described as *la divina commedia*. I quote Wittgenstein: "Within Christianity it's as though God says to men: Don't act a tragedy."

Having set forth a Christology, I offer a philosophical intermission in which I discuss the general nature of the religious voice. One might follow through the liturgy to the beliefs that the liturgy assumes but then conclude that the whole religious business is merely "subjective." The voice of religion is an emotional outcry. "Subjective" is a very slippery term and may be used by critics to dismiss religion—not objectively true—and by enthusiasts to praise religion—as a matter of the heart. I reject the subjectivizing of religion either negatively or positively. Religion—Christianity for sure—is made of sterner stuff; it makes a claim on truth and reality.

If Christianity—like all religions—makes a claim on truth, how does that claim sit with other ways toward truth? In part 2, I examine that issue by examining the "teaching" function of the Church as exemplified in the office of the Pope, *the* official voice of Catholicism. In chapter 6, having rejected certain false constructions of papal teaching, I attempt to locate the proper understanding of the papal teaching voice as "patriarchal"—absent, I hope gender bias and false domination. In chapter 7, I offer an extended analysis of this patriarchal voice as a basis for affirming the traditional marks of the Catholic Church as hierarchal, infallible, and teaching. My strategy here is what Marx called "immanent critique." Instead of rejecting traditional concepts, as is often the tendency of ultra-liberal critics of the Church, I prefer, as Marx says, to "make these petrified relations dance by singing them their own tune."[4] The patriarchal voice may be "infallible," but not in the mode normally assumed as the teaching authority of the *magisterium*. Having discussed the possibilities and limitations of infallibility of papal pronouncements of faith, in chapter 8, I turn to the papacy as the infallible voice of morality. I argue that the Church may well be infallible in the arena of sin, but morality and sin are not the same notion. Chapter 9 sums up and attempts a general characterization of the voice of the Church. Chapter 10 concludes with some practical suggestions about how to increase the possibility that the genuine voice of Christianity could be heard within the institutional structures and practices of the Church.

Finding the Voice of the Church

# CHAPTER ONE

# Is There a Voice for the Church?

*For last year's words belong to last year's language*
*And next year's words await another voice.*

—T. S. Eliot, *Little Gidding*

## Liberal and Conservative Voice

In the wake of the recent clerical sex scandals in the Catholic Church, a significant reformist movement has been initiated within the Catholic community under the title Voice of the Faithful (VOTF). Based in the Boston area, the epicenter of the linked problems of priestly pedophilia and episcopal failure and fumbling, the group has taken the slogan "Keep the Faith, Change the Church." The advertised intent of the organization is to change the governing and bureaucratic structures of the Church while maintaining traditional teachings. It is envisioned that greater participation by the laity in such matters as Church finances, policing of clerical moral lapses, and lay participation in the selection of bishops would be a proper check on the closed clerical culture that covered up the misdeeds of errant priests. Lay participation of this sort is generally regarded as a "liberal" argument within the Church.

Benign as such reform might seem—particularly to Americans with their tradition of democratic governance—VOTF has been viewed with deep suspicion by Catholic "conservatives." A counter group in the Boston area labels itself Faithful Voice. In contrast to the zeal to change governing structures and practices in the Catholic Church, Faithful Voice proclaims utter loyalty to papal teaching authority, the *magisterium,* and specifically to the direction and teaching of John Paul II and now Benedict XVI, who as Cardinal Ratzinger and head of the Congregation for the Doctrine of the Faith was regarded as the enforcer of John Paul's orthodoxy. Faithful Voice believes that the VOTF slogan is a sham because it contains an inherent contradiction. To "change the Church" *is* "to change the Faith." Peter received the keys to the kingdom, so that the one who holds the Petrine office is the final determiner of our religious duties and destinies. He is the voice of the Church. Peter was given authority by Christ, and hence no different group be it other apostles or VOTF could or can establish, replace, or qualify the unique capacity of Peter and his successors. Local bishops and episcopal structures gain whatever authority they may have as extensions of the office of Peter, the sovereign teacher of Catholic truth.

I have used the conventional labels "liberal" and "conservative" to characterize these two groups. Timothy Radcliffe, O.P., notes the inadequacy of various polarizing labels: liberal/conservative, left/right, or progressives/traditionalists. These terms, imported from the political realm, tend to distort the actual issues involved within the Church. All Catholics are, after all, conservative in the sense that they reflexively argue from the given of biblical witness. Radcliffe offers an astute characterization between Kingdom Catholics and Communion Catholics. The former see the people of God on a pilgrimage toward the Kingdom, the latter see themselves within an institution of fellow believers.[1] Radcliffe believes the Church needs the insights of both views—and I agree. Not only do I agree, I hope in this book to offer a synthesis of these apparent tendencies, a synthesis that transcends the fault lines in either position taken by itself.

Having said, that, I will not shy away from the liberal label for my work. Imprecise as it may be, the label is widely used and does capture tendencies that should be marked. To lay my ideological cards on the table, I am clearly on the liberal side of the splits in the Church. As it happens, I am at the time of this writing the chair of the Board of the *Commonweal* Foundation which publishes the lay-edited magazine of that name. "*Commonweal* Catholic" has been and continues to express a middle-of-the-road liberalism somewhere between *First Things* and *Crisis* on the pugnacious right, and *The National Catholic Reporter* on out to *Call to Action* on the aggressive left. *Commonweal* tends to pick and choose from the holiness agendas of the right and the democratic reformist impulses of the left, while maintaining what almost anyone would call a general liberal cast within the spectrum of Catholic opinion. As a *Commonweal* Catholic, my sympathies in the current crisis of Catholicism are clearly with VOTF. I do not find their arguments or their agenda at all threatening to the central tenets of Catholic faith. Many of their suggestions about changes in day-to-day governance of the Church are not only modest alterations but can be validated by historical precedent. Selection of bishops, for instance, has been an exclusive papal prerogative only for the past two centuries. When Leo XII died in 1829, of the 646 Latin-rite diocesan bishops only 24 had been directly appointed by the Pope.[2] Prior to that time bishops were often appointed by the state authorities or by the clergy of the diocese. One may think that papal appointment was an improvement in governance, but it is not a practice steeped in history.

## Whose Voice for the Church?

Voice of the Faithful or Faithful Voice? Both groups make a claim for the *voice* of Catholic faith. What is the proper voice for faith? Can one *lose* the voice of faith? One could say that the sex scandal has discredited the voice of the Catholic bishops in the moral arena. Who will listen to what they say on a whole range of moral issues given their own duplicitous role in the cover-up of sexual abuse of minors? Authentic voice assumes a harmony of words and deeds. The sex scandal is only the latest failure to match word and deed that has done so much to discredit Christianity down its long history.

If American bishops may have lost their public voice because of scandal, Catholicism—and Christianity in general—seems to be losing its voice on a broader scale. We read about a de-Christianized Europe. Even such traditional Catholic countries as Spain and Ireland appear to be suffering a crisis of faith. While the Catholic Church in America still enjoys extraordinary levels of participation by European standards, there is a significant crisis of the next generation, the turning away of youth from traditional Church practice and attendance. One could attribute the falling away from Christian belief solely to the discrepancy between preaching and practice, but it is the thesis of this book that the problem is deeper than a split between moral instruction and immoral action. There is something quite wrong with the official voice of the Church, the presumed voice of faith. Of course there are many voices of Christianity, and the present day is not without saintly folk who speak with the voice of faith. The loss of voice that is the concern of this book is the voice of the Vatican establishment, the voice of the papacy and a host of others who make claim to speak *the* official, authentic teaching of Christianity. From local preaching to the papal encyclicals, there is something amiss in the voice: a presumptive tone, an over-assurance of attitude, which fails as the vehicle of faith.

To criticize is not to say that the voice of faith is easy to come by. I search for the proper voice to speak, for example, my love and trust of the other. A perfunctory "Trust me" won't work. How many times do we say "I love you" as routine, while the mind strays, while we say to ourselves "in my fashion" or "when you please me." Voicing Christian faith is at least as complicated as voicing our daily loves and duties—a task at which we repeatedly fall short. The saving grace of daily intimacy is that we so quickly sense the inauthentic; it is the stuff of every modern novel of love, marriage, and betrayal. In the case of the official Church we are not so certain about the proper voice. In fact, we may come to think that the more officious the voice the better, a situation we would never accept with friends and lovers.

The quarrel between VOTF and Faithful Voice is itself a quarrel over a certain type of voice. It is not wholly misleading to characterize it as either a liberal and conservative voice, open to dialogue or strictly committed to valued tradition. These are not simply ideological beliefs in the abstract, they come as voice with tones, attitudes, ironies, and pieties that are part and parcel of the positions advocated.

But for all VOTF's innocuous suggestions for good order in the Church, I think that its slogan is wrong. The conservatives are on to something: to change the Church *is* to change the faith. The conservative critique of VOTF's slogan is based on impeccable theological reasoning: Christian teaching and its mode of promulgation, the Church, are essentially linked; changing the mode of propagation changes the message delivered. The flaw in Faithful Voice's criticism lies in failing to explicate the notion of Church. The ministry of the pope may be related to the very essence of Church, but that is a far cry from equating the elaborated historical papacy with the commission to Peter in the Gospel of Matthew. Rosemary Radford Reuther quipped that if you believe that Jesus Christ created the Roman *curia,* then you should believe that Sitting Bull created the U.S. Bureau of Indian Affairs. The merest glance at the history of the Church suggests that there might be more (or less) going on in the current configuration of the papacy than can be justified biblically or from the tradition. Cardinals and the curia are late inventions, which suggests that the Church could exist without them because, after all, it did so for centuries. When Paul VI decided to forgo wearing the traditional tiara (the papal crown) it would hardly seem that the faith of the Church was in jeopardy. So if VOTF's urge to "change the Church" deals only with various historical accretions, encumbrances, and distractions, it would seem relatively harmless to the faith.

But if historical context should give pause to any simple equation of current papal trappings and modalities with the essential nature of the Church, there is a profound truth buried in the fundamental relation of Church and faith. As one regards the nature of Church so one defines the meaning of faith. Or the reverse: different views of faith will create different meanings and modes of Church. Marshall McLuhan's slogan that "the medium is the message" (or its counterpart: "the message should determine the medium") applies. A mismatch of medium and message can be fatal. In the terms of this book, speaking the faith in the wrong voice obscures the Church. Since the Church (with or without curia or cardinals) is the medium that transmits the message of the Gospel, McLuhan would suggest that as the medium is structured, so is the message affected. Is the medium (Church structure, practice and preaching) appropriate to the message, does it distract from the message, or might it utterly subvert the message? Paul VI's gesture of refusing a diamond tiara was an attempt to avoid a distraction. The pope should not be viewed as crowned monarch. Papal teachings are not royal dictates. No doubt there exists a plethora of extinct symbols and practices that could be jettisoned by the Catholic Church not only without compromising faith but as means of clarifying faith.

VOTF's agenda for bureaucratic change does not go far enough. Checking diocesan fiscal and moral accounts is a worthy goal but does not address the real malaise of the contemporary Catholic Church. The change that is needed is much more fundamental and goes to the core of faith and to the Church as the medium of faith's proclamation. Faithful Voice is correct: Church and faith are correlatives; *deep* change in the Church changes faith because the meaning of "faith" dictates ways of being Church. Faith and Church are interlinked in definition. The question raised by this book is whether certain current structures and practices in the medium of the Catholic Church *subvert* the faith. Such was the implicit claim of the Protestant reformers. Their core conceptions of what it meant to be a faithful follower of Jesus Christ led them inevitably to demand different structures for the Church from the prevailing Roman structures of papacy, episcopacy, and priesthood. The reformers' emphasis on faith as direct experience of God through the Bible easily led on to the nonhierarchal, nonpriestly Church structures of the Baptists and Congregationalists.

In the current Catholic controversy about changing or not changing the Church, those on the far left make democratic demands that could, their critics charge, remake Catholicism as Congregationalism. Those on the farther right with their enthusiasm for vested hierarchy create what their critics charge: a Church embedded in "popolatry." Democracy or "popocracy" are different ways of being Church, and they are also different ways of defining faith. I do not mean that the propositions of faith differ—all branches and sects recite the creed—but what it means to recite a creed or the relation between creed and "performing the faith"[3] may be radically different. What is needed is a fundamental theology of Church. And one cannot get the theology of Church right without getting the right theology of faith. It is just such a fundamental look at "changing Church" and "keeping faith" that this book hopes to accomplish.

## The Voice of Vatican II

If the Churches are emptying and vocations are disappearing, at least part of the problem is the failure of the official Church to learn, preach, and teach an appropriate and compelling theology. Nor are such theologies difficult to discover. The last century—particularly the period after World War I—was one of the most illuminating and exciting periods for Catholic theology since the middle ages. After centuries of retreaded scholasticism, Catholic theologians and philosophers produced profoundly important constructions and reconstructions of the meaning of Christian existence. These efforts were augmented by the flowering of Catholic biblical scholarship after Pius XII's *De Afflante Spiritu* liberated that discipline from catechetical fundamentalism. In short, we have the tragic paradox that the last seventy-five years could well be regarded as a "golden age" of theology and biblical scholarship, but a flowering that, as far as I can determine, has had little effect on the style or substance of "official" Catholicism.

It did appear for a short time during the heady days of Vatican II that a deeper theology would emerge to reconstitute not the propositions of faith but the *meaning* of faith and thus the meaning of Church as faith's medium and expression. Theologians like Congar, Rahner, Murray, de Lubac, and others who had been under official suspicion or outright ban were recruited as *periti* to the assembled bishops. The council became an exercise in intense theological instruction. Unfortunately theological dialogue seemed to come to a crashing end with Paul VI's encyclical *Humanae Vitae* upholding the traditional teaching on artificial contraception. The shock of *Humanae Vitae* was not only on the issue of contraception, it was the fact that the pope unilaterally reversed the overwhelming recommendation for change of two special commissions, the second of which was his own hand-picked committee. What point theological dialogue when nothing can change?

Critics of the papacy of John Paul II charge that for all that he referred to certain themes from Vatican II he failed to heed the "spirit" of the council.[4] Quarrels about "the spirit" of Vatican II are often mere partisan positioning, but an exchange in the Jesuit publication *America* between Cardinal Avery Dulles and John J. O'Malley, S.J., illuminates the issue.[5] Dulles, who tends to side with conservatives on various Church issues, carefully extracted the doctrinal conclusions of Vatican II and noted that they do not in any way stray from traditional teaching. O'Malley, who is a Church historian, countered by comparing the "style" of the Council of Trent with Vatican II. Traditional councils like Trent formulated their documents in doctrinal proclamations and anathemas. Vatican II's style of presentation was in sharp contrast. Vatican II's style was discursive not doctrinal, persuasive not proclamatory. To be sure, one can extract doctrinal views from the documents, but that is like believing that all paintings of the Crucifixion from kitsch to Rembrandt convey the same value and meaning. *Humanae Vitae* aside, Paul VI spoke from the *spirit* of Vatican II when he said that the Church's aim was *"pas vaincu, mais convaincu,"* not to conquer, but to convince. For O'Malley (and Paul's *convaincu*), Vatican II displayed a different way-to-be-Church. In the terms of this book's presentation, it changed the medium, the way in which the message was to be delivered. Changing the medium does not change the verbal content of faith—Dulles can well extract traditional statements of faith—but it changes the meaning of being faithful.

The council was an experience of *learning* because of the openness to debate and discussion, listening to the many voices assembled, from bishops to theologians and the outside Protestant and Jewish observers. On the whole and with some happy exceptions, the papacy of John Paul II was not a learning papacy, it was a *didactic* papacy, obsessed with the assertion and reassertion of teachings. The role of the Congregation for the Doctrine of the Faith (CDF) under Cardinal Ratzinger fit the model of a didactic Vatican authority.

The two marks of John Paul's papacy and the work of the CDF that seem most out of tune with the spirit of Vatican II were closing discussion and creeping infallibility. Vatican II was if nothing else a place of open discussion with sharply divided opinions from the assemblage of bishops. The final documents often reveal these fissures in undeveloped arguments, unclarities, and the different tone of the various documents. Once the council closed, the spirit of dialogue evaporated. John Paul II and the CDF under Ratzinger seemed particularly anxious to avoid the "scandal" of having any issues regarded as open for discussion. Vatican II's call for a synod of bishops meeting regularly in Rome was intended to maintain dialogue, but the actual conduct of the synods held has been deeply disappointing. The bishops usually have been asked to approve schema already set forward by Vatican officials. Closing dialogue has created a sense of creeping infallibility: the supposition that any Papal statement from a solemn proclamation to an off the cuff remark is *de fide*. Creeping infallibility is directly counter to history and canon law—there is not even an infallible list of infallible truths available for Catholics—but it is part and parcel of the papalization of Catholicism that has marked the time since Vatican I.

The long argument of this book runs counter to the didactic style of the papacy, but I would suggest even at this early point in the text why one can have some legitimate concern. To anyone who would emphasize the "spirit" of the council, a comment by Ratzinger is illuminating: "Where the spirit of the Council is turned against the word of the Council . . . this spirit becomes a specter and leads to meaninglessness."[6] Ratzinger quotes with appreciation Gregory of Nazianzus' refusal in 382 to attend the second session of the Council of Constantinople: "To tell the truth, I am convinced that every assembly of bishops is to be avoided, for I have never experienced a happy ending to any council; not even the abolition of abuses . . . but only ambition or wrangling about what has taken place."[7] The problem with open discussion and dialogue is that one may come to believe that the teaching of the Church is perpetually uncertain, subject to the back and forth of opinion. The Church begins to look like a university faculty meeting haggling over the content of the core curriculum. Surely there must be more certainty to faith than the continuing quarrels of the philosophers. I agree, and in this book I opt for the surpassing truth of Christian faith but not on the didactic model.

Now that Ratzinger has succeeded John Paul II as Benedict XVI, one might reasonably expect a continuation of didacticism. One should be cautious, however, about drawing a negative prediction about the style of his papacy. His initial encyclical, *Deus Caritas Est,* was anything but didactic, demonstrating instead a pastoral style. In the course of my presentation, I quote frequently from Ratzinger because he says many things that conform to that style and to the argument of this book.

## We Need More than Mitres

At a recent meeting I had a conversation with a well-published Catholic ecclesiologist, a person who specializes in understanding the theology of Church. I commented to him that studies in ecclesiology were urgently needed. His rejoinder was disheartening. "No, the work has already been done, it is just that the officials in the Church are either unaware of the work or choose to ignore it." Second anecdote: at a Common Ground conference I attended in 2002, a monsignor who had spent ten years at the North American College in Rome commented on "what Rome thinks." "You have to realize that there are *three* Romes: the Rome of the universities [the Gregorian, the Angelicum], the Rome of the generalates of the great religious orders [Dominicans, Franciscans, Jesuits], and the Rome of the Vatican. *And they do not talk to one another.*"[8] The lesson that I draw from these anecdotes and from my general experience with officers of the Church from parish priest to cardinals is that precious few of these individuals have the least interest in or acquaintance with the importance of modern Catholic theological or biblical scholarship and the implications of that work for traditional assumptions about the meaning of "Church" and "faith."

The distinguished theologian Nicholas Lash summed up the abysmal failure of bishop-theologian dialogue in Great Britain. In a brief article with the provocative title "We Need More than Mitres" he recounts the efforts shortly after Vatican II to establish a commission to maintain dialogue between bishops and theologians. The theologians were to act as a "consultative body" to the bishops. In the first five years of the commission's existence the theologians were asked to comment on only two issues: the appropriate age for confirmation and whether people could receive communion more than once a day. Lash concludes:

> What continues to be quite lacking . . . is any sense from the bishop's conference of its recognition that the grave cultural and pastoral crisis in which we find ourselves has, ineluctably, profound and far-reaching *theological* implications for every aspect of the Church's structures, life and mission.[9]

Lash's comment about the local dialogue with bishops replicates the exasperation that many have expressed about the post–Vatican II synod of bishops mentioned above.

Given my confessed liberal leanings, it would be all too easy to imagine that the demand for dialogue is a special concern of liberals and the democratic left in the Catholic community. Not so. Germaine Grisez, an influential, learned, and deeply conservative moral theologian is as much exercised about the lack of dialogue between theologians and bishops as radicals from Call to Action. He laments not just the fact of deep disagreement and dissent among Catholic theologians, but even more the failure of the hierarchy to admit that there is dissent and to address the crisis entailed by conflicting views. His remedy (speaking to a bishop at a conference):

First you [the bishops] must face up to the disagreement. Then give me and those who disagree a chance to come before you and the Holy Father . . . and present our views and argue with each other. Sit still and listen until you learn what the issues are, and what you think about them. Ask us questions, and make us answer until you've heard all you want to hear. When that's done, both sides will have had a very fair opportunity to tell you what they're thinking. Then throw us out. Send us home.

Then sit down with the Holy Father. And ask yourself this very important question: What is the Catholic faith here?[10]

Grisez is suggesting a learning session like Vatican II where bishops and theologians dialogue. "Sit still and listen," *then* you send the theologians home. It often seems that the Vatican prefers to throw out the theologians straight off. Rome bars the door to dialogue so that there is not even the *appearance* of disagreement or dissent. The garment of the Church is not only spotless, it isn't even fraying at the edges.

The Vatican's desire to avoid controversy and the appearance of controversy seems to govern the present appointment of bishops. Doctrinal orthodoxy—often on the controverted issue of artificial contraception—has become a litmus tests for episcopal appointment. Speaking from the conservative side, Grisez rejects such a strategy.

I have heard the line, "The Holy See seems to be following a policy of trying to appoint 'better bishops.'" That strategy isn't going to work. . . . [B]ishop appointments don't answer [dissenting theologian] Charlie Curran's questions. They don't answer my arguments. They don't answer anything. And the questions have to be answered. The modernist controversy should have taught the Church one thing: Questions must be faced up to and answered. They won't go away.[11]

## The Apostolic Voice

The argument of Faithful Voice would seem to reject Lash's title. That organization might well proclaim: "We need no more than mitres." The rationale seems clear: apostolic succession is the vehicle of transmission for faith and is attested to by scripture and tradition. Apostolic succession may indeed be central, but the problem that Faithful Voice and similar conservative Vatican centralists fail to appreciate is that there are at least two quite different apostolic voices clearly marked in the New Testament. One can argue both from present day reality and biblical background that a strategy of leave-it-to-the-bishops (or the pope) won't work.

The late Raymond E. Brown, S.S., perhaps the most respected Catholic biblical scholar of his day, recounts the New Testament background to the problems with understanding the apostolic voice. There were two senses of "apostle" in the earliest Church: the twelve who, as those who witnessed Jesus in the flesh, were the guardians of orthodoxy. In addition there was the *missionary* apostle represented by Paul, "the apostle to the Gentiles." Beyond the distinction in apostleship there is the fact that none of the apostles were bishops—including Peter who, though he may have gone to Rome, was certainly not in any manner "bishop of Rome." In the early Church, bishops were the leaders-left-behind. Thus, after one of Paul's missionary forays he would move on and sometimes leave behind someone to guard the teaching preached. *Sometimes* because it seems clear that in Corinth, where Paul spent an extended period of eighteen months, no "bishop" was left behind, which caused Paul to write back to the Corinthians cautioning them on how to practice the faith.

Over a period of time, the two apostolic functions (orthodoxy and missionary preaching) devolved onto the bishops though that was clearly not their original function. Fr. Brown's assessment of the coalescence of apostolicity on the office of bishop is telling:

> The unexamined claim of apostolic succession [in the office of bishop] can cause confusion about the theological role of the episcopate in several ways. Excellent bishops have put themselves in vulnerable and even ludicrous position by making dubious theological pronouncements, not because they were proud men, but because they felt that as part of their apostolic office they must supply the answers to the dogmatic and moral problems of the time. On the other hand, precisely because the bishops are considered the successors to the apostles on doctrinal matters, they are often criticized by "advanced" clergy and laity for not taking the initiative in bringing Christian thought to bear on the problems of contemporary civilization and for not providing theological leadership.[12]

Fr. Brown goes on to offer a possible solution to the "overload" of function on the contemporary office of "resident" bishop:

> Perhaps then it would be wise for Catholics to affirm explicitly, and not merely implicitly, that in the modern Church some of the principal activities of the Pauline apostolate, especially as regards offering leadership to face new religious problems, have been taken over by men and women who are not bishops — by theologians, by enterprising priests and religious who by circumstances are thrust into new situations, and by perceptive laity with their manifold competencies.[13]

The ultra-conservative construction of Church collapses all the apostolic functions into the hierarchic office of bishop, centered ultimately in the bishop of Rome. Further, and most damaging, is the construction of the apostolic office as solely concerned with guarding orthodoxy. Guarding orthodoxy may be the long-term task of apostolic succession, but challenges to current practices and pronouncements from the missionary apostolate may be necessary to maintain a continuously *living* orthodoxy. The Church lives from tradition, but as has been well said: tradition is the living faith of the dead, traditionalism is the dead faith of the living. The importance of missionary apostolicity for contemporary Christianity could not be more obvious. Paul, the original missionary apostle, had to find preaching and practice that would speak to a non-Christian (pre-Christian) world. The Church of the twenty-first century — at least in the developed world — must find a way of speaking to a world broadly regarded as post-Christian.

Fr. Brown's modest suggestion changes the sense of Church by locating missionary apostolicity in the work of theologians and even the competencies of perceptive laity. The dialogue between bishops and theologians that Lash and Grisez advocate is not a mere exercise in tidying up arguments for papal positions already taken: it is a fundamental examination of the way in which the faith can be present to the present. Likewise, taking theological dialogue seriously is more than auditing the books: it transfers direct apostolic function outside the vested episcopal hierarchy. To be sure, Brown sees a continuing dialogue of theologians and resident bishops, but he concludes that only through such dialogue "drawing on the larger resources of the Church can [apostolic succession of bishops be] realistic."[14]

The thesis of this book builds on Brown's distinctions and recommendations, but suggests that in changing the messengers from bishops
alone to theologians and the laity, the sense of how one goes about being
Church shifts in a significant fashion. Changing the messenger changes the
voice of faith. The voice of the missionary apostle is not the same as the
voice of the guardian-apostle. An obsession with guarding orthodoxy sup-
presses missionary engagement with contemporary problems. Of course, a
bishop may well be a theologian displaying missionary engagement, but
that is not the current norm or practice. It is more likely that new appoin-
tees will be experts in canon law like Law, Bevilacqua, and Rigali. The voice
of canon law is not necessarily a voice infused with theological perception
and missionary outreach.

## A Forgiving Voice

The change in the Church must go to fundamentals about the nature of
*who* is "Church" (not just bishops but missionary theologians and laity).
*Who* is Church will change both *what* is Church and the message conveyed.
There will be change in what it means to be faithful. It is not that one will
tear up the Apostle's Creed and proclaim some quite different doctrine:
Jesus was really only a man, or really only God in disguise, or an angel. (All
of the above have been tried and found wanting as statements of Christian belief.) No, the notion that I want to present for changing the faith is
expressed in Wittgenstein's notion of a language game: the pieces on the
board are the same, but the underlying rules of the game are profoundly
different. There may be infallibility for the voice of the Church, but not if
the Church is playing the natural science game (more on this later).

The "style" of Vatican II was no more an irrelevance to conveying
faith than tone of voice is in conveying a message of love or command
or indifference. George Lindbeck noted that when the Crusaders cut down
the "infidel" Muslims with the cry, "Christ is Lord," the statement was
false. "Christ is Lord" cannot be said truly as a statement of conquest and
slaughter. It seems all too clear that more and more people in and out of
the official Churches hear the words of faith spoken in the wrong voice.
The spirit of the Council of Trent, the voice of Trent, was *anathema sit:*
the voice of condemnation. Whatever the wrangles of Vatican II, it was

clear that the fathers did not wish a document that was a voice of condemnation. This did not mean that the fathers meant to capitulate to the modern world—one of the conservative complaints about the interpretation of the council. It is more reasonable to think that they thought it worth listening to the modern world first as a way of finding the voice of faith that would speak to the world. Starting a conversation with the declaration that your interlocutor is mistaken is a poor way to foster communication.

Bad enough that the secular world misses the message, I was having dinner with a well-placed and well-respected priest whose entire life had been spent working with individual pastors across the United States. In the course of the conversation he opined that maybe half the priests with whom he worked *did not believe* the faith they preached. In terms of this book, they uttered the words of religion but in the wrong voice, an unbelieving and unbelievable voice. I think my informant was correct; it would certainly go far to explain everything from the sex scandals to the empty pews and vacant seminaries.

Uttering the propositions of faith in the wrong voice takes many forms from boredom to bluster. Paul VI was within range of the right voice when he said that the Church's task was to speak in a *convincing* way. There is a tone of voice that carries sincerity and conviction. Interestingly enough, it is a tone of voice that is also permeable, open, even tentative. I will end this entire study by characterizing the voice of faith as a listening and forgiving voice. There is, of course, the sense of forgiving voice as the forgiveness of sin, and I shall concentrate on that as the Church's essential mission and voice. For now, however, I suggest the sense of forgiving as I learned it in various architectural projects in which I have been involved. It was frequently the case that an architect would choose a natural wood surface because wood is "forgiving." In a high traffic area, subject to significant scarring and stress, wood is an excellent material because it maintains visual and structural integrity despite a variety of nicks and scratches. Forgiving wood is superior to a hard surface such as tile, which, when it is scarred, shows every wound. The whole surface is compromised by a scratch. I would commend "forgiving" for the Church in this sense: the ability to maintain integrity while open to stress.

A person who is convinced can afford to be forgiving. She is not afraid to listen to criticism and contradiction; she believes that her views are wide, deep, and capacious enough to understand and encompass critical questions. Speaking from conviction, the speaker continually seeks new modes of expression, a different formula for a truth that she knows is deeper than any formula can quite capture. One must be suspicious when religious discourse simply repeats stock phrases from some catechism. The more one falls back on pat phrases, the more one falls into religious chatter.

This chapter has been taken up with the voice of the Church as the voice of proper theology, preaching, and proclamation. In a sense, these are derivative voices. Without retreating from concern about how the Church presents itself to the world, I want in the next chapter to consider the primary voice of the Church: the liturgy. The liturgy, one might say, is how the Church presents itself not to the world but to God, how it presents itself as *worship*. Theology and the forgiving voice are, as it were, voices *to the outside*—even to ourselves as "outside" the deep mysteries of faith. The primary voice of Christianity is an *insider's* voice, the voice of prayer and sacrament. Christianity is not a theological school and does not express its inner life in argument. The Church is a community of worship, and it is from the fact of worship that all the other voices are derived and receive their justification.

# Part I

*Lex orandi, lex credendi*

# CHAPTER TWO

## Extra ecclesiam nullus

---

*The task of the Church in a world like this is to be a big place,
where those bits of humanity that can't find a home anywhere else
can flourish: a place where people [can] . . . be human in a way
they never realized before.*

Archbishop Rowan Williams
at Westminster Cathedral, 2005

Since the issue in this book is the voice of faith, it seems appropriate to start off with a brief account of the primary voice of the Catholic faith: the liturgy. Liturgy is the fundamental way Christians "voice" their faith. Of course people may go to Church and recite, kneel, bow, and even receive communion without having any idea what they are doing: mere routine. Because of the possibility if not prevalence of liturgical routine, all sorts of liberal thought in and out of the Sunday pews suggests that true Christianity is somewhere else. Peace, justice, and love are what Christians do — or should do — and all those special Church doings are anywhere from irrelevant to dangerous to *real* Christianity. Discounting ritual would

A version of this chapter appeared in *Pro Ecclesia* 13, no. 2 (Spring 2004) under the title "Church: *Extra Ecclesiam Nullus*." It appears here with permission.

seem to echo the Hebrew prophets who disdain temple sacrifice, and it certainly comforts secular liberals who are happy to have nuns as peace pickets as long as they don't pass out sectarian tracts. Peace, justice, and love are, one hopes, universal moral imperatives that are pursued by all persons of good will. It would be relatively easy to legitimate Christianity as an institution dedicated to fostering these high human ideals. The Church would be comparable to the United Nations or the Red Cross. But the Church's task is stranger and deeper than morality. It is a fundamental argument of this book that Church is involved in something other than instructions and encouragements to sound morality. Prayer and sacrament are not well understood as moral symbols, which is why many honest and earnest pursuers of the good regard them as unnecessary if not distracting. Picketing for peace, justice, and love are laudable Christian practices, but they are grounded in distinctly different suppositions than those that obtain under "secular" movements for these ends. Christians strive for world peace among nations but believe that Christ offers "the peace that the world cannot give." Prayer and sacrament express a unique Christian grounding for peace, justice, and love.

The ground of peace and the nature of one's hope for peace have a decisive effect on the meaning of peace. I offer two quite different examples. Thomas Hobbes believed that the natural state of human interaction was perpetual war: the war of all against all. His solution was to overcome "nature" through the artifice of a social contract in which humans handed power over to a single supreme authority. For Hobbes, peace was the best bargain in a bad situation. There was no *summum bonum,* highest good, for humans, only avoidance of the *summum malum,* the worst evil. In sharp contrast to Hobbes, there are many modern "new age" thinkers for whom "nature" is a realm of peace. It is "artifice" that leads to human misery. If humans would live in the peaceable kingdom of simple animal nature there would be no war. Christianity disagrees with both views. Unlike Hobbes, Christians believe that there is a *summum bonum,* God's peace. Christians also believe that in a sense peace is *already given,* not as the placidity of the natural world but in the action of Jesus who establishes the Kingdom of God. The sacramental liturgy reveals the special Christian ground and meaning of peace, justice, and love.

If sacramental liturgy expresses the Christian meaning of peace, justice, and love, what are the essentials of liturgy? Gordon Lathrop argues convincingly that Church practice consists of three things: baptism, scripture, Eucharist—water, word, meal. Lathrop rests his argument not only on common liturgy throughout the ages, but on the very earliest evidence of Christian practice.[1] Following the ancient formula, *lex orandi, lex credendi*—the law of prayer is the law of belief—I propose to consider the meaning of these ancient and persistent rituals. The rituals are peculiar Christian actions—the secular peace picket does not partake in baptism, scripture, and eucharist—and it is these rituals that ground and define peace, justice, and love for Christians.

## Baptism: Twice Born

Several years ago I visited Yad Vashem, the official memorial in Israel to the victims of the Holocaust.[2] By far the most moving memorial was the recently constructed remembrance of the children who died in the Nazi concentration camps. The distinguished Israeli architect Moshe Safedie constructed an underground chamber into which one descends along a stone ramp. Above the entrance to the chamber are broken pillars representing the lives cut off by Nazi persecution. The interior of the underground chamber is completely dark except for five candles. The interior walls, ceiling, and floor are constructed of half-silvered glass so that the candles are reflected and re-reflected in all directions. Walking through the chamber is like walking through a star cluster. As one proceeds through the space, a voice intones the names of the children who died.

One of my companions on the visit to the memorial was Jewish. He had been there in a previous year with his teenage daughters. As one of the daughters was proceeding through the darkened chamber of flickering light, she heard *her* name being called. Of course, it was not the American teenager who was being called, it just happened that she had the same name as one of the victims. His daughter was, my companion said, "completely undone." I offer the experience of this young girl at Yad Vashem as a type for "baptism."

To understand "baptism" one must recognize that everyone is "twice born."[3] First we are born *biologically* into the world of nature, then we are born *historically* into the world of history. Biological birth frames us in the world of male, female, sexuality, sickness, aging, dying. Historical "birth" frames us as Americans, wealthy, scientists, Republicans, Christians, Jews, and so on through all manner of categories and contrasts. Nature and history, while ontologically separate, are not kept in airtight compartments. I am a biological male by nature, but what it *means* to be male is deeply determined by history and culture. Parents not only procreate their offspring, they inevitably create a scenario for them. "Boys don't act like that! That's girlish!" and vice versa. Male or female children cannot avoid interaction with gender history either positively or negatively. Parental maxims about history abound: "How lucky you are to be an American," "It is not what you know, but who you know that matters," and so on. Christian baptism is the formal sign of being born into history *as Christians view history*.

When the young woman heard her name being called at Yad Vashem, she was being called by and from Jewish history. The American young woman's response to *her* name caused a Holocaust victim to be "reborn." Reciprocally, the American teen was "born" into Holocaust history. She realized that, as a Jew, the destructiveness of the Holocaust was her history. The Holocaust was not only her history as a matter of record but as an always present, perpetual danger to herself as Jewish. *This* Rachel could have been *that* Rachel. The motto of the Holocaust memorial is "Lest we forget." That admonition is not an exercise in archival memory, it is a warning that for the Jewish people, for any Jew, for this protected American teenager, history is a profoundly dangerous and destructive place. For Jews, the Holocaust could well be regarded as *the* marker of their history. When the young woman heard her name called in the Children's Memorial, when the victim was reborn in the present consciousness of one who shared her name, the teenager was "baptized" into Jewish history. At Yad Vashem one could believe that Holocaust *is* Jewish history.

Before proceeding one word further, I want to emphasize that Holocaust is *not* Jewish history for religious Judaism. For an observant Jewish believer, Exodus is the marker of history. History is the story of God's *rescue* from slavery in Egypt, from exile in Babylon, even from the destruction of the Temple in 70 BCE, and finally from the Nazi Final Solution. Christianity and its "good news" grow from this profound Jewish tradition of God as one who rescues. Keeping the religious commitment to Exodus in mind, nevertheless I want to continue contrasting a Jewish-Holocaust view of history with the Christian view—a view that is at one level deeply Jewish!

It is not only Jews of the Holocaust who may regard history as destructive. James Joyce's fictional alter ego, Stephen Daedalus, says that history is a "nightmare" from which he hopes one day to awaken. Barroom sages and profound philosophers agree. "It's dog eat dog out there!" Hegel characterized history as the "slaughterbench" of great states and peoples. Holocaust may not be a marker only for Jews, it may be history for one and all. Given the projection of history as the ultimate arena of death and destruction, how should one understand Christian baptism?

Christian baptism is entry into history. The Jewish teenager was called to history under the sign of the Holocaust. In the dark chamber at Yad Vashem she walked "through the valley of the shadow of death." What is the sign of history for the Christian? The child is born in baptism "under the sign of the Cross." In the traditional rite the celebrant traces the sign of the cross on the initiate's forehead. The Cross as *the* sign of history is one which could be accepted well beyond the reaches of the Christian faith. History is a nightmare, a slaughterbench where the good and the loving are betrayed. Like the Holocaust, the Cross could be a warning sign about universal history: danger—proceed with extreme caution.

The shock of Christian baptism is that the Cross is not a warning sign for history, it is a sign of triumph and hope. Holocaust announces "bad news" for the Jews; the Cross announces "good news" for the Christian. In my Yad Vashem example, the young woman is called in the name of a victim. The living girl places herself in Holocaust history as the victim is reborn in her, reborn as a sign of danger and death, a sign that she too may be a victim. In Christian baptism, the initiate is given a Christian name, and is led into history *in the name of the Father, Son, and Holy Spirit.* In the Christian name the individual is called in the name of Jesus, the Son. The baptized is given the name of a Christian saint: the name of an individual whose life was defined from within the story of Christ. As the present girl was called *by* name *in* the name of the past victim, when my *Christian* name is called, I am called to the story of Jesus. Christ is "reborn" in me as past Rachel was "reborn" in present Rachel. Christ, the victim, is reborn in me as victim. But then the "miracle" of Christianity: this victim reborn in me is victorious. When this victim is reborn in me, *if* this victim is truly reborn in me, then I am identified with the whole story: Cross and Resurrection. Sharing in His death, I also share in His victory over death.

There is then a radical difference between a Rachel called to Holocaust history and a Christian called under the sign of the Cross. It is all too easy to see Holocaust, unrequited suffering, as the given course of history: history is a nightmare and we do not awake from it. The Cross calls to history but radically denies the apparent nightmare course of human events. Moreover, history has a sacred dimension: it is somehow not just human history, it is sacred history, God's history. At the very point when one would be most inclined to denounce history and its cruelties—the cross of the innocent as history's persistent paradigm—we are told that this is a Cross like no other, a Cross of triumph, a Cross *beyond* death, a Cross that signals the end (apocalypse) of human history.

The very act of naming is itself an entry into history because it designates the singular trajectory of the one named. As a biological entity born into the species, I am, as the ultra-Darwinists claim, only a means for continuing the species. I (singular) die, but that is not a very interesting event because the species endures. On the other hand, as the one named, the unique singular, I have a history; I do not endure. As named singular I will be no more and that is very concerning to me. When Christian baptism gives me a name, it gives me a history and my unique death. Immersion in water is the sign of death and destruction. But since this is Christian naming, one is reborn in the name of the Resurrected. Being called in the name of the Holocaust or Christ are both insertions into history, but they may be seen to differ as victim or victor in history.

Christian baptism names not only in Christ but also in the Father. The idea of "God the Father, Creator of heaven and earth" (as the Creed says) is the ultimate ground for the logic of naming singulars and of history as the story of singulars. "He determines the number of the stars; he gives to all of them their names" (Ps 147:4) The notion of God-the-Creator is *the* basic notion on which all else rests in Jewish and Christian faith. Creator-God will be a theme to which we will return again and again in this book, so it is imperative even at this stage to sketch in the logic of Creator-God.

My view of God-as-Creator differs from such classic designations of God as "first cause" or modern arguments about God's role in the Big Bang of cosmic origin or the issue of "creationism" vs. evolution. The biblical God does not relate to creation primarily as an order of many *kinds* of things: tables, chairs, people, and stars. God's relation is "singular-to-singular." One could say that in a certain sense the relation is "personal";

he knows the things of creation *by their name*. Plato's demiurgic creator imprints form onto chaotic matter rather like the grand watchmaker of the old argument for the existence of God from design. The biblical Father Creator is not a God for forms and general sorts of things, he is a God who calls each by name — even the stars. Calling by name relates to the unique and singular.

Consider how different it is when I regard the *other* under some general category. It is not just *a* woman but *this* woman whom I love. Even with "personal" categories, it is not *a* daughter that I speak to, but *this* daughter whom I call forth by her name. Names can be simple devices for locating an item, picking someone out from the crowd. But when God calls by name it is not just for identification as if He were taking the cosmic roll call. God calls by name in the solemn manner in which I may be summoned by friend or lover, by duty and commitment. Instead of the image of the potter shaping material, the watchmaker designing his machine, the idea of Father-Creator projects a universal "dialogue" of love between the Father and all that He calls by name from stars on down to the sparrow that falls. "My will and my desire were turned by love, / The love that moves the sun and the other stars" (Dante, *Paradiso* 145). In that sense, even if the cosmos were in some sense "eternal," regenerating by some "natural" process in a succession of Big Bangs and Busts, there would still be place for a Creator who knew it through and through by name.

There is a long argument that could be taken up here about the "metaphysics of Creation." I think I am saying in terms of naming and singularity what Aquinas means when he argues for God as a pure act of *esse*, of to-be-ness, of existence. I leave development of such technicalities to the scholars. All I wish to show is that when we give a name (singularity and history) in Christian baptism, we place the initiate within the meaning and ground of history. If I exist in the name of the Father, then the reality of my history is grounded in Creation itself, the work of the Creator. If there were only the Jesus of Resurrection, one might regard his miraculous return as a one-time event. Resurrection would show Jesus to be a figure of utterly unique character, but would it be a sign of hope for history overall? Because the Father-Creator raises Jesus from the dead He signs history with re-creating hope. Resurrection reflects humanity's deepest reality, our hope and salvation. The creating action of the Father was from the beginning and will be forever, that is the promise of the Holy Spirit. Christians give glory to God the Father, Son, and Holy Spirit, who was from the *beginning,* is *now* and ever *shall be.* What God names he does not forget; what exists in the name of the Father shares in his life.

Holocaust's ultimate message: beware of history, remember the past so as to guard the future, be prepared to defend yourself because the enemy abides. Christianity under the Cross also sees history as a dangerous place: remember the Cross. But then Resurrection says that we can have hope in history even unto death. This resurrected one is not an isolated religious hero, he is the Son of God, Son of the Father who knows me by name. Because we have hope, because history is the realm of those whom God has named, defensiveness is not the last word for life. Love your enemies.

I have been assuming that everyone is twice born, baptized into history. At some high level of generality I would be prepared to defend that claim. However, it is important to note that societies and individuals may well seek to escape the terrors of history. Stephen Daedalus was immersed in nightmare and hoped one day to awaken from history's bad dream. Noble religions and great philosophical systems have mustered powerful arguments for refusing reality to history. A "nature" religion that casts human life within the cosmic cycle of the seasons may offer a wholesale discounting of any unique, unrepeatable history. The example of nature religions and philosophies illustrates again why Christianity cannot be reduced directly to simple advocacy of peace, justice, and love. I recently participated in a ritual conducted by a group called "The Peaceweavers." The Peaceweavers are a small community dedicated, as the name implies, to peace and nonviolence. The leader explained that they found their inspiration in Native American religions and in Buddhism. I greatly admire the earnestness and dedication of the Peaceweavers and can only feel abashed when I consider my own reticence in contrast to their activism. The problem I have with the Peaceweavers and a host of such groups is that the "peace" that seems to underlie their efforts is the peace of nature. Nature can be seen as the realm of peace. The calm of the forest, the self-balancing economy of nature, the placidity of animals all suggest a realm of peace far from the rancid ambitions of humanity. This vision of peaceful nature is, of course, something of a myth—Tennyson saw nature "red in tooth and claw"—but like all myths it has a core of truth.

Any appeal to nonviolence that is successful in a violent age should be valued, but the peace of nature is not the peace that emerges from Christianity. Christianity is firmly planted in history, in the crucial event of Cross and Resurrection, an event which the Scripture claims is *apax,* once and for all. The Hebrew Bible, the Christian Old Testament, is a ferociously warlike document and cannot be suppressed or ignored. If there is to be peace it must be in the milieu of strife and war (the realm of sin) that is the stuff of human history. Christian peace is not a "return to nature," it is a peace that emerges within the arena of ambition, arrogance, selfishness, and sin, which are marks of humanity and history.

The peculiarity of Christian peace can also be seen in contrast to the Buddhist background of the Peaceweavers. Buddhism is an enormously powerful and attractive spiritual wisdom, but it originates in quite other suppositions than those of the Bible. As I read the basic teaching of the Buddha, peace emerges through a detachment from desire that deconstructs the self. Good or bad as it may be, biblical religion is anything but deconstructive of "self." This would seem particularly true of the "earthy" tradition of the Hebrew Bible. There is a tradition of "self-denial" in Christianity, but it is not so much to deconstruct the self as to wash away a false self so that the true self may achieve loving communion with Christ.

In sum, the peace, justice, and love that Christians advocate and pursue exist under the sign of the Cross. Christian peace—which believers hold to be *true* peace—cannot occur by a social contract, return to nature, or detachment from desire. It comes from recognizing the reality of the Cross (history as conflict, sin, and death) and Resurrection (God transcending conflict, sin, and death so that history is redeemed and recreated). Explicating the contradictory complexity of Christian peace is not at all obvious. I have only offered here a sort of *via negativa* toward Christian peace. Nature religions and Buddhism in their very different ways deconstruct the historical self, dissolving the singular in universal Nature or the Buddhist *anatta* (no-self). Biblical religion maintains the self—and thus the perpetual sinful breakdown of self into "selfishness" and the strife that flows therefrom. Rather than suppressing self, the Bible seeks a communion of true self to true self, a communion that is possible only because each singular self is loved wholly by God. The great commandment is to love God, and, in loving God who loves each and every one, I find my brother and sister in the stranger.

## Gospel: The Good News

The claim that all humans are baptized or twice born—once into nature, again into history—needs to be qualified in two respects. First, though history is an embedded reality of distinctly human existence, history may be recognized only to be avoided. Having been born into the burdens of history, individuals and societies may create an ideology that rebirths them back into nature. That is the background hope of the Peaceweavers. Second, although birth into history is inevitable for humanity, it is more often than not un-thematized. The lesson of history may come piecemeal, scattered in common sense and popular anecdotes: "It's a tough world out there," "A bird in the hand is worth two in the bush." Christian baptism is noteworthy because it is a self-conscious, ritually enshrined, thematized second birth. Christians are not to blunder into history without a self-conscious signpost about what is ahead.

The focus on the *self* in the naming of the baptismal rite is carried forward in the liturgical progression. The next act of the liturgy, Gospel, proclaims the meaning of the self within the Christian story. Thus, the liturgy begins with a washing as a reminder of baptismal rebirth even if that "washing" is as minimal as Catholics dipping into the holy water font at the entrance door of the Church. The liturgy continues by telling the story of history: the reading from scripture. In the case of the Jewish young woman at Yad Vashem, remembering history can be "bad news"; in the history of Jesus, Christians are given "good news."

Mark, the ur-Gospel, announces the Christian lesson in the first sentence: "The beginning of the good news [*euaggelion,* gospel or good message] of Jesus Christ, the Son of God" (Mk 1:1) "The good news of Jesus Christ" is a formula open to easy misinterpretation. If not understood correctly, both the earlier part of liturgy (baptism) and the later (Eucharist) are fundamentally distorted and devalued. The most common distortion of "the good news of Jesus Christ" is that Jesus *delivers* good news. To be sure, he does deliver good news in announcing the Kingdom of God, but if he were merely delivering news, Jesus would be understood very differently than he has been understood by the canonic tradition. A *prophet* delivers news, he is God's spokesperson. Jesus does not just deliver news, *he* is the news. As a prophet, Jesus would not earn the title given straight off by Mark: Christ, Son of God. Theologian Paul Lakeland put the contrast exactly: the New Testament is not the *revelation* of Jesus, it is the revelation of *Jesus*. Jesus does not merely announce the Kingdom, in his life and death he realizes the Kingdom. When later Christians attach all the high Christological titles to Jesus of Nazareth, they are saying in effect that Jesus not only proclaimed God's Kingdom, he was — and is — the Lord who reigns. (The next chapter on Christology attempts to spell out in detail how these strange statements are to be understood.)

The notion that Jesus *delivers* news recasts him as prophet or teacher, and neither role fits what Christians have said about him from the very beginning. Prophets and teachers deliver news, truths about something "out there." The prophets tells us about God, the teacher presents a subject. The aim of prophet and teacher is that the listener and student should pay attention to the message, not the messenger. Mohammed is a prophet, the last of the prophets. The Qur'an is the message, it is the actual words of God. Allah commands Mohammed to "recite" as one might recite a memorized lesson learned. (The literal meaning of Qur'an is "the reciting.") Muslims revere Mohammed but do not worship him nor confuse him with the God who delivered the words of the Qur'an. They consider Christian exaltation of Jesus idolatrous.

Buddha is not a prophet, he is a teacher. He teaches us the Four Noble Truths, and the Noble Eightfold Path. The last thing the Buddha would wish is the veneration of himself. Buddhism — at least in its pure form — is not worship of Gautama, it is following the teaching. In contrast to prophet or teacher, Jesus says: "*I* am the way, and the truth, and the life" (Jn 14:6). What teacher would say "*I* am the truth!"; teachers want students of the subject "out there," not disciples. Wittgenstein is powerfully perceptive when he distinguishes Jesus from the teacher by focusing on the central importance of Resurrection:

> If he did not rise from the dead, then he decomposed in the grave like any other man. *He is dead and decomposed.* In that case he is a teacher like any other and can no longer *help*. . . . So we have to content ourselves with wisdom and speculation. . . . But if I am to be REALLY saved — what I need is certainty — not wisdom, dreams or speculation — and this certainty is faith. And faith is what is needed by my *heart*, not my speculative intelligence. For it is my soul, with its passions, as it were

with its flesh and blood, that has to be saved, not my abstract mind. Perhaps we can say: Only *love* can believe the Resurrection.[4]

Simply put, the Jesus of the Gospel is not a teacher-of-truths, he is himself the Truth. The truths of a teacher may outlive the teacher as the teachings of Plato have had continual life for two millennia. But the followers of Jesus did not proclaim the continual life of Jesus' teachings, they proclaimed the continuing life of the Teacher. For Christianity, as Wittgenstein states so powerfully, salvation must be through a living teacher, not by a *teaching* however noble and profound.

We have gone from baptism and washing to reading scripture, which is claimed to be the Word of God. "Word of God" is subject to the same misunderstanding we have seen about "truth." Jesus does not *deliver* the Word of God, he *is* the Word of God. Let us say, as Christians do say, that salvation is through the Word of God. A common "fundamentalist" reading is that the Bible contains truths and moral injunctions that I am to accept and follow. But that is not the New Testament lesson. Christians are not saved by following a Biblical rule book, they are saved by the suffering, death, and resurrection of Jesus. It is important—and should be recognized as curious—that the Jewish and Christian scriptures are "histories." If the point of Judaism and Christianity were obeying some set of divine commands, one might skip the history of the patriarchs in Genesis and most of the New Testament except for the Beatitudes. As N. T. Wright notes, although the Protestant reformers wanted to rely on scripture alone, they concentrated on "'timeless' doctrinal and ethical teaching" derived not from the Gospel story of Jesus but from the epistles.[5] The fact that we know next to nothing about the history of Plato does not detract a moment from his teaching. Nor is it proper to argue that all the miracles of Jesus up to and including Resurrection were just so much evidence that he knew what he was talking about. Salvation is not getting some "facts" straight, for example, about the seven days of creation or even following the ten commandments. Jesus makes that explicit when he counsels the young man who keeps the law to sell all he has and come follow him. Why is attachment to Jesus, selling all and following him, "salvation"? Wittgenstein has it right: "[I]t is my soul, with its passions, as were with its flesh and blood, that has to be saved." I want a "word" which saves my life. What *word* would be commensurate with my *life?* No doctrine however elevating, no set of moral commands however noble, can finally encompass or enclose the fullness of life as lived. The word that would be commensurate with my life must be another *life*. The Bible *as history* is set alongside *my history*.

Several years ago there was a squib in the *New Yorker* quoting the introduction to a newly published atlas. The text pointed out that there were different types of map projections. The familiar Mercator projection flattens the surfaces. Better, the text went on, is a globe because it replicates the actual shape. Even that, however, it concluded was a distortion because it wasn't "the right size." The *New Yorker*'s comment: "In that case, the hell with it!" The atlas author had wandered into an absurdity. A map is not a replica of the original; one penny does not *map* another. The whole point of a map is to distort by flattening or diminishing so that one can get some limited understanding of positions. Normal words are like maps: they abstract to create understanding. The word "cat" hardly grasps the slumbering, secret feline purring in the corner. I do not want a word (abstraction) for my life that is less than my life at the full. Any "word" for my life must be nothing smaller than another life. If my *life* is to be saved, "with its passions . . . with its flesh and blood," it will be saved in relation to another life. We call that relation "love": the meeting of life and life. Salvation, then, in the Christian meaning, demands Jesus alive, a life to my life. "[L]ove can believe the Resurrection." As in the anecdote of the map, a Jesus who teaches truths, who delivers the word of God, is too small. Jesus does not offer truths, a moral map for life, rather *he* is "the way, the truth, and the life."

In sum: having been reborn into history under the sign of the Cross, in the name of the Father, Son, and Holy Spirit, the next liturgical moment proclaims the good news that the Savior "was born, died, and was buried, descended into hell, and arose on the third day *according to the scriptures*." If the gospel is not read through the lens of birth-death-resurrection, it is not the good news of Jesus Christ. Scripture assures us that the Creator knows us in our singularity. In the life of Jesus, God shares our life in the fullness of life, the density of existence. In a paradoxical reversal of Jesus-as-teacher-of-truths as too small, incarnation says that God is not so large that He cannot be small: he empties himself to become human. Finally, Jesus is more than a fellow sufferer who can show compassion, who can know my life alongside his life, can sympathize with my suffering and death, be the world alongside my world. Jesus is more than compassionate: Jesus' life goes beyond death into God's life. If I live in Christ, if the relation is love, life to life, I live in God's life. There is salvation.


## Eucharist

The final action of the Christian liturgy from time immemorial has been the meal. Starting at least with the Emmaus story, Christians have known the presence of Jesus in the breaking of bread. As ritualized in the Eucharist, breaking bread becomes the climax of the liturgy and its theology. From baptism to Gospel to Eucharist, Christianity claims that history is good news because something definitive happened in the history of Jesus. The young Jewish girl at Yad Vashem comes to know that she lives in a special history because of what actually happened at the Holocaust; Christians come to know that they live in a special history because of what actually happened in the event of Jesus. As the Holocaust makes threat present in history, so Resurrection makes salvation present in history. History is eternally shadowed by the presence of Holocaust and Resurrection. The Holocaust is a "real presence" for the Jewish people; Jesus is a "real presence" for Christian believers. Christianity is not a speculative philosophy, a doctrine of edifying truths, or a set of righteous moral commands. All those worthy endeavors are finally too thin, too small, too abstract for the fullness of life. When Yahweh commands Ezekiel to eat the scroll of law, He is acting in character. If Jesus is present to us, life to life, something more than talk and teaching anchors and expresses that reality.

There is a famous exchange between Catholic Flannery O'Connor and ex-Catholic Mary McCarthy. McCarthy was generously opining that the Eucharist was an effective "symbol." O'Connor snapped back, "If it is only a symbol, the hell with it." Symbols are maps, they offer "lessons," and what O'Connor wanted was "the real thing," Jesus present, not referred to. The Eucharist as symbol makes the same mistake as reading the Gospel as the good news *reported* by Jesus. Jesus as reporter, prophet, or teacher devalues what happened from reality to symbol, from living Teacher to a teaching. Relating to Jesus present, Jesus as our history here and now, something more "bodily" than words and symbols is the proper mode.[6]

Having opted for real presence, for the fullness of the Teacher over the symbol of teachings, there is the danger of physicalizing the real presence. One will hear Catholics repeatedly insisting that in the Eucharist one has the "real body and blood of the Lord." Of course, it is a "miracle" because to all appearances the bread remains bread but is transubstantiated into Christ's body. The term "transubstantiation" is derived by Thomas Aquinas from Aristotle's natural science and metaphysics. As I will argue in the next chapter, I have grave reservations about the use of Aristotelian terminology in theology. However, if one is not misled by the quasi-scientific cast of "transubstantiation," Aquinas' formula can be helpful. Within Aristotelian science the notion of trans-substantiation is simple nonsense. For Aristotle, "substance" is what remains the same while "accidents" change. Socrates is the same substance even if he becomes bald. In the theological doctrine of transubstantiation, this common sense Aristotelian notion is completely subverted. It is the substance that changes while the accidents (the appearance of bread) remain. One should credit Aquinas not with *explaining* the Eucharist via transubstantiation but enshrining it in mystery as a process that makes no sense in Aristotelian science.

There is a use of "transubstantiation" that can be adopted to help explicate the Eucharist. Consider Eucharist within the initiatory moment of baptism, Eucharist as the culmination of the meaning of baptism. "Transubstantiation" says that the bread and wine of the sacrament are radically transformed from their natural state as everyday items of food into "the body and blood of Christ." The bread and wine become new "beings," new substances. All this sounds mysterious and miraculous, but one should recognize that something like a transformation of being has already happened at baptism. Transubstantiation in some sense happens to all humans in so far as they are twice born. Humans are *natural* beings who are transubstantiated into *historical* persons. As *historical* beings we do not lose our *natural* reality; I remain a biological male even as I assume the historical role or fashion of masculinity. Natural appearance as male remains while historical reality as masculine becomes my lived reality. As in the transubstantiation of the bread in which appearance remains while being changes, so my natural sex designation remains while my historical gender role defines my singular historical life.

If one accepts the notion that a second birth into history creates a new being, a new reality that is incommensurate with natural, biological being, we are compelled to ask about the character of this new form of existence. We know about natural biological life and its destinies. Biological life is guided by biological facts and necessities: eating, sleeping, procreating, aging, death. These natural suppositions do not apply to the new *historical* being. Assume, then, that Christians accept the lesson of baptism: that they are new beings born into history, a history marked by Cross and Resurrection. Baptism is "the first transubstantiation" in so far as the natural being, *homo sapiens,* is now living in a nonnatural reality: the reality of history. The Resurrection says that this transubstantiation into history is deeply grounded in the Creator God's reality. History is not a "dream," Stephen Daedalus' *nightmare.* The Eucharistic ceremony replicates the move from the being of nature to the being of history and then assures us that history is finally *sacred history.* The priest offers the bread "which earth has given and human hands have made. It will become for us the bread of life." The progression is from nature ("what earth has given") to history ("what human hands have made") to what God is doing in history: offering us the bread of life. The natural elements of bread and wine are made personal, become a person, Jesus Christ. If we feed on nature, we die; if we feed on the person who signs and saves history, we live.

The exposition offered here is primarily intended to draw discussion of the Eucharist away from a metaphysical miracle that happens to the piece of bread toward a re-insertion of Eucharist into the immersion in history which commences in baptism. There is "transubstantiation" from the beginning in the transformation from natural being to historical being. Eucharist reveals the final meaning and hope of this primary transubstantiation. For the Catholic, it is significant that Eucharist is the climax of the liturgy. Word, yes, for there is a teaching to be given about sacred history. But finally God is with us bodily, more intimately than teaching. Christians do not just learn lessons from Scripture, they are radically transformed into new beings. In nature I am sustained by the bread of the earth, in history I can only be sustained by sacred bread, by the Word of God: Jesus, whose resurrected body is the food that sustains my life in history.

I don't wish to go any further into the metaphysical intricacies of the Eucharist and real presence. I am content again to take the *via negativa* and indicate why symbolic presence won't finally work for Christian faith. The progression from baptism to scripture to Eucharist constitutes a ritual expression of human history. The ritual is deeper than an expression, it is an *enactment* of that history: emergence into sin and death, rebirth into the story of Jesus, recognition of the Word, sharing by anticipation in the banquet of eternal life.

## Extra ecclesiam nullus

Given this brief sketch of the specific Christian acts — washing, word, meal — I want to conclude this chapter with a general characterization of the idea of "Church." If successful, this characterization of Church will underline why Christian pursuit of peace, justice, and love is critically different from other religious or secular pursuits of these goals.

One might think of the Church as an organization like the Rotary Club. The Rotary Club is a voluntary association promoting a sense of comradery and sponsoring a variety of benevolent activities. There are individual clubs organized around towns and cities but linked nationally and internationally to Rotary Clubs throughout the world. Weekly meetings are held locally, and there is a strong obligation to attend. There is a meal with speeches and communal singing. The local, national, and international Rotary sponsor philanthropic work, such as the international Rotary Scholarships.

At a surface level, Rotary looks in many ways like the Church. There are those obligatory weekly fellowship meetings complete with meals and song. The organization is national and international so that one can participate in Rotary in Houston or Hong Kong. Finally, there is a benevolent purpose of promoting international understanding. The comparison may seem persuasive: the Church as a voluntary association promoting peace, justice, and love. After all, Churches are "voluntary philanthropic organizations" in American law. But for all the common perception and legal precision, the Church is not at all like Rotary and similar benevolent enterprises.

Consider as a secular contrast to Rotary the recently organized group using the acronym SNAP: Survivors Network of those Abused by Priests. The essential distinction between SNAP and Rotary is that the "survivors" do not *choose* their class designation. I may choose to belong to Rotary or not, I did not choose to have been someone abused — that just happened as a fact of my history. The given fact of being a "survivor" explains why the organization is called a "network." SNAP is not a group of disparate individuals united by the act of joining for a common purpose, it is a group of common sufferers pursuing disparate strategies of healing and reform. One of the purposes of SNAP is to get individuals who have been abused to acknowledge their history. Recognition and acknowledgment will help victims to escape the burden of their history of abuse. By making public the facts about abuse, SNAP hopes to rescue the abused from the denial and shame that often accompany the trauma of abuse. SNAP says to the abused: you are not alone, speak up, help us to obtain restitution and re-structure ecclesiastical governance to minimize the possibility of future abuse and concealment.

I offer SNAP because when one looks at the theological grounds of the Church, it is more like SNAP than like Rotary. I have even con-structed an acronym for Church: SNAPF, Survivors Network Accepting and Preaching Forgiveness. One should start any analysis of Church with something like "survivors" as a powerful reminder that the Church at the deepest level is not a voluntary association, a class of folks to which you could choose to belong. No, the existence of Church is first of all a state-ment about the condition we are already in. Like survivors of abuse, Chris-tians are what they are because something was done to them, not some-thing that they did. If the Church consists of survivors, survivors of what? Survivors of sin. Sin is the universal condition of human kind. Christians proclaim "original sin," a concept that I will explicate in chapter 8, but for now I ask the reader simply to accept this gloomy and not wholly unrealis-tic account of the human condition. Christ's action saves humankind from sin; his action is as universal in its scope as the universality of sinning. The problem is that while in one sense all have been "saved" and could be sur-vivors, not all recognize sin, salvation, and survival. Not all who have been sexually abused are prepared to recognize it as such, and not all have "sur-vived" the experience. Christians have a self-conscious recognition of sur-vival from sin as a reality from which they have been forgiven. Whether they can completely live up to the fact of forgiveness is a very different issue. That Christians or anyone can *survive* sin is due to what was done for us and to us in the life and death of him who was without sin.

Analogizing the Church to SNAP should seem odd because it means that all humans can be seen as part of the deep Church. I am prepared to stick with the notion of the Church universal—really universal—

amending the old slogan to *extra ecclesiam nullus:* outside the Church, nobody. As James Joyce said about Catholicism, "Here comes everybody!" The public, visible, "official" Church would be constituted by the "A" and "P" in my acronym: *Accepting* and *Preaching* Forgiveness. Presumably, the worshiping Church is made up of those who recognize that they are sinners, acknowledge forgiveness in Christ, and want to share the reality of forgiveness with all humans by preaching the Good News.

The visible Church is only a rough and ready location of the body of the saved. Many outside the visible Church live as "forgiven sinners" though they have never heard of Christ or even of the notion of "sin." One need not be a member of SNAP to have survived abuse. On the other hand, there are lots of folks in the visible Church from pew to papacy who (1) do not really think that they are sinners or (2) don't really accept (or want) forgiveness. The first group fails to understand the depth of sin. "Oh my, a few faults, of course. I mean we are all human after all. But on the whole — considering what *those* people do. Well . . ." The second group knows the depth of sin but either does not wish to escape or just can't believe there is a forgiveness deep enough for survival. There are the obvious cases of people who don't want to be forgiven because they are enjoying their "sin" too much, but a deeper case are those who cling to their sin as essential to self-worth. I recall dealing with a very bright student who for no obvious reason managed a spectacular flunk out of college. Why? When he was in high school, every high grade, every athletic trophy he obtained was a *family* affair. Failure was the one thing that would be his alone. Because everyone shares my virtues, sin anchors my self. As President Kennedy said after the disaster of the Bay of Pigs: "Victory has many fathers, defeat is an orphan." I may cherish my orphan self because defeat is mine alone. Finally, there are those like Ivan Karamazov who refuse the idea of forgiveness. He will not forgive the Russian landowner who sets his dogs on a child. There is no way that the suffering of the innocent can be "rescued." A God who would forgive the appalling evil of the human race is unworthy: Ivan believes there is a God, but he "turns in his ticket."

The old slogan *extra ecclesiam, nulla salus* — outside the Church, no salvation — is ambiguous. On the construction here offered "outside the Church, no salvation" would be an analytic statement: the Church is simply the class name for "survivors"; everyone has been saved whether or not that fact is recognized or accepted. Historically, the slogan was used to damn those who failed to partake in the public rituals or professions of the visible Church. With that understanding, there were many who were *not* saved. There is one possible interpretation for the latter, more restrictive notion that one will not be saved without public allegiance to the Church. Unless one comes to self-consciousness about sin-and-forgiveness, one will not have a *sense* of being saved. Lacking a sense of being saved, one may not recognize the forgiveness which has been offered. There is then the darkest possibility: one will self-consciously refuse to accept a God of forgiveness. Ivan Karamazov *demands* "No salvation!" and for that reason he is visited by the Devil during a descent into madness.

By categorizing the Church as survivors accepting forgiveness, one shifts the sense of Church preaching from setting forth laudable ideals like peace, justice, and love to bringing the other to self-consciousness of who he or she is (a sinner) and that forgiveness is at hand. The task is analogous to that of a psychiatrist bringing a patient from denial to self-recognition—a theme that I will explore at length in the conclusion of this book. In abuse cases, we allow the individual to admit the abuse and deal with it at the conscious level. In the Church case it is reversed, over-coming the denial that one is an abuser—a sinner in the myriad daily ways we abuse love and human dignity—and then finding a way of forgiveness out of the cycle of abuse.

Viewing the Church as the universal class of survivors explains why I choose "network" in the acronym. It is obvious that as survivors (of abuse or sin) commonality is created *ab extra*. We are all in the lifeboat together after the wreck. "Network" in the SNAP case suggests that we are stitched together from those who consciously acknowledge and those who suppress or deny. Unlike Rotary, which approaches us through our ideals and benevolent urges, SNAP and SNAPF approach us from the stand-point of our deeper, darker, wounded selves. This makes all the difference in the kind of peace, justice, and love pursued and hoped for. Christian peace is *already given*. For the Christian, peace is not a human ideal that may be realized if we work hard enough, it is recognizing a condition already established. Jesus both announces and realizes the kingdom of God. If we accept our condition as sinners forgiven, peace emerges as our ac-complished state. Of course, for the reasons suggested above, humans are loath to accept sin and forgiveness of sin, so we live in a world of war and injustice. But there is a profound difference between peace as human idealism and peace as the given, but repressed, condition of mankind under God.

Christians exist first as sinners, and they emerge only as *forgiven* sinners. As forgiven sinners the Christian's view of the other, of all others, is inclusive: they too are, after all, sinners and have been forgiven if they could come to know such. As forgiven *sinners* Christians do not face the world from a position of superiority. The World Bank grants loans to impoverished countries on the condition that they reform their social, political, and economic systems. Grand schemes of social amelioration, communism, for example, often end by forcible "reeducation" of the "impoverished" so that they can permanently emerge from their false ideologies into a just society and be deserving of the brave new order. Christians do not demand forced "reeducation," there are no "undeserving poor." Christians are themselves undeserving; they give from deep gratitude because in their sinfulness they have received undeserved love and forgiveness.

## From Liturgy to the World-Play

The reason for initiating a discussion of the voice of Christianity with liturgy is that liturgy is the Church's fundamental voice. This is especially true of Catholicism in contrast to Protestant denominations where preaching tends to dominate over sacrament. As stated at the beginning of this chapter, Christians apparently want to say something more about peace, love, and justice than secular morality deems either necessary or useful. This "more" is expressed in the common liturgical gestures that Christians have practiced from the very beginning. Faith and liturgy are interdependent. *What* is believed is expressed uniquely in the act of worship. While it is true that we can learn much about the *what* of belief by the words and formularies of prayer and worship, one can still miss *what* is believed if the ritual is carried forward in the wrong voice—if one places liturgy in the wrong "language game," such as doctrinal instruction or moral exhortation.

The voice of the liturgy is highly complex. Consider the following comment by theologian David Ford about Eucharistic language:

> Eucharistic language embraces many genres: praise, lament, confession, exclamation, narrative, proclamation, petition and all the other genres of the Bible. It also unites the oral and written, escaping many of the restrictions of both. Above all, it is a language which is performed, and resists discursive overviews in a somewhat similar way to good drama.[7]

Ford is correct in pointing to the *drama* of the liturgy. Christianity resists "discursive overview," a set of theological truths or moral commands, it instead invites participation in the drama of history where history is the World-Play of a divine Author. The next two chapters seek to explicate this drama.

CHAPTER THREE

# Author! Author!

---

*All the world's a stage,*
*And all the men and women merely players*

Shakespeare, *As You Like It*

In the previous chapter I approached Christian belief through its primary expression: the liturgy of baptism, Gospel, and Eucharist. In the next two chapters, I want to move to the theology that grounds the liturgy, though in another sense theology is also derived from the gestures of liturgy. In traditional terms, these chapters offer a Christology: an analysis of the meaning of the Church's proclamation about the historical Jesus and the rationale for the "odd" practices of Church liturgy. The Christology outlined is a *theo*logy since the Christ I describe is the one proclaimed by the Church as "son of God"—something more than a moral exemplar or even a prophet of the most high. Liturgy as *worship* only makes sense if the focus of the action is on what-is-worthy-of-worship: God, Son of God— and not any old god at that! On the basis of the *what* of Christological theology, I will in the second part of the book proceed to *how* Christ is conveyed in the voice of the Church.

## Theological Voice

Because I will be presenting a theological Christology, I reiterate earlier comments about the theological *voice*. Much elegant theological argument can remain in a state of mental suspended animation. How did we get into this thicket of theological talk? Just *what* are we talking about? Most readers of theology are, I would assume, believers of some sort. They are accustomed to hearing talk of "grace" and "salvation" and "the Holy Spirit." I am not certain, however, that the average church attendee has much understanding of the deep meanings of these terms. This is what we say in church, but what does it all mean? For all that I would like to speak to the nonspecialist, I also want to address professional theologians. I want to find the "cash value" of technical theology. *"Perichoresis"* and "transubstantiation" are elegant refinements that are more like to dazzle with erudition than enliven the heart. The presence of technical vocabulary when accompanied by the structuring of arguments characteristic of traditional scholasticism suggests the voice of a deductive philosophy or a special sort of elevated, supernatural "science." I believe that the voice of strict philosophy is seriously misleading as a background for theology — certainly for Christian theology.

I offer an example of how choice of philosophical terminology can be misleading. In the very first section of the *Summa Theologica,* first question, second article, Thomas asks "Whether Sacred Doctrine is a *scientia?*" *Scientia* is a term that seems bound to be translated as "science" — and so it is in the standard translations.[1] Thomas concludes that sacred doctrine is indeed a *scientia*. Read carefully, Thomas's theological *scientia* depends on revelation, which is not at all how moderns think of science. "Science" as the term is used today in, for example, "natural science" is impersonal, something that any neutral, rational person should be able to grasp. If Christianity were that sort of science, it would be a philosophy of sorts along with Cartesianism or Kantianism. I do not believe that Christianity is any such endeavor. Aquinas's use of "science" may be acceptable if one understands his special meaning of a *theological* science, but to modern ears theological *science* sounds like a contradiction. Thus, I prefer to leave "science" to the physicists while seeking a different, if no less revealing (I hope *more* revealing) background terminology for theology.

There are historical reasons that Aquinas uses such terminology. In so far as he takes Aristotle as "the philosopher," he is saddled with two problems. Aristotle's philosophic manner was *expository* and his terminology was "scientific." Expository argument assumes a certain neutrality in the reader being instructed. Since I don't know much of anything about Antarctica, I accept with relative passivity the explorer's exposition about the subject. Aristotle, an excellent natural scientist, was a model for expository presentation. Plato, by contrast, (particularly in the early dialogues) embeds his arguments in some existential crisis of the interlocutors. Euthyphro in the dialogue by that name is rushing off to accuse his father of murder. The dialogue is framed by Euthyphro's rash life decision. My assumption is that Christian teaching occurs within a life engagement or crisis, and cannot be well appropriated by exposition.

Concomitant with expository style was the adoption by Aquinas of what for lack of a better term I would call "scientific" terminology. Aristotle's philosophy is dominated by the schema of the four causes. Given Aristotle's causal language, a Christian philosopher-theologian like Thomas would naturally be tempted to discuss the biblical doctrine of Creation as a causal process and God as *causa sui,* self-caused. Of course, Thomas will assert that the causal process of Creation is not like any other causal process and that God is not "cause" in any ordinary sense.

"Cause" was used by Aristotle and Aquinas in the broadest analogical manner, but, as it has filtered down through the rise of modern science, "cause" has taken on a restricted sense. Thus, God as *causa sui* risks misreading the doctrine of Creation in some quasi-scientific mode. It is risk that has not been avoided. I want to offer an alternative terminology from that of "cause" and "science." I will adopt terms from the structures and practices of *art,* by which I mean the fine arts. Reading Christian theology from our understandings of art offers only an analogy to divine action, but reading theology from categories of science is no less an analogy. I will talk analogically about God as an author, but God as first cause is no less an analogy. My contention is that, given present understandings and overtones of terminology, the science analogy is more prone to mislead than that of art. For instance, science demands "proof," but I think that there is no transferable sense of proof into the truths of Christianity. I am not at all trying to "prove" the truth of Christianity by changing the analogical model. I think that the notion of proof is a scientific import into religion that should be banned at the border. Nevertheless, though science may be banished, truth is a paramount issue in my discussion. Shifting analogies away from science to art does not constitute an abandonment of truth for Christianity. To discover the truth of Christianity requires a different modality of truth which I hope to explicate and justify.

The ultimate aim of this revisionary Christology—sketchy as it may be—is to advance the problem of the entire book: what is the proper voice of the Church? My argument is that the Church is not an accidental by-product of the shape and meaning of Christ's life. It is good fortune that Plato recorded Socrates' philosophical musings, but there was nothing in the latter's inquisitive career that demanded a follower. In the case of Jesus, to understand him as Christ is to become Church. Transformed by Christ, the Church speaks to the world in a unique voice; it speaks in a voice that could only arise as a result of Christ's presence and action in the world.

## Art as Background

If abandoning theological science is not abandoning truth, it is necessary to consider, however briefly, various modes of truth. As suggested, "truth" in the modern world seems to be best established by the modalities of natural science. The Galileo case is an emblem of the superiority of scientific truth over supposed religious truth. What are the assumptions that seem to make scientific truth so superior and secure? In the realm of science, truth is universal, intended to be open to any observer and rational thinker. Newton's theory of gravitation is not something only Newton could know or something only appreciated by seventeenth-century English savants. There is an ascetic transcendence of personal self and historical placement in the processes and theories of science. The objective observer can know objective truth. Some modern philosophers of science deny that such transcendence is possible; all science is finally colored by the personal position of the investigator: man, woman, liberal, conservative, and so on. However that may be at some deep, deep level, the simple fact is that scientists at least play the game of impersonality. Ascetic science may be as metaphysically impossible as ascetic sainthood, but it is the aspiration of the enterprise.

In contrast to the impersonal game of science, there is the intensely personal attribution of art. When we appraise a work of art we contact the personal vision of a particular artist. The work is Mozart or Rembrandt or Shakespeare and none other. So convinced are we of the specific personal vision of the artist that when we do not have a name for ascription we attach a definite description: the Master of the Fiesole Epiphany, the Eleusis painter. Just as some modern philosophers of science have suggested that there is something finally (or fatally) personal in scientific endeavor, so former commentators on art like Vasari thought that art proceeded in the manner of science, plotting out new general truths about reality. Vasari waxes eloquent about the "discovery" of perspective in Renaissance painting as if perspective was a forward looking revelation of truth from which subsequent painters would, of course, build. In short, modern philosophers have suggested that science is more like (personal) art, and Vasari suggests that art is more like (impersonal) science.

I have no intention of entering into these complex quarrels about science and art. The views that I am working with—impersonal science, personal art—have enough significant warrant and currency to justify my account. I give a special designation to the personal in art: *signatured* truth.[2] There could be sophisticated quarrels about the notion of signatured truth. If one is obsessed with the notion that only impersonal science can deliver truth, then signatured (personal) truth is nonsense, a contradiction like a round square. On this issue, I am not prepared to offer any quarter to the critic. It seems clear that Shakespeare reveals truth about the human condition. It is also clear that this truth is specially attached to his vision. His world is the general human world, even while it is also the Shakespearean world. Harold Bloom talks about Shakespeare as "the inventor of the human."[3] Bloom does not say that Shakespeare invented idiosyncratic Shakespearesque characters, he invented *the* human for all that Hamlet and the rest are Shakespeare's unique creations. Finally, *the* human that Shakespeare invents is not some generality like "rational animal," it is the human as a dazzling array of particulars. We learn that we are human particulars, unique persons, somewhere among the array of Romeos and Rosalinds that cascade from his creative genius.

So much for an initial and, I believe, plausible indication of the special capacity of art: the capacity to present signatured truth. My contention is that Christianity is best understood under the idea of signatured truth: God as author and artist, God as inventor of the human. To get to the special Christian sense of God as signaturing author I need, however, to offer a transition from art to religion. I begin with an astute observation from Henry James about art and life.

## Art and Life

In the preface to his novel *The Spoils of Poynton*, Henry James describes how he came across the "germ" from which he constructed his novel. At a London social occasion, he overheard a story about a messy inheritance. It presented a set of complications from which he formed the plot. As the conversation continued, however, the actual events were quite different from James' narrative. It led him to reflect on the difference between life and art:

> Life being all inclusion and confusion, and art being all discrimination and selection, the latter in search of the hard latent *value* with which it is concerned . . . the artist finds in his tiny nugget washed clean from awkward accretions . . . the very stuff for a clear affirmation. . . . At the same time, it amuses him again and again to note how, beyond the first step in the actual case . . . life persistently blunders and deviates. . . . The reason, of course, is that life has no direct sense of the subject and is capable, luckily for us, of nothing but splendid waste.[4]

Much as we value art and its signatured truth the fact is that art is *signatured,* encompassed and ordered by the perceptive eye of a Henry James. *Life* finally escapes the named artist's clarified vision and is capable "of nothing but splendid waste."

Reflection on something like James' distinction between art and life has been a powerful motif in the development of many significant strands of modern art. Various artists in various media have attempted to jump the gap between Jamesian art and the fullness of life, creating a sort of anti-art art or, if one prefers, an art that transcends art. One need only turn to the "grandada" of modern art, Marcel Duchamp, to prove the point. The beginning of a radical turn in the arts can be dated to the New York Independents show of 1917. Duchamp, who was already notorious because of his cubist *Nude Descending a Staircase,* purchased a urinal at a plumbing supply house and submitted it to the show under the title *Fountain.* It was the first of what Duchamp called *objet trouvé,* found objects. Duchamp did not shape or craft the object, he simply found it, gave it a title, and declared it a "work of art." Much of the modern art scene since has been Duchampian. Pop, minimalist, conceptualist, installation, and performance art are often "non-arty," deliberately crude, awkward, often erotic. Why? A critic summing up several of these trends points out that these efforts are a "drive to wrench art from its normal subject matter and materials so as to bring it closer to the chaotic vitality of everyday life."[5] Post-Duchampian art seeks to transcend art toward "the chaotic vitality of everyday life," to give the artistic expression of life as "splendid waste." Depending on one's taste, it is not always clear whether such "avant garde" works transcend or trash art, but either way there is a message!

I accept James's distinction between art and life. We certainly learn about human life from great artists, but there is a sense in which real life never quite shapes up to some orderly plot. If you decide to live your life as a work of art you may end up like Emma Bovary trapped in a romance novel or Don Quixote tilting at windmills. I think we need to be constantly reminded that life goes beyond art into "splendid waste" or "chaotic vitality." And the lesson of life is not always splendid. Jean Améry, a concentration camp survivor bitterly sums up the failure of art. "No bridge led from death in Auschwitz to *Death in Venice*."[6] The sensitive and tragic prose of Thomas Mann's novella about death in Venice fails to reach obscene death in Auschwitz. Life may not be *splendid* waste.

I make this distinction between art and life, between order and waste or chaos—splendid, vital, or obscene as it may be—because one must proceed on into life to understand Christian faith. There is no artistic bridge from death in Auschwitz. Humans may signature art, they cannot signature life. Life escapes us in manifold desires and manifest death. The pop artist takes something at hand—a urinal, a snow shovel, a pile of rocks, her dirty breakfast dishes—and signatures it, transubstantiating it into the realm of art. But it is a trick. The pop artist does not signature life, he calls attention to the *irony* of art (or irony of life) by the signature, to the fact that life in its chaos *cannot* be signatured. Duchamp, the supreme ironist of art, did not sign the urinal with his own name but, as was his universal custom, with a pseudonym. Duchamp's preferred "name" was Rrose Selavy derived from the French *arroser c'est la vie:* a sprinkling of life. *C'est la vie* cannot be signatured!

The shock of Christianity is the proclamation that there is one who *signatures life itself,* one who can appropriate chaos, waste, misery, sin, and death. Jesus says, "I am the way, the truth, and the life." Using James' distinction between art and life, one can understand Oscar Wilde's characterization of Jesus as the *supreme* artist.

To the artist, expression is the only mode under which he can conceive life at all. To him what is dumb is dead, but to Christ it was not so. With a width and wonder of imagination that fills one almost with awe, he took the entire world of the inarticulate, the voiceless world of pain, as his kingdom, and made of himself its eternal mouthpiece. Those of whom I have spoken, who are dumb under oppression and "whose silence is heard only of God" he chose as his brothers. He sought to become eyes to the blind, ears to the deaf, and a cry on the lips of those whose tongue had been tied.[7]

The claim that Jesus signatures life itself, that he is the supreme artist, is extravagant but has the ring of a genuine Christian claim. Wallace Stevens called poetry "the supreme fiction." For the Christian, the life of Jesus Christ is the supreme fiction of the supreme artist—except that this *supreme* fiction transcends *mere* fiction. Given this sense of art and life, I want then to offer an elaborated analogy relating Christianity to the ways of art—with the fundamental proviso that we are talking about *supreme* art and the *supreme* artist; not the artist of fiction, the artist of form and expression, but the artist of reality, the one who signatures life in all its fullness.

## The Supreme Shakespeare

Imagine God as the Supreme Shakespeare.[8] The Supreme Shakespeare will incorporate not only the special genius of the actual Shakespeare, but aspects of Chekhov and Pirandello. Why these two will be explained as the story develops. The historic William Shakespeare is the creator of the characters in his plays. Let us assume that he creates these characters because he loves to see them strut and fret their hour upon the stage. He is not only enchanted by the actions of his characters, in some profound sense he comes to love them—*all* of them. He loves his Macbeths and Iagos as he loves his Cordelias and Katherines. Why does he love them? What does he love in them despite their villainies or foolishness? He loves their sense of genuine *life*. Shakespeare is a great author because his characters are more than manikins for a didactic purpose. No, in their aspirations and passions, their buffoonery and heroism, they express an energy which is unique, the very spark of life. Harold Bloom comments that in the best of Shakespeare's plays characters like Hamlet and Falstaff seem to expand beyond the confines of the play, taking on a reality that the drama itself cannot quite contain.

What can we infer about William Shakespeare in the light of his great characters, his Lears and Juliets? It would seem necessary that one who can create such life, character, and persona must himself have life, character, and persona. He may not live the dissolute life of Falstaff, but he knows that life deep in his heart, it is what makes him capable of bringing Falstaff forth in all his glorious foolery. If that is how it is with William Shakespeare, what should we assume about the Supreme Shakespeare? In my analogy He is the author of life for all the *real* personae in the historical World-Play. The life He creates is not merely biological existence, it is the unique energy of particular persons just as the actual Shakespeare limns the unique and differing characters of Richard II and Richard III. Whereas Bloom sees Falstaff expanding beyond the play, for the Supreme Shakespeare expanding personal vitality is potential in each and every character, in every human being. Like any good author, the Supreme Shakespeare does not create puppets. The Supreme authors his creations in their vital reality and He loves them as William Shakespeare can be said to love all his characters.

What is the special value in regarding God as the Supreme Shakespeare? Considering creation under the analogy of authorship suggests what can be misleading in the traditional language of God as cause. Do we really want to describe William Shakespeare as the cause of his characters? To be sure, in some sense he is a cause, but the notion of cause carries an aura of generality, of *types* of characters rather than live *individuals*. In the language of cause, the same cause results in the same effects. This kind of DNA causes this kind of being; horse DNA produces horses. The relation is from generality (horse DNA) to generality (horses). The point of *authorship* is that the signaturing author creates signatured characters. The connection is not universal and general, but individual, particular, and personal. As discussed in the earlier sketch of biblical creation, the relation of Creator God to the world is not primarily to forms but to the particular. Creation is more like a personal conversation than an exercise in divine pottery. In turn, Shakespeare, the playwright, and the Creator make personal interaction the heart of the play.

Authorship removes a temptation toward causal necessity in creation. Nothing compels William Shakespeare to create his characters; he creates them freely as he imagines them in the exuberance of their lives. It seems best to describe the relation between Shakespeare (William or Supreme) and his characters as stemming from love and fascination with the hurly-burly of life that the characters present. An author who is predetermined by some moralistic conviction, a Marxist scenario, or sheer fancy will not create *live* characters but tokens. Since the author is not predetermined by a didactic philosophy, so too the characters created are not determined. The characters are invested with an inner spontaneity, a freedom that identifies them as rounded life, not abstractions. It is more than mere hyperbole when a human author says that a character in his drama took on in the writing a "life of her own." For all that he is Shakespeare's creation, Macbeth is just that troubled soul, uniquely Macbeth, not an empty shell, a stock villain at whom the audience can hiss and boo.

Imagine, then, that the structure of creation is the structure of authorship as the Supreme Shakespeare might carry it forward. The Supreme's sheer delight in all those individual, idiosyncratic, living characters is the root of His creative action. He imbues these characters with liveliness because He is himself supremely alive in His creativity and in the love that He lavishes on the characters of the World-Play. Suppose now that William Shakespeare comes to think how wonderful it would be to have a tankard of ale with Falstaff. He loves the character he has created so much that he wants that love to be real and mutual. Charming thought, but fancy only; it is the Pygmalion temptation. The Supreme Shakespeare, however, is not dealing with fancy. The Supreme creates realities who actually live upon the historic stage of the World-Play. The persons in the World-Play, because they are characters busy playing their parts, do not know that they are creations any more than Macbeth in *Macbeth* is meditating about Shakespeare. If the characters in the World-Play do not come to know the Supreme Shakespeare, then His love cannot be fully realized. Because he loves his real creations, He wants to be "be real" with them. He wants them to know His love, which means they must come to know Him. The Supreme wishes to fulfill the mutuality that is the core of love. He wants a real tankard of ale with the real Falstaff.

The Supreme Shakespeare does not *need* the love of His creatures. As the author, the fount of love and life, He is complete, all in all. He would be the same Author whether He created or not. William Shakespeare would have been the same William Shakespeare, the same "being" if he never wrote a single play, just as he remained the selfsame William Shakespeare when he gave up writing and retired to Stratford-on-Avon. He does not need some relation to this or that character whatever his fancy in that regard. His head is full of characters, but they are *only* characters and he can easily turn away from one who seems tiresome to some more entrancing creation. The Supreme Shakespeare having created the World-Play is more deeply involved because his "characters" are not imaginings but real. While He does not *need* mutuality with His characters, failing to reveal His reality once they come to real existence frustrates the love that created them in the first place. It also keeps the characters in a state of unreality and delusion: they do not know that they are authored and so believe falsely that they are self-authoring. The Supreme Shakespeare seeks a real relation with His real characters. For Him to accomplish this end—or for us to describe how it is done—is anything but simple.

## Pirandello and "Metaphysics"

At this point my tale of the Supreme Shakespeare takes on a Pirandellian air. Pirandello's best known play is called *Six Characters in Search of an Author*. It is a "metaphysical" drama in which a play rehearsal is interrupted by a set of characters who burst into the theater claiming to be "real," not actors. They are in search of an author who can explain the painful "plot" in which they are enmeshed. Given the Supreme Shakespeare's desire to share his love with his characters he wants to write a World-Play in which the characters—His creations—are in search of the Author. But revealing that there is an Author of the World-Play is no simple task.

Suppose that a playwright writes a play in which some character in the play tells the other characters that they are creations of an author. If the characters accept this startling revelation, the play is ruined. Macbeth disappears to be replaced by "Macbeth." "Oh, it was only a play!" In ordinary drama, authorial revelation creates the play within a play. In the play *Noises Off*, the curtain opens on what appears to be a dopey sex farce. Five minutes into the performance a voice is heard from the audience. It is the director of the "play" we have been watching. We realize that we have not been seeing the play, but a play about a play. The play within the play is the real farce. (There is a significant danger that a divine playwright who reveals his authorial hand will turn the World-Play into farce.)

If the Supreme Shakespeare wants to solve the dilemma of loving His creatures in mutual intimacy, He has no other choice than to somehow insinuate Himself into His own World-Play. He can't just send a third-party messenger, a prophet who bursts on the scene to announce "it's only a play!" as might happen with Pirandello. Even if the characters were to believe the messenger, the Supreme Shakespeare's wish to *love* his characters would be placed in jeopardy. As numerous fairy tales have pointed out, if the king wishes to assure himself of the humble maiden's love, he cannot arrive in superior splendor. As king he may gain the maiden's awe and gratitude, but will he be loved as himself? Thus, in the tale, the king arrives in disguise. There is something of that in the Christian story of Incarnation, except that Jesus cannot be regarded as God-in-disguise. The plot is more complex. The author-in-the-play must be on the one hand humble and ordinary, and yet be recognized in that very humbleness as king. Humility is not God's disguise, it is somehow His reality; his humility is his kingship. The author-in-the-play must be "ordinary" and yet be accepted as "author."[9]


## Chekhov and Sin

The Supreme Shakespeare writes Himself into the World-Play, the author himself is in the play as an "ordinary" character. Entering the play remains a monumental paradox: He needs to enter the play as author without ruining the play. How is that possible? There is an absolute gap in reality between being creative author and being a created character such that putting the author *in* the play seems to fatally shift the reality of the drama in progress.

In the World-Play, however, there are *two* problems of reality. On the one hand there is the problem of *ontological* reality. How does the author appear *in* the play without ruining the play, turning it into "only a play," a fiction of the (divine) author. But there is a second reality problem: the *spiritual* reality of the characters in the play. If the entrance of the author threatens to reduce the ontological reality of the play to illusion, the failure of the characters to see themselves as authored leads them into a life of spiritual illusion. Being ignorant of the fact that they are authored, the characters believe that they are their own authors. They think that they self-determine themselves. Macbeth thinks that he has written his own script. Being fully *self*-determined is, of course, something that only the Supreme Shakespeare can manage; he is the one and only Author. Believing that they are self-determining, the characters in the World-Play become fatally "overdetermined"; they become the authors of themselves as "fictions." The World-Play proceeds with a cast of humans acting as if they were each their own author—which is, after all, the definition of a god. Humans playing god are bound for disaster. The human characters come to inhabit their lives with a guardedness and rigidity, which mask the density and openness of life. The original meaning of *persona* is "mask": the mask worn by actors in the ancient theater. In the theater, the real human being is masked. In short, as a merely *human* story, the World-Play is "unreal," a masquerade, a clash of personal fictions.

Etienne Gilson , citing the philosopher McTaggart, raised the question whether Dickens' Mrs. Gamp is "real."[10] He comments that "Mrs Gamp and her dram of whiskey . . . are to all [Dickens'] readers incomparably more 'real' than hundreds of people whose actual existence we hold as absolutely certain simply because we happen to meet them on the street." Mrs. Gamp is more real than passers-by because she has a "wonderful self-identity and perfect internal homogeneity." One of the reasons we are fascinated with fiction is that the characters have this flawless self-identity. They are Henry James' good fiction and quite unlike the "splendid waste" that he identifies as actual life. The spiritual malaise of the World-Play is that the characters aspire to be fictional, to have the sort of self-identity that makes Mrs. Gamp "real." But the Supreme Shakespeare's characters are not fictional characters, they exist in the realm beyond art, in *life*. By aspiring to the self-determination and flawless self-identity of fictional characters, human beings close in upon themselves. Jean-Paul Sartre's mordant analysis of human existence posits the human self in just such inescapable fiction, a form of self-deception that he labels "bad faith." From the standpoint of the Supreme Shakespeare, when His characters think that they are self-authoring, they live falsely, they exist in bad faith, they live "as false gods." The Supreme's wish and will is that they should live in good faith, in the truth of the Author. Humans are to live not as gods, but as humans!

If Pirandello writes the ontological script, Chekhov writes the spiritual script. Confined to some remote country house, Chekhov's *dramatis personae* exist within an atmosphere of inescapable tension. Unlike Shakespeare's dramas where mighty kingdoms are at play, in Chekhov the conflicts are intimate, understated, and repressed. The heart of conflict comes from the overdetermined, fixed nature of the characters who play off one another, unable to understand or act upon the lives and desires of the others. In a Chekhov play the characters continually miss connections within the stifling intimacy of the assemblage. Because they are so locked into their character, life and vitality slip away. In *Ivanov,* the first of Chekhov's plays, when the curtain rises we find one of the female characters idling her time at the piano. Her opening line virtually defines the theme of all Chekhov's plays: "I'm so bored." Boredom reigns when life dies and one reiterates a tired routine. The conflicts, for all that they are modest, are nonetheless deadly in the lives of the protagonists. Vanya is as broken in the end as if, like Macbeth, his bloody head were carried in on a pike.

The Chekhovian moment in my analogy of the Supreme Shakespeare depicts the course of the World-Play proceeding in irresolvable tension and conflict because of overdetermination. The self-determined character believes that he is his own "cause": like a god he is *causa sui.* Acting as *causa sui* is the source of ruin *in* the play and can be ruinous to the *performance* of the play. I saw a performance of *Uncle Vanya* starring the distinguished British actors Derek Jacobi (Vanya) and Roger Rees (Dr. Astrov). Despite—or because of—the presence of the two superb actors, the overall performance was a disaster. The problem was that the rest of the cast had been recruited from actors in soap operas, who simply could not respond to the powerful performance of the leads. It is absolutely essential for the successful performance of Chekhov that every character from lead to walk-on perform at the same level. Ensemble performance is the only way to play Chekhov. Chekhov's plays cannot work as what show business calls a "star turn." A "star turn" disaster can also describe the action *in* a Chekhov play. In *The Sea Gull,* Madame Arkadina, a famous actress, is spending a holiday in the country. Her son, Konstantin, has written a play, which she views with a certain comic indulgence. Playing the star actress, Madame Arkadina bypasses the passion that drives Konstantin. In the "real life" of the play, they do not act as an *ensemble* or, better, one could say that they act as an ensemble of destruction. Madame Arkadina's failure to acknowledge the other because of her own self-absorption becomes the root of the tragedy that ensues.

The Supreme Shakespeare did not create his characters to act out a Chekhovian script where self-determining protagonists fail to act lovingly with others. True, the Supreme's characters are radically particular but they are all bathed equally in His love and are meant to live in the ensemble of that love. The Supreme Shakespeare loves *all* his characters. Presumably neither William Shakespeare nor the Supreme loves the villainy of Iago, but they cannot help loving his sheer vitality. We are all more attracted to the lively rogue than the pedantic prude. Villainy is itself a product of overdetermination, of self-authoring. It arises from the need to defend the (false) self against the enemy whether it be armies in the field or the subtle assaults on self-esteem that enervate the characters in Chekhov. Madame Arkadina is the witless "villain" of *The Sea Gull.* Othello is no villain and yet he is brought to destruction by his own overplayed sense of honor. Even the "best" of human roles from lover to saint can be false and overdetermined if we are acting out some *idée fixe,* some predetermined view of lover or saint that is closed to the shocks and openness of life.

From the standpoint of the Author, the World-Play is suffused with love and open to life in a manner that the characters in the play fail to perceive. If the non-communicating, quarrelsome, murderous humans in the play could realize that they are all the work of a single author who intended them to live *life,* not fiction, peace would reign. This is often stated in secular terms by urging us to realize that we are all part of the "human family." But like peace, love, and justice, the assessment of "human family" differs in Christianity from that appeal in various secular humanisms. *Humanly* stated, appeal to "family" is an idealistic piety. Family quarrels have been the deepest stuff of tragedy from the *Agammenon* to *Hamlet* to *Uncle Vanya*. It is the *dys*functional family that is the heart of tragedy and the ongoing story of humanity. It is no good preaching "family values" to the collection of Chekhovian characters that we are. The World-Play played as *human* family is bound toward tragedy. Played as God's family, it is "comedy." I do not mean "comedy" as a metaphysical farce—the passion of the play as mere illusion. The Author writes the World-Play as a comedy not as humorous, but as *comity,* as loving resolution. In Shakespearean comedy, Act V resolves all the lovers' quarrels, usurpations, and menaces, which seemed so tragically bound in Act III. When the characters come to know themselves in the life and love of the other, the potential for tragedy is resolved. The World-Play is the Supreme Shakespeare's *divina commedia.*

## Saving the Play

The Supreme Shakespeare wants to love his characters and by so doing change their status from self-determining to Author-determined. They are to realize that they are all and each the result of His loving, free creation. Realizing that they are authored within the divine comedy solves the tensions of the Chekhovian assemblage of humanity. To effect this change in the characters from self-authored to authored, to solve the anxieties emerging in Act III, the Supreme Shakespeare inserts Himself into the World-Play. If the author enters the play as the author of the play he will change the *reality* of the play. In the ordinary case, the entrance of the author changes the ontological reality of the play. The characters who took themselves seriously—or whom the audience took seriously—are seen as less-than-serious, as fictions over whom we need not weep or wail. The Supreme Shakespeare cannot wish to reduce the World-Play and its characters to illusion. He wants a real tankard of ale with a real Falstaff. There must then be a radical difference between a stage play when the author shows up in the play and how this occurs in the World-Play. In a Pirandellian play, the entrance of the author throws all the characters into the fictional category. In the theological case at hand, the Supreme Shakespeare seeks just the reverse. By entering the World-Play, the Author moves the characters from fiction into life.

The Supreme Shakespeare must on the one hand maintain the ontological reality of the created characters authored while at the same time transforming their spiritual reality from self-determining to authored. One obvious way to affirm the ontological reality of the characters created is for the Author to enter the ontological reality of the characters in the World-Play. He does not stand above and outside, a *deus-auctor ex machina,* who simply descends on the scene to tidy up some impossible plot complication. Coming on stage in that manner would reduce the characters in the play to puppets of the author's imagination or the *deus'* manipulative solution. If the Supreme Shakespeare is to maintain the reality of the characters, the reality of the World-Play, He must be fully in and of the world. That means that He must have normal human existence, an existence that is unique and historical, flesh and blood. Being unique and historical, flesh and blood, is the fundamental reality of characters in the World-Play. If the Author is to change the reality of the play from self-determining to authored, He must accomplish this fact *within* actual history, not by some transcendent metaphysical reversal from outside.

The Supreme Shakespeare's strategy differs radically from a variety of deep spiritual philosophies that posit reality *beyond* the illusions of everyday existence. "Salvation" in such spiritualities occurs when we come to recognize the vanity and emptiness of this life in contrast to an eternal reality "above." This dichotomy between God as real and the world as illusion is not the biblical view. The biblical doctrine of Creation rejects the model of reality (God) vs. appearance (world). The relation is between God as uncreated reality and the world as created reality. To be sure, the world depends for its reality on God's gift, but the fact of origin does not diminish creation to a phantasm. In so far as my dramatic scenario is an analogy to Christian theology, the author-in-the-play is the creator of reality in created reality. *Reality* applies both to Author and the World-Play into which the author enters. When the Author enters the play, he does not diminish the reality of the play as such; rather, he shows that the reality present is a gift, not self-grounded.

The Christian strategy as I am analogizing it to the work of the Supreme Shakespeare calls for salvation *within* the play. The work of the author-character must be effected within the on-going course of the action. The author-character does not preach a message to the characters that they are only characters, fictions of the Author for whom he speaks; he must transform them as characters who remain within the play. He must be more than a messenger who comments on the World-Play: he *acts* in the play, he *does something* that changes the course of events on the ground. Something happens in his historical existence that affects the rest of the play.

It is extraordinarily important to chivy out this tangle of reality and appearance because, if improperly understood, the notion of Jesus as "the author-in-the-play" will be misconstrued in the direction of ancient but persistent heresies that elevate Jesus to such a divine level that the notion that he is truly human fades. Jesus is God in disguise. A spurious high

Christology says that at no time and in no way does Jesus cease seeing things with God's eyes. He is like the author-in-the-play who knows in Act II exactly how things will work out in Act V. Elevate Jesus to that level of authorial prescience and it is difficult to assert that he is human. Ignorance of the future defines human life as anxious struggle. The chanciness of the future makes us flee to roles and causes that we believe transcend the unpredictability of life. "It matters not how strait the gate / How charged with punishments the scroll / I am the master of my fate / I am the captain of my soul." Only a boisterously confident Victorian could write such lines. It is precisely what Jesus does *not* say. In the garden of Gethsemane he does not master his fate, he says "thy will be done." Jesus is not master of his soul, the Father is master of his soul. Jesus accepts life fully in its joys, passions, and uncertainties as God's gift.

The sense in which Jesus is the author-in-the-play is not, then, like the Author who knows how the plot develops. He is not the author-in-the-play in the sense that, should he perceive an ill conceived piece of action, he can rewrite it. The all-knowing, all-revising author-in-the-play ruins the play. The rest of the cast are his puppets: he knows their lines before they speak them, and if he doesn't like the action in Act III, scene 2, he will stop the action and rewrite on the spot. Jesus as actor-in-the-play is none of that. He is as ignorant of the future as anyone; he is powerless to change the dreadful course of events. He fears the fate that awaits him to the point of tears and bloody sweat. Jesus is the author-in-the-play in the sense that he alone lives out fully, to the depth of his being, *the reality of human being as gift.* For Jesus there is an Author, the loving Author, from whom he accepts his life and destiny as gift. Because he lives his life wholly as authored gift, he is proclaimed *Son* of the Author, one whose life is at one with the Author. High Christology depends upon and flows from Low Christology.

The fact that the World-Play is as real as real can be does not mean that there is no problem of "fiction" in the course of human history. *The* problem of the World-Play is, in fact, a problem of fiction. The actors in the play, because they fail to accept their reality as gift, as the work of an Author, fancy themselves as self-created. The result of self-creation is that humans construct themselves as fiction, overdetermined in a manner that closes them off from what the Bible calls "the fullness of life." I posited Jesus as the "artist" of life, the one who can signature life itself in its fullness. He is *the* real human being in the World-Play because he accepts his life and destiny as the gift of the Father. Because he avoids self-creating fiction, he can say "I am the Life."

There is more to Jesus' story than acceptance of life as gift. This *attitude* to life may be common to many saintly men and women. Acceptance could be regarded as a life lesson, a teaching that Jesus offered and that his life exemplified. But consider again Wittgenstein's comment about the importance of Resurrection. If Jesus did not rise from the dead, "he is a teacher like any other teacher and can no longer *help*. . . . So we have to content ourselves with wisdom." Because of resurrection, the full story of Jesus does more than offer *a lesson about* life and history, the event of resurrection *changes history itself*. The Christian marking of history into BC (Before Christ) and AD (*Anno Domini*: The Year of the Lord) is not a mere calendrical piety. I may admire Socrates as a teacher—I might even say that I love him—but he cannot love me in return. Wittgenstein goes on to say, "Only *love* can believe the Resurrection." It is love that cures "my soul, with its passions, as it were with its flesh and blood, that has to be saved." If the story of Jesus is a story of my salvation, then he must be alive, the one who "flesh and blood" speaks to my flesh and blood, the teacher who loves me without fail.


## Life as Gift

Life as gift sounds splendid, but is it? On the basis of the historical record, humans seem to have decided that life is too much, fiction is better. Given manifest human suffering and disaster, one might even come to think that if there is a God who gives life, He does so out of malice. God would be like a sadistic playwright who created his characters and plot to work out some dark fantasy. This view is not implausible. There are those who, considering the gross suffering of this world, regard God either as such a menacing presence or as a weak power who injects just enough love and aspiration into humankind to make actual life a perpetual disaster. Better that such a God had never meddled with nature's metabolism of birth and death. When Jesus accepts his life with all its failures and ignominy as total gift, when he accepts his life as authored not self-authored, he trusts the Author. The Author is not a sadist or incapable of writing my part, tragic as it may seem, without a loving intent for my good and that of the all others in the play. In the Christian story, Resurrection affirms that God gives life, love, and immortal longings not as forms of sadistic torture or utopian intent, but as His deepest will and power.

If I emphasize that Jesus as "author-in-the-play" does not enjoy the knowledge held by the Author-outside-the-play, there is the obvious counter problem of retaining a sense of why he is at all identified with the Author. Lacking foreknowledge of the plot or the ability to rewrite the action, in what way does he differ from all the rest of us? In Christian terms, why is he "son of God" rather than a mere "holy man," one who trusts in God? Karl Marx famously said that all previous philosophies had tried to understand the world, his aim was to change the world. One can use this distinction between understanding and world-historical change to frame the special claims about Jesus. Jesus' sense of his life as gift was more than a powerful spiritual insight on his part. He not only saw his life as gift— perhaps saints and true believers can come to that insight—beyond insight, his life itself was gift. The author-character in the play is a gift to the play and its characters. The gift of Jesus is not just the message that life is a gift. The Hebrew Bible tells that story. The message of "being authored" has to be conveyed beyond the message. The author-character in the play changes history. What he does, what he suffers, and what happens to him changes the tenor and meaning of the play.

By living life as authored, Jesus rejects the human temptation to become a self-creating fiction. Jesus lives the fullness of life, he signatures life, he *is* "the Life." In our everyday dealings with other humans we play our fiction off their fiction. Novels and plays are instructive because we are able to see the clash of characters so clearly, for fiction clarifies role and character. Madame Arkadina is always her grandiose self so that her presence can precipitate the multiple frustrations and tragedies of the play. Suppose, then, that one introduces into the play a character who does not play as self-creating fiction, a character who is not fiction but who is the fullness of life. It is like placing a Duchamp *objet trouvé,* a snow shovel, in the center of a gallery of Renaissance paintings. The *objet trouvé* calls into question the character of the paintings, it speaks to a different reality, it drains away the "arty" reality of the carefully crafted world of the paintings. (Or, conversely, the formative reality of the paintings drains away all "artistic" meaning from the snow shovel. *That* item should be in the garage, not the gallery.) Life is an *objet trouvé*. We take great care in the world of art to exclude life-as-found. Children are not to play hopscotch in the gallery of Dutch landscapes. Silence of all noise and bodily functions is required at the concert—unless it is a John Cage concert in which case the more life noises the better!

I suggest that Jesus has the same effect in the World-Play that an *objet trouvé* has in the well-ordered gallery. He throws the art works, our self-fictions, off kilter. He reorders spiritual reality. In Flannery O'Connor's grim short story "A Good Man is Hard to Find," a sociopathic criminal kills off the members of a family excursion gone astray from the highway. He calls himself "the Misfit," and he sees Jesus as a misfit. "Jesus thrown everything off balance. It was the same with him as with me except that he hadn't committed any crime." [11] Just before he shoots the cranky old grandmother, she looks at him and says that he has the face of her children. He immediately shoots her and then allows that the old lady might have been a good woman if someone had shot her everyday of her life. It takes the face of instant death for her to see her children in the enemy. Jesus is the misfit who throws the World-Play off balance. Faced with Jesus, the enemy looks like one of our children. Like the Misfit, Jesus faces us with life and death, with the fullness of life and the radicalness of death. He is the corpse in the art museum, the balloons at the funeral.[12]

A result of saving the play *in* the play is that whether the other characters acknowledge the reality or the message of the author-character, once the author acts in the play the reality of the play is once-and-for-all changed. The author-character not only preaches a message that can well be forgotten, ignored, and misconstrued (the history of the Christian Church), he *does* something in the World-Play, to actual history, that marks it forever. If I believe that the author-character acts in the play, *what* he does (how he acts or suffers) changes my view of how the play is meant to proceed. To understand Christianity, one must see what happens when life enters the World-Play of fiction. How will the other characters play against the character who is not fictional, who lives the fullness of life? The playing out of the relation between the author-in-the-play and humanity is the story of the New Testament—and of the next chapter.

# CHAPTER FOUR

# *La Divina Commedia*

___

*Within Christianity it's as though God says to men:*
*Don't act a tragedy . . .*

Ludwig Wittgenstein, *Culture and Value*

In the previous chapter I sketched the complications that will structure the strange play where the "author" appears. I place "author" in quotation marks here to indicate that the character *in* the play cannot appear as "Author" (capitalized) because that would ruin the play by shifting its metaphysical reality. For all that God/Author is the source of reality, his reality does not turn the World-Play into appearance, illusion, or fiction. The character who I identify as "author-in-the-play" is at one with the Author in the limited sense that, unlike the other characters, he refuses self-authoring and lives his life—and death—as total gift. Jesus is thus "Son of God," one who lives in the World-Play not in the self-enclosing fiction of human sin, but with full openness to God's gift, a life fully graced. Other humans live their personal and political fictions—Jesus is Life.

How would one expect the action of the World-Play to develop if one introduces a character who lives life as gift? How will the action as played out determine the course and meaning of the World-Play? The full Christian answer would be the whole course of the New Testament in detail and nuance. That is a task well beyond my capacities and the purpose of this book. My account here of the author-character (Jesus), his words, life, and death is, as earlier stated, merely a sketch. Nevertheless, I think that it presents the basic lines of the high Christology that has emerged over time from the New Testament writings. The scenario offered revolves around the twin themes of the metaphysical gap (how can the author appear in and not ruin the play?) and the spiritual gap (how would the players react to the author-character and his revelation?).

In the Supreme Shakespeare analogy, the author-character announces that all the characters and their goings on are authored, all exist under the reign of the Author. (Jesus proclaims the Kingdom of God has come.) If the players accept that message, they come to view their reality differently. Once again, the obvious change would be for the characters to regard themselves as scripted fictions. This interpretation has hardly been avoided in strands, sometimes pervasive strands, of Christian piety. Yet it is a profound misinterpretation. The messenger in the World-Play comes to deepen the reality of the characters, not to erase it.

The characters in the World-Play are not at all predisposed to believe the message that there is an Author, however it is delivered or by whom. The characters believe that they are self-scripted. In human history, maintaining the self inevitably means defense over and against the other. Hegel more or less created the subject "philosophy of history," and for him history is generated only by the conflict of master and slave, self and other. The history of world literature could be cited as evidence of the conflictual reality of humanity. We are surrounded by pushing, jostling others who continually challenge our self composure. It is only a small step from the tangle of small jealousies and failed aspirations that mark a Chekhovian "tragedy" to the outright slaughter of enemies. On the human plane, Sartre is correct: Hell is other people. The Supreme Shakespeare's author-character delivers a message that is deeply disturbing to characters enmeshed in a self-authoring world of self and enemies. He forgives the characters for their sin, that is, he releases them from the illusion of self-determination. The message is not well received. "Forgiveness" releases the characters from their most cherished possession, their *self*-possession. We thought we were "gods" (self-determining), and we are not happy to be reduced to being all too human. Under such assumptions, forgiveness is *not* good news.

Forgiveness of sin is intended by the messenger to open the characters in the World-Play to the Author's life and thereby to *real* life beyond
their fictive selves. It may seem that no message could be more welcome.
Being released into the Author's life and love can be misunderstood sen-
timentally as some sort of celestial valentine. But recall Henry James' point
that, beyond fiction, life is "splendid waste." Release into *life* may be anything but sweet. It may be "splendid" or "chaotic vitality," but it may also
be the obscenity of Auschwitz, which fiction cannot contain. Life opens
up to splendor but also to suffering. Life *always* goes beyond our best self-
defenses. Opening to life defeats my *self*-defense; it opens me to loss of
self in madness, disdain, and death.

Forgiving sin, releasing the characters in the World-Play from *self*-
defense into life means "love your enemies." For the Author there are
no enemies. Since all are bathed in His love and delight, there can be no
final enemies. How will the message of forgiveness, real life, love, and "no
enemies" be received? The human scenario seems obvious. I am too invested in my self-determination to accept the message. I am not at all certain that I need to be forgiven — well, maybe a few faults here and there —
but totally reoriented from my self investment in my self. No way! Besides,
there certainly are enemies! This message of life is utterly unrealistic and
certainly too risky. I prefer the safety of fiction. The message of authorship and all that it entails is to be rejected.

Repeating: the function of the author-character in the World-Play is
not to diminish the reality of the *dramatis personae* but to deepen it. This is
accomplished by reversing the conditions that obtain in the Pirandellian
play in which the characters of the play who believe they are "real" are revealed as fictions of the author. In the World-Play, the author-character
reveals to humans acting fictional, self-authoring, and self-enclosing roles
that they are more than these roles: they are immersed in the density of
reality. But "Human kind / Cannot bear very much reality." (T. S. Eliot,
"Burnt Norton," from *Four Quarters*). Humankind will happily flee to fiction. In the Chekhovian analogy, they must forgo the illusion of acting a
"star turn" and act in the real world of humanity's great ensemble.

If all there were to the story was the rejection of the *message* of life,
the World-Play would be read as tragedy. The lesson of such a World-
Play would be that humanity is unsalvageable in its taste for fiction over
life, enemies over love. If the World-Play is not to be a continuous display

of universal human sin, the author-character must not only deliver a message that is sure to be rejected, he will have to *do* something that changes the course of the play whether or not the characters understand or accept his message.

What does happen to the author-character in the World-Play? Since the natural course of the play is committed to self-and-enemies, the author-character preaching the message of "no enemies" will be regarded by the rest of the players as the ultimate enemy. He is the *ultimate* enemy because he denies the reality that there are enemies. Accepting his message would destroy the universal construction of the defensive self and subvert human history—or save human history! As ultimate enemy in the action of the World-Play, the author-character then becomes the ultimate victim. The author-character whose life and message is "love of all" is the very one who cannot in any way be an *enemy*. Thus when he is persecuted as an enemy, he is also the pure (ultimate) victim since unlike all humans he has no enmity in him, he has no enemies. The action that the author-character plays in the World Play will be as ultimate enemy and ultimate victim.

If humankind can eliminate the ultimate enemy, history can continue on its normal conflictual course. When the author-character dies repudiated and abandoned, the world of self-and-enemies is reasserted as the one and only "real" world. The author-character was, as we suspected, just another of those starry-eyed idealists who arise in history preaching a dangerous utopian fiction. To the message of "no enemies," humankind says "be realistic!"

The death and abandonment of the author-character should rid the World-Play of its ultimate enemy and his message. He does not fit in this "realistic" play. But the New Testament play does not end with a tragic defeat. The author-character returns to the World-Play and the message is still forgiveness. Having suffered all the defeats that the world can muster, having become ultimate enemy and ultimate victim, the messenger is not excluded from the play, he is not enclosed in history's dark self-understanding. The Author of Life "transcends" the human World-Play and writes the author-character, life, and forgiveness back into the play. Realism is not sufficient to destroy his presence. It is essential that the author-character reenter the play (the Resurrection is "real") because it is his returned presence *in* the World-Play that constitutes history's marker and final meaning. As suggested, history is radically reevaluated in the manner in which an *objet trouvé* revalues the well-ordered, formal gallery. If the messenger only "rises into the message," the World-Play remains locked in tragedy. The life and death of the messenger would then be only an idealistic message. It is only because the author-character enters the play, allows himself to be destroyed as ultimate enemy and ultimate victim, and yet returns to the play as forgiving presence *in* history, that history is redeemed.

When Martin Buber accepted an invitation to lecture in Germany shortly after World War II, he was bitterly criticized by many Holocaust survivors. His presence seemed to suggest that the horrors of the past were forgotten or forgiven. He wisely said that his appearance in Germany did not signal a forgiveness of Nazi persecutors. Only the victim had the right to forgive. Only the ultimate victim could possibly forgive history, and that means he must return to the World-Play. *The ultimate enemy/victim is the only one who can offer release from the historical cycle of enemies and victims.* The rejection and resurrection of the author-character is the event which marks *the* meaning of the World-Play.

In the earlier discussion of baptism, I suggested that the event of the Holocaust could be understood as *the* marker for Jewish history. Something happened that darkens forever the fate of the Jews — even for a casual American teenager visiting Yad Vashem. Suppose that the Holocaust victims did return. Suppose that they embraced the members of the *Judenrat* who in their concern and confusion cooperated with the oppressors because they thought that it was better that some should die lest the whole nation perish. Suppose the victims went on to embrace the *Gauleiters* and guards at the extermination camps. In the light of such a miraculous event, we would not by any means erase the horror of the Holocaust as if it were simply some breach of manners that one could overlook. No, the Holocaust would remain as a deep marker for history. Nevertheless, the return of the victims as the forgiving would open a way of life and love that would transcend viewing the Holocaust as an everlasting threat and unforgivable sin. Perhaps it was this "transcendence of the Holocaust" that Anne Frank sensed when she wrote, "I see the world gradually being turned into a wilderness, I hear the ever approaching thunder, which will destroy us too, I can feel the suffering of millions and yet, if I look up to the heavens, I think that it will come out right."[1]

In the New Testament the author-character returns to those who abandoned him. They are the first forgiven. The disciples become the *forgiven community,* become the Church. As the forgiven community, they are compelled to tell everyone how the World-Play has been changed, to live in the peace that the world cannot give. The apostles are not so much commissioned to preach the good news—though they are specifically instructed to do so in the New Testament—as compelled. They preach forgiveness because they have been changed by forgiveness. Imagine the *Gauleiter* embraced in love by his victim. If he appropriates that embrace he is born again in the sense that his history is transcended. He can begin life again beyond the stain of sinful history. Humans must be reborn, baptized under the sign of the Cross (as humans we refuse Life) and Resurrection (our great refusal is not accepted, it is forgiven). Life is reasserted, refusing to abandon the World-Play to the realists.

In chapter 3 I offered the notion of Jesus as the one who, unlike the ironic pop-artist, signatures life itself: "I am the way and the life and the truth." Signaturing life is forgiving sin. Jesus, the one who signatures life, releases us from the protective shell of self into the splendid waste or chaotic vitality or abyss that is life in the depths of suffering and the highlands of joy. Forgiveness may sound like a welcome notion, but if forgiveness is release into life I may well refuse the risk. But in Jesus I am assured that life itself has been signatured. Jesus is the Lord of life beyond all risks including death itself. If I believe in Him, if I live in His name, I can bear to be released from sin into life.

### "His performance was a revelation!"

How can we understand the action of a single character on all of history, Jesus, as a unique "revelation" who affects the actual course of history, the World-Play? Imagine sitting at a play, say *Hamlet,* which is being tolerably well acted. The actors know their lines and recite them with cadence and precision. Some emotional tension is being created so that the performance is not at all inadequate. Then, in Act III, an actor appears for the first time, say the Player King in the troop of itinerant actors. Suddenly in that performance—and I deliberately chose a "minor" character—the play comes alive. This actor is so "into" the part that he moves beyond good acting to a gripping reality that throws the performance of the other actors, as good as they may be, into shadow. It makes no difference that the time on stage of the Player King is minimal, that he has relatively few lines, it is that we see in his performance what is really going on in the play, the level on which it was meant to be played. I recall seeing a performance of *The Merchant of Venice* in which the Duke of Venice received rave reviews. The Duke's part is small, and his lines are hardly the great poetry of the play, but in his speech and gesture there was an authenticity of performance that was remarkable. Suppose that his performance had been the only one to reach that height: it would have devalued all the other earnest efforts of the major players. It happened that the great Edmund Kean was performing *King Lear* at the same time as another distinguished performer, John Phillip Kemble. It was said of Kemble's performance that he was "every inch a king" but that Kean was "every inch a King Lear." Coleridge said that seeing Kean act was like seeing Shakespeare performed in "flashes of lightning." One could say that in Kean's performance Lear was fully realized, fully "alive" before the audience. Kean echoed this sense when he said of his Lear, "I could not feel the stage under me."

Shifting to the World-Play, the Christian claim is that, among all the actors in that play, there is one who played his part to the full, who in his performance revealed the sense and depth of the World-Play. This one performer revealed the deep sense of the play. Karl Barth is famous for saying that Jesus is *the* man (*the* human). In my dramatic analogy, he is *the* actor who establishes in his performance how the play is to be performed. The rest of us are like the other actors—our performance is diminished in the light of his performance. If we are sensitive to the discrepancy we try to act *up to* the level of that performance.

How does one authentically perform the World Play? What in Jesus' performance singles him out as the unique actor who despite his brief ministry, his minor role, illuminates the world scene as in a "flash of lightning"? The Christian claim is that Jesus lives as full reality. He is the actor who "comes alive" in the World-Play, who shows how the play is to be played. In the case of Kean and King Lear, Kean plays the *part* to the full, we think he realizes Shakespeare's meaning, the sense of the play. He is Shakespeare's Lear. At the same time that Kean is Shakespeare's Lear—what the author really intended for the character—Kean's Lear is certainly Kean's and fully alive. If we sense a fully "alive" Lear, we do not sense the author "pulling strings" in the background. Kean does not feel the stage beneath him because he is acting a "real" Lear.

In terms of drama, Jesus' appearance in the World-Play is a "star turn." (*Jesus Christ, Super Star* is not wholly off the mark!) There is, however, a profound difference between Jesus' star turn and a case like the miscast *Uncle Vanya* already mentioned. The powerful performances of the stars in that production when set against the pedestrian performances of the other actors ruined the play as a performance, ruined it *for the audience.* There are certain philosophical idealisms, like ancient Stoicism, that regard history from the standpoint of an audience. From such a point of view, history, the World-Play, is badly played. There are a few saints whose sorry fate only demonstrates the essential tawdriness of history. The sage rejects history for contemplation of the divine. Christianity is different. The star turn in Jesus' case ruins the World-Play in one sense: it shows the hollowness of how humans play their fictive roles. Jesus is the misfit who throws the World-Play off balance. But Jesus as the star of the World-Play does not ruin history in the Stoic sense because in the Christian World-Play I am not audience, I am an actor. I am in an analogous position to the soap-opera denizen cast in a production of the Royal Shakespeare Company's *Vanya.* I cannot luxuriate in critical disdain for the performance, I try to act up to the level of the star. I might hope that I could learn to act up by following a set of drama lessons, mastering the Stanislavsky technique. That would be dramaturgical Pelagianism: salvation by works. Drama lessons won't hurt, but still one must catch the spirit of the thing, somehow move into something like the life revealed in the star's performance. Even on the stage, salvation is by grace!

The Christian interpretation of the World-Play is relatively pessimistic about the capacity of the human actors to act up to the full life revealed in the "star." It is at least one way of regarding original sin: original sin is failing to live according to one's *origin,* that is, as the loved creation of the Author. Only Jesus lives the life fully from the true origin, he is the one character who lives the Author's intent. Nevertheless, Jesus' star turn if it does not lift the others to his level, reveals the meaning of the World-Play. Mediocre actor that I am, I thought that we were playing tragedy, but now I see that it is a comedy. "Within Christianity it's as though God says to men: Don't act a tragedy." Knowing that this is the trajectory of the play, I am charged to alter my performance toward a comedic resolution. I cannot manage the star turn, I cannot identify with the Author as Jesus does, but now I exist as a new being in a different play: a character in *All's Well that Ends Well.*

## Playing My Role

In William Shakespeare's plays, the characters breathe real life, they are not mechanical puppets. This is revealed in the creative challenges that Shakespeare's great characters present to actors. The relation between an actor and his character in the performance of Shakespeare is an apt analogy to the essential mystery of my self and the Supreme Shakespeare. In the theater the actor relates to a role, say, Richard II. Richard II is a definite character with particular lines and set pieces of action. But for all that there are fixed speeches, Richard II is a mystery, a character so deep as to defy any realization an actor might give to the role in any given night's performance. If he is a great actor he discovers shades, nuances, hints that illuminate, enrich, lead him on to even further penetration of the role. I recall Laurence Olivier asking Ronald Pickup how he, Pickup, planned to *walk* as Richard II. Is there a Richard II walk? For a great actor there is, just as there is a level of voice, a gesture of the wrist. It is a continual process of discovery because Richard II is a mystery, a "living" character.

Actors in Shakespeare are charged to enter into the role creatively because the character they portray is meant to be living. In the World-Play of the Supreme Shakespeare I am meant to be "alive." I will, however, be alive in some "role." Everyone starts life, after all, in the "role" of son or daughter. There are roles that are, as it were, precast by nature (son or daughter) and roles that are cast by history (American or Catholic). Roles precast by nature are a particular source of drama because they so often conflict with the historical meaning or historical circumstance of that natural role. King Lear, for example, does not recognize the good daughter and precipitates tragedy.

The times in which I live will cast me in a variety of historical roles and scripts whether I like it or not. I will be a citizen of this or that country, choose or be stuck with this job, attest this faith or cause, be married or unmarried. I inevitably exist in what the philosopher F. H. Bradley called "my station and its duties." If I believe I have been authored by the Supreme Shakespeare, I am charged to play my part creatively, not as a caricature. It would be an offense against the Author to "walk through" my part. Sin is walking through your part! Since actual life is not, however, a stage play, I do not need to play a role for which circumstance has left me utterly miscast. I may finally refuse the part I have been handed. I refuse the part because it is impossible to play *that* historical role in *life,* with *life.* It is doubtful that one can play "the tyrant" as a life. As Plato himself demonstrated, playing tyrant is the ultimate illusion whether it is played on the throne or in the small dictatorship of an abusive marriage. The meaning of tyranny is that one self-controls life: that role cannot be played and is the essence of sin. It is the tyranny built into the variegated major and minor villainies of life that must be rejected as unplayable. Fortunately, complete tyranny is rare if not quite beyond actual human capacity. The ordinary villain, say Iago, reveals a painful emptiness, which drives his action. There is a thwarted urge toward love, which is revealed negatively in his destruction of Othello's love for Desdemona. Iago is not a stock villain, he can be played as a live character.

In the World-Play, while we end up cast in some part, life always exceeds the script. Consider the role of parent—a role to which I will pay extended attention later in the book. There is a "script" for parenting, which I inherit from my culture and my parents. I may even have embellished it with some reflections of my own. Parenting already has some good lines and appropriate gestures. Am I fully prepared to play the parent? Alas, life keeps going beyond the script. I have to parent not by the book but in life itself. No script! I improvise. My loving-parent role goes beyond formula as I strive to parent in all the chanciness of children. How do I shape parental love around teen-age angst or the forgetfulness of adult children? How do I love them in their essential independence, their wholly other mysterious lives? How much easier it was with diapers and bedtime stories.

If life is splendid waste or chaotic vitality, humans have the choice between seeking a fixed form beyond life or losing all sense of self in a flux of desire and chance. In neither way are we masters of life: we either avoid life by crafting a fictive self, or life masters us in passion and death. I really want to be *a-self-in-life*. This, I have claimed, is what Christians say about Jesus. He takes on life fully in chance, passion, and death and is not destroyed. He is *the* master of life. He who could play such a role is someone who is at one with life itself, with the very ground of reality. That one is the Author. If one thinks that Jesus can accept death and yet master death in resurrection, He would be indeed very man and very God.

## Christology and Liturgy

To say that these few paragraphs are a simplification of the New Testament is itself a simplification. Nevertheless, I think it highlights the crucial turns in the New Testament account of Jesus and his ministry. Assuming that the Christology presented is basically correct, such that the good news revealed must be spread to the whole cast of characters in the World-Play by the post-Resurrection forgiven community, how will that community go about its task? I return to the specific liturgical performances by which the community of disciples, the Church, comes to express the meaning of the Christ event. Liturgy is the primary voice of the revelation. The liturgy is the enactment now of the World-Play as anticipation of Act V. The German historian, Reinhart Koselleck, wrote an extraordinarily interesting book, *Vergangene Zukunft,* which was translated as *The Future's Past.*[2] It is a study of how cultures have shaped their present through their visions of the future. The cultural tale of Christianity that is enacted in the liturgy expresses history from a vision of the future. In the World-Play, what do we expect in Act V? Someone has remarked that Christians have a "nostalgia for the future."

*Baptism.* We enter the Church in baptism when we are born again. We reunderstand our selves from being self-authoring to existing under the signature of the Author. We live in the name of the Father, Son, and Holy Spirit. We are reborn from a performer in our own play to a performer in the Author's play. Under the sign of the Author we renounce the fictive self-protection that constitutes sin and creates enemies. In baptism we are born into *life,* the gift of the Author. This life goes beyond the form and fiction of self-authoring into actual history itself with all its reality of suffering and death. Entering history and life is the ultimate threat to our self-possession. However, because we enter history and life *in the name of the Author of Life,* we have hope in the midst of history and life. It may be no more clear to me in Act III how the tangles of history can and will be resolved than before *except* that I trust in the loving author who writes a comedic finish in Act V. Tonight we play comedy!

*Gospel.*  If baptism is the entrance into life, what is life's message? The young woman at Yad Vashem who was "baptized" in the name of the Holocaust victim was baptized into a history where the message is danger. To be a Jew in the Holocaust world is to be surrounded by enemies. History as the story of enemies is chillingly realistic not only for Jews but for anyone who has taken a sober look at the human record. The psalms of the Hebrew Bible continually place the psalmist in the midst of his enemies. Humanly we are besieged. The New Testament could be read in this manner: a history of death and defeat, the Cross as the symbol of a despairing and tragic world. The shock of Christianity, as noted, is precisely in *not* reading the Cross as bad news, but as good news. Having entered into life in baptism, having thrown away sin and self-protection, we are asked to believe that life has a saving message: life is a divine comedy. The Cross, a symbol of complete historical defeat, death, and abandonment, becomes the deepest sign of divine love.

The author-character in the World-Play is more than one of history's desolated victims. When I am baptized in the name of the author-character, when I take on a Christian name, I am reborn in his life and he is reborn in me. In the course of the World-Play I will certainly be cast both as enemy and victim; that is the way of the world. But, in so far as I play my part in the name of him who was the ultimate enemy and ultimate victim and thus rose above the world's script of enemies and victims, I rise above the World-Play's inevitable defeatist script. If the author-character did not go to the extremities of life, if he did not become the ultimate enemy and ultimate victim, his love would have remained benign paternalism from above: the author is never *in* the play, always above it. If the benign author were to resolve the World-Play from above it would be as a *deus ex machina* who radically devalues the passions of the players: my own real life as the creator of enemies and victims, myself as enemy and victim. I do not want a heavenly message delivered from above, I need someone who stands by me, life to life. (Recall the earlier quip about the map that fails because it is not "the right size.") The message of Cross and Resurrection in the New Testament is that God is in the play, in life to the full, and yet is not truly defeated or destroyed in the play, in history. That is the fundamental good news of the Gospels that follows our baptismal birth into the Author's life.

Because salvation remains *within* the World-Play, Christianity is essentially eschatological, connected to an Act V, a last judgment. As long as the revelation that there is an Author does not devalue the play, turn the World-Play into God's fiction, history with all its nightmares and delights remains. The resolution, like the revelation, is a validation of history in which we come to believe in an Act V of judgment and mercy that will show that the World-Play has been both real and comedic. There is an Author who created the play, the same author-character has appeared in the play. His action in the play as ultimate enemy and ultimate victim radically revalues the direction of the play from tragedy to divine comedy. The author-character has his "hour upon the stage" but, unlike all the other historical characters who are "heard no more," we believe that this author-character will come again to write a final act that saves the tragedy into comedy. He was before as Author, came in Act III as author-character, and will come again to judge and resolve matters in Act V which is yet to come.

*Eucharist.*    How do we live out the reality we enter in baptism and the promise we hear in the Gospel? By sacramentally feasting with the Lord, partaking in the Lord's supper. (Recall the fancy that William Shakespeare loved Falstaff so much that he wanted to share a tankard of ale.) Table fellowship is an expression of the Christian story that works at many levels; it is a common theme of the Gospels. (Someone remarked that one could read the New Testament as Jesus' *Tischreden*: his table talk.) We are to be com-panions with the Lord, those who take bread ( *panis*) with the Lord. Given the presumed metaphysical gap between author and character, it would certainly be reassuring about *our* reality if we were to share a meal with the author. Author and authored feed off the same real earth!

There is, however, a limit to this common earthly table. In his duel in the desert with the Prince of this world, Jesus says "man does not live by bread alone." But we do! We live by consuming the things of this earth. Of course, if life is only consumption of bread, then we will eventually be consumed by the earth from which bread has been derived. By contrast, in the World-Play, the characters live only by the words of the author.

They live "by every word that comes from the mouth of God." "Every word that comes from the mouth of Shakespeare" would be a proper reminder to an actor in *Hamlet* who somehow fancied that he had improved his lines. If humanity's final reality is dependence on the Author, nothing would be more powerful and appropriate than to reverse the act of consuming bread of the very earth that will eventually consume us in death. We consume the bread of "eternal life," which is the Word of God. The analogy to the actor who believes he is improvising Hamlet fails in the case of the World-Play. The actor in Shakespeare's *Hamlet* is, after all, constrained by the poetry of the script. The actor may make Hamlet "come alive," but it is Richard Burbage who takes the curtain call. Actors would be in scarce supply if Hamlets had to be poisoned and stabbed in the last act. In the World-Play of reality, we live by every word that comes from the Author, but the "word" that comes is not a set script, it is a life: the life of the Word who says that he is the Life.

## The Preaching Voice

Liturgy is the primary voice of the Church, but there is more to be said about the Christian voice than what is contained within the direct expressions of baptism, Gospel, and Eucharist. One must be *inside* Church understandings to turn all these goings-on from empty ritual and fanciful story into "reality." One needs "faith" that we are in an authored World-Play to properly perform baptism, Gospel, and Eucharist. What is the Christian voice to the outside? How does one preach the faith to all nations?

The initiation moment for Christianity is baptism. I have interpreted baptism as a second birth: the birth into history after biological birth into nature. Christianity only makes sense if there is some recognition of second birth. The problem of communicating Christianity to the "outside" is that many individuals, whole tribes, and nations live outside of history. They cannot really live outside history, but they may delude themselves in that regard or undertake elaborate rituals to erase history. Mircea Eliade's *Cosmos and History*[3] is a classic treatment of societies that ritually reject history. Not only whole societies but single individuals may easily fancy in the urges of biological desire that the meaning of their existence is ahistorical.

One withdraws from history into the bedroom. Withdraw from history and Christian preaching makes no sense. Believing in history, however, does not by itself lead toward Christianity. As discussed at various places, one may be all too conscious of the reality of history as a fundamental threat. It is the threat of history that makes retreat into nature in the manner of the Peaceweavers so attractive. On the other hand, one may be determined to guard against the threats of history or even to eliminate them altogether in something like the Communist vision. Andre Malraux was attending a party conference in Moscow. The party hack who was speaking said that "after the revolution there would be no more suffering." Someone asked what if a child ran into the street and was run over by a tram car. The speaker without hesitation said that after the revolution that would never happen!

Assuming that Christian preaching speaks within and to the reality of history, I will simplify the "voice to the outside" around three themes that emerge from the Christology I have presented: peace that the world cannot give, drama, and comedy.

*Peace.*   To preach to those "outside," the Church must first of all come to understand itself as the peaceful community. It is peaceful in promise if not always in fact. The Christian community believes, despite the obvious antagonisms of the day, that for the Author of the World-Play there are no final enemies. It is the Author's peace as gift that defines the character of the Christian community. Most emphatically it is not a peace that is created by the efforts of the humans who make up the Church. If the Church exists as a community for whom there are no final enemies, then one must understand in preaching *to the outsider* that there is no one "outside." No one, absolutely no one, is outside the gift of peace that the Author has accomplished in the play. The primary Christian voice to itself and to the "outside" is the voice proclaiming "no enemies." This "peaceful" voice applies everywhere and all the time: to other religions, atheists, secularists, heretics, dissenters, sinners. One would expect from the universality of sin that at least some of the outside voices will reject the Church's message in terms of the same self-defensiveness and need for an ideological enemy that characterized the response to the historical Jesus. Still, as He forgave his enemies from the Cross of their triumph, so must the Church forgive if it is to live by its own Gospel.

The voice of forgiveness must not be confused with an attitude of indifference. One may listen to a child's wildly inaccurate talk with an air of "forgiveness" because in the long run we judge that not much is at stake. We indulge her fantasies. All too often Christian apologists "forgive" their interlocutor opponents with the same sort of unexpressed dismissal from above with which we treat the discourse of children and fools. There is a fatal error in any easy dismissal of difference whether conscious or unconsciously expressed. The Christian speaker—from pope to peasant— is never inside the truth in a manner that makes his position the clear, distinct, and only discourse. Christians may be "inside" the true Church, but they do not cease for all that to be sinners—forgiven sinners perhaps, but a *forgiven* sinner is like a person with a prosthetic limb: repaired, but definitely with a limp. No one is finally outside the Church and no Christian is fully inside—at least "inside" as a personal assured achievement and possession. Christians are never wholly inside the truth, others are never wholly outside the truth. The conclusion is that Christian preaching to the outside has to begin with deep *listening*. Failure to listen creates an arrogance in the speaker, which blocks him from whatever truth is stirring in the outsider.

*Drama.* The notion of drama that has guided this discussion gives a further structure for understanding the relation between Church and the world, between "inside" and "outside." If there are no final enemies, what should a Christian make of the obvious fact of human diversity: the diversity of moralities and the diversity of religions, which often stand in apparent opposition to Church teachings? What should a Church that believes that no one is outside its truth make of these differences? One popular answer is that in the long run all these differences are merely varying expressions of the same thing. All religions are at heart the same in their search for human transcendence. There is some truth in this idea of a common Truth, but it bypasses the irreplaceable value of difference and diversity. While apparently accepting difference, it makes difference superficial. I want to emphasize the reality and importance of genuine difference.

In my dramatic analogy, the Supreme Shakespeare scripts a profusion of differing lives. Difference is his love and his delight. Enjoying difference and diversity has become the watchword for a variety of fashionable current philosophies. There is a radical difference in difference. The Supreme

Shakespeare is writing a drama, he is not just running through the variety of human types, one sensational lifestyle after another. This Author is not an aesthete or a fashion designer. As a Christian, I go beyond aesthetic enjoyment of humanity's "innumerable choreographies" to a drama moving toward resolution. The World-Play is an ensemble drama: all the characters play a vital part, moving with or against another either toward tragedy or resolution. As in Chekhov, there are no minor roles. Christianity's special care for the World-Play's "minor characters"—the poor, the sick, the imprisoned, the hungry, and the dying—follows from the imperative of a single great ensemble drama. Because the poor are so often discounted, cast as servants and walk-ons, the author-character in the World-Play highlights their reality.

In the ensemble of the divine comedy, the burden is on the believer to see how the other is not-other, the outsider is part of the ensemble moving toward resolution. If my first duty is to listen to the deep message of the other, it is not listening for agreement, it is listening for disagreement, for genuine difference. All comedy, including the divine comedy, depends on genuine differences among the *dramatis personae.* When the reconciliation comes, the splendid differences in the characters are not dissolved into some bland commonality. When the conflicts are resolved in Act V as in Shakespeare's *Midsummer Night's Dream,* the lovers maintain their personal characters, but the right lovers are finally matched up after the confusions of the night.

*Comedy.*    If a Christian character in the World Play believes that all the characters in the play act under the loving signature of the Supreme Shakespeare, does she proceed differently when encountering the "other"—the enemy or the merely dissimilar? In one sense not at all, in another profoundly changed. Immersed in the play, it appears that the conflicts and tensions make impossible demands. The world appears as locked into loneliness, misunderstanding, and boredom as the ensemble in Chekhov's remote country estates. If, however, the Christian character believes that there is an Author and the direction of the Author's intent is toward resolution, she comes to believe that, despite it all, she is acting within a comedy. Chekhov attended a rehearsal at the Moscow Art Theater of *The Three Sisters.* At the end of Act II the actresses playing the sisters were weeping at the sad scene they had just enacted. Chekhov protested: "But it is a *comedy*—a *comedy!*" In the World-Play, "Chekhov-in-the-play" brings that assurance.

For the sake of brevity (and probably shock value) let me suppose that "comedy" is the revelation that comes to the disciples in the life, death, and resurrection of Jesus. They come to believe that there is a final act on the way in which judgement and mercy will be dispensed. As Julian of Norwich was to proclaim centuries later: "All will be well, and all manner of things will be well." Supposing that they are in a comedy, how do Christians speak their lines? A skillful actor in a comedy will deliver his lines—however harsh and antagonistic they may seem on the surface—with an undertone of resolution, of comedy. Yes, he is enraged at the other character and yet there is a touch of something in the delivery which allows us to think that there is something more and different in the offing. When the final resolution occurs, one can see how this precise delivery shadowed the "happy ending." There must be within every clash the undertone of final reconciliation.

The fourteenth-century English mystic Richard Rolle talked about "mirth in the love of God." Dietrich Bonhoeffer praised *hilaritas* as a special Christian virtue. He mentions a variety of individuals from Luther to Rubens, Hugo Wolf and Karl Barth who "have a kind of *hilaritas*, which I might describe as confidence in their own work, boldness and defiance of the world and popular opinion, a steadfast certainty that in their own work they are showing the world something *good* (even if the world doesn't like it) and a high spirited self-confidence."[4] Bonhoeffer stresses "confidence in their own work." One who acts with *hilaritas* does not undercut the force of the moment, making every gesture ironic, as if one absented onself from the moment into some superior intellectual perspective. Managing the paradox of complete involvement and "comedic" undertone is vital in avoiding the danger in Christian talk of devaluing my genuine and immediate love for spouse, child, friend because it is *really* the love of God at which I am aiming. No, I play to the hilt my part as lover or parent but with the clear sense that life goes beyond my best scripting of the role. I parent beyond the script and I do so with *hilaritas*.

I commend comedic talk as the way of the Church to the outside world—and to itself. (A comedic touch in the Vatican might constitute fundamental reform for the Church.) The Church is first of all—and maybe last of all—a way of evaluating self and other, especially the other who to all appearances is the enemy. In comedy there are no final enemies. The Church offers an invitation to all performers in the World-Play to regard their interaction within the reparative realm of the comedic, as interactions that a loving Author is moving to resolve in Act V and which his action "on stage" in Act III has already realized and forecast. As Chekhov said to his actors: "It is a comedy!"

It should be obvious from the complexity of the account of the author-character in the play that conveying this message is no easier for the Church believer than it was for the original messenger-author. All the metaphysical and moral resistances are there to bar the message. If one appreciates the problem of the message, then it should be clear that many Church voices are inherent failures. Simply asserting some list of things-to-be-believed because they are written in the Bible or in a papal pronouncement seems the least convincing of all methods, yet that sort of didacticism seems all too often the chosen mode of Christian instruction to the world. Similarly with moral imprecation and condemnation. Didactic statements on both "what to believe" and "how to behave" fail because they are delivered from above the human exchange of the World-Play, as if one had some purchase above one's own status as a character in the play from which he could instruct the other characters. Converting the other characters in the play — and it is *conversion,* a recalibration of reality that is at issue — must occur *within* the play, in the interaction of character-to-character. To put the matter in an often stated Christian truth, people are converted because of human contact, some vital exchange with an other that leads into a vision of life, love, and a world without enemies.

Understanding the Christian voice as peaceable, comic, and caught in the interchange of an ensemble drama certainly suggests a style and tone for Church discourse. In part 2 of this book I will look at specific expressions of the Church voice: papal pronouncement, dogmatic teaching, and moral instruction as they may be affected by the scenario of the World-Play that has been sketched in this chapter. Before turning directly to official Church-talk, however, I offer an intermediate chapter on religious discourse in general. Setting forth the notion that Christianity presents itself as signatured truth opens up a general question about the relation between what Christians may say, such as telling a tale about an authored World-Play, and how things *really* are. Projecting an Author may give subjective comfort but it is, after all, only a pretty fable.

Life as authored may seem only a pretty fable, but it is in fact quite fashionable these days. Humanity is, for example, not authored by some Supreme Shakespeare who delights in laying out a comedic ensemble of human persons, but by the Supreme Gene for whom individual human persons are just a means for perpetuating the Genotype. Not Father God but Mother Nature is writing the script. When the script is written by the Super-Gene, then humans in the World-Play are puppets, mechanically following the machinations of their DNA. The Creator God of the Bible has precisely the reverse intent: to convert puppets into life. It is a scenario worth considering.

# Philosophical Intermission

*Turn to the Subject*

# CHAPTER FIVE

# Exorcizing the Subjective Voice

*Religion is having an intense attitude
and no time off.*

Iris Murdoch

The topic examined in this book is how Christianity is to be conveyed both to its believers and to the world. If the Christian message is to be authentically delivered, what is the mode of that delivery? What sort of messenger is capable of speaking the truth of faith, speaking truthfully of faith? I have focused the problem of messenger on the *voice* from which and in which the Christian message is conveyed. A messenger in the wrong voice will distort the message beyond recognition. Speaking in the wrong voice, he or she will not be believed. On the other hand, even the right voice, speaking with the tongue of angels, may not be believed because of the fantastic nature of the story told. One might think my tale of the Supreme Shakespeare a charming tale quite beyond belief. A sophisticated modern view holds that religious belief is subjective without any clear access to common reality. If someone says "I believe [some religious claim]," all one can say is "So you do, but that proves nothing." Some people believe in astrology, but I can remain deeply skeptical about destiny spelled in the stars. Faith seems fatally beyond access to those with different subjective urges. In short, faith is given over to a subjective voice that, while it may record my emotional state, fails any and all tests of truth.

Before turning directly to specific voices of the Church—pope, Creedal dogma and moral instruction—I want to exorcize the subjective voice. There is no use writing a long book as an extended venting of emotion. There is no use talking about a *proper* voice of the Church if one is convinced that all that is being voiced is my personal emotional state. Getting straight about what is subjective about faith is not only important for secular understanding it is also important within the Church. "Subjectivity" can be taken negatively as a ground for the secularist's prompt dismissal of faith but also positively as a source of religion's highest value. The possibility of opposite appraisal rests in the ambiguous characterization of religion as "personal." Positively, "personal" points to the profound importance of religion to the individual believer; negatively, it can serve to discount religion as *merely* personal: a subjective peculiarity of the believer.

The strength of the negative consignment of religion to the subjective rests on a common perception that faith claims are not verifiable by generally accepted objective tests. Despite failing the test of objectivity, people persist in expressing faith in statements and ceremonials that they regard as of the greatest importance. The sceptic regards these nonobjective affirmations as expressions of feelings and emotions which may tell us something about the believer but not about reality and the world. The voice of religion is the voice of emotional expression, a revelation of feeling, a cry of pain or delight. The person who makes a religious claim is not talking about the world (objective), he is registering his subjective state. Not "Lying is bad," but "I dislike lying," or "Lying. Ugh!" For obvious reasons this has been called the "emotive theory" of value (ethical, religious, aesthetic). Relying on this assumed subjective/objective distinction can place religion clearly into the subjective, personal, emotional side of the dichotomy. I want to rescue genuine religious talk from blanket submersion in subjectivity either by adherents or critics.

## What Is "Subjective"?

The relegation of faith to subjectivity is the product of a long philosophic and scientific process that created a particular construal of "objective" and "subjective." It is worth touching on that history in order to indicate that the distinction between objective and subjective requires significant interpretation. Slicing the world neatly into objective vs. subjective with no remainder is not as simple as it may seem. It is generally agreed that serious philosophy has undergone a profound revolution since the time of its origin with the Greeks; that change is referred to as a "turn to the subject." Plato and Aristotle in their differing ways considered that they were examining the nature of things: what Plato called the "really real," or Aristotle, the nature of being. This metaphysical direction of philosophical thought continued more or less through the high middle ages. For various historical reasons philosophers in the modern period rejected that classical approach and concluded that we cannot address the nature of things directly, first we have to examine our human capacity to reach the "really real." The nature of the knower, the knowing *subject,* must be ascertained before one can talk about what could be known.

Depending on how one regards the nature of the subject, one will evaluate this philosophical revolution differently. If you are of a scientific bent, you will start with Descartes placing "I think" as the center of knowledge: the one thing that one cannot doubt since to doubt thinking is to think a doubt. From that base, Descartes hoped to build a complete scientific edifice of truth. The reason for his optimism was that Descartes' subject, "I think," was a detached subject capable because of its detachment of reaching objective, dispassionate truth. Emptying the subject of personal idiosyncracies like gender, nationality, specific culture, and so on creates the "objective" mind, which can apprehend objective reality. A contrasting view of the subject occurs in Hegel. What we know is linked to the state of our concrete self embedded in differing historical cultures. Because he believed that history progressed, Hegel thought that we progressed in truth. One can, however, derive quite different conclusions from the historical placement of knowledge. Contemporary deconstructionists and multiculturalists accept the historicity of the subject without the progressive aspects. Cultures are not better or worse then or now, further or closer to "reality," they are just differently placed in historical perception. This last position is true subjectivism in which there is no escape from the relativity of cultures or personal position.

There would be no need to be concerned with the stratospheric arguments of philosophers, but like the greenhouse gases a collection of philosophical doubts above has obscured the possibility of receiving the light of truth even on more down-to-earth issues. (This metaphor is not scientifically correct; though atmospheric gas does not block light, it raises temperature on the ground. That certainly is true about religious controversy.) If we come to doubt that the table we see is really real—that it may be only a collection of subjective sense data—one can imagine what philosophical doubt does to the precarious status of religious belief. At the extreme with the deconstructionists, we are left with the subject and his or her local historical perceptions and spiritual enthusiasms. "Knowledge" becomes a species of personal memoir. Religion can be "saved" by deconstructionist efforts but only at the price of subjectivizing everything from physics to faith.

It is that latter turn to the subject as the basis of relativism and scepticism that so exercised John Paul II in his encyclicals *Fides et Ratio* and *Veritatis Splendor.* Cardinal Ratzinger's sermon at the opening of the conclave that elected him to the papal office reiterated in the strongest terms the condemnation of relativism as the besetting sin of the modern age. Given the commitment to the realism of medieval philosophy and a defense of *the* truth of Christian dogma, John Paul II and Benedict XVI's position is not at all surprising. The popes are, however, battling a powerful trend in modern thought, particularly in the realm of religious belief. We do after all come to some rough and ready common sense views about the objectivity of tables *pace* elegant philosophy, but in religion searching for objectivity seems a hopeless cause. Bother the epistemological problems, there is also a deep political advantage to subjectivizing religion as the ground of tolerance—not a virtue much adhered to in the history of religions. Modern epistemology and liberal politics are only too happy to send religion off into the realm of subjectivity.

In opposing a retreat of religion to relativistic subjectivity, Church apologists frequently fall into the trap of implicitly accepting the common distinction of subjective/objective and then arguing for the truth and objectivity of religious belief. The Church apologist is onto something in his opposition to relegating religion to personal idiosyncrasy, but the term objectivity has been so captured by science—the modern paragon of objectivity—that tying religion to that sort of objectivity, to that sort of "truth," will be unconvincing at best and disastrous to the proper truth of faith that one wishes to defend. The Church lives by truth, but truth that is not at all in the mode of scientific claims. Confusing Church-truth and anything like scientific objectivity is the fatal turn of fundamentalism, biblical or papal as the case may be. My argument is that Christian belief statements are neither subjective nor objective in the way those terms are commonly used. What else is there?

## What Is "Inner"?

It is fashionable either because of high philosophy, common opinion, or a desire to prevent religious war to think that religious belief is not *really* true, that is, testable by any objective standards. You may never have heard of deconstruction and yet be persuaded of the irresolvable nature of religious opinion. I am convinced that this retreat to subjectivity in religion is thoroughly mistaken. Critics and believers should have more stringent standards for accepting or rejecting belief. The problem is to discover the standards for such stringency.

I agree with the modern slogan that we need to "turn to the subject," but only if turning to the subject does not subjectivize truth and reality into untestable personal opinion. What do we usually mean when we refer to something as "subjective"? The standard example is the statement "I am in pain." The "I" in that statement calls attention to something uniquely rooted in *my* consciousness. "I am in pain" points to something "inner," my *subjective* experience. "I am in pain" is, in an odd way, an infallible claim. It is infallible in the sense that rejecting (falsifying) such a statement is quite different than falsifying "it is raining." Claims about the state of the weather are settled by looking out the window, not "into my head."

That there is something unfailing in an "honest" first person report can be seen by considering how to verify a third person statement: "Smith is in pain." We would proceed as we would in checking on the weather by making observations. He grimaces, we see the wound, we take his temperature. Finally we can ask him whether he is in pain. If he says, "No, I am not in pain" and if we discount lying, acting, or just being brave, then we may conclude that he is in shock and is, in fact, reporting accurately about his lack of pain. The honest reporter is an infallible witness to his own pain experience. The problem with such "infallible truth" is that it does not tell us about the objective world, it only tells something about the patient's inner state. There are experiences that are peculiarly mine. While these experiences can be said in some sense to be true, they are *dismissed* as subjective in the sense that they do not tell us about the objective state of the world. I may well have the subjective sensation of pain but under conditions where there is no objective reality to be discovered. Amputees have "phantom pain" when they feel pain in a severed limb. There is an objective *explanation* for the pain—amputation—but the pain is wrongly ascribed to a nonexistent limb.

If I say "I am in pain," given the proper safeguards about lying, and so on, that is true enough, but my report of pain says something only about *me* not about the objective world. It may not even say anything about the objective world of my body, phantom pain, for example. So, if someone says that she believes in God, well, she does (though it may be very difficult to know quite what claim or emotive state is expressed). Having granted the religious person her subjective state, I can say that the belief is like a phantom pain. She has this *feeling* that her life is guarded over by some supernatural being, but there is no such entity any more than the amputee still has the limb where he feels the pain.

## Persona

Religious truth is certainly subjective in some sense. If it does not affect the inner life of the believer it can hardly be a *religious* belief. One might hold that Aristotle's rational proof for the existence of an unmoved mover god was quite sound, but then attach absolutely no personal significance to the existence of such an entity. The fact that religion must affect the subject is what leads to the view that religion is true but in a manner that makes no claim upon the world. The issue is to understand religion in a manner that affects me, the subject, but not because it is "merely" subjective.

Religious belief is not like reporting some inner states like "I am in pain." Religious belief is not a feeling that comes and goes or even a more permanent feeling that we can discount like phantom pain. No doubt a good deal of religiosity has a transient, episodic character; no doubt there are people who have strong religious longings but discount them as lacking an objective basis. But genuine religious subjectivity is quite different than either type of subjective sense or feeling. In a fictional Platonic dialogue, Iris Murdoch depicts a young "seeker," Anacostas. He characterizes religion thusly: "religion is having an intense attitude and no time off." Murdoch's "Plato" expands on Anacostas' comment:

[Religion] has got to be the magnetic centre of everything . . . it's beyond us, more real than us, we have to come to it and let it change us . . . we're not volunteers, we're conscripts . . . it's about what's absolute, what can't not be there . . . it's happening all the time. If it's not everywhere, in the air we breathe, it isn't what I mean . . . It's to do with life being a whole and not a lot of random choices . . . If it's anything it must be everything . . . It's not retiring from the world, it's knowing the world, the real world, the world as it really is, in all its details . . . everybody knows this.[1]

The views of Anacostas and "Plato" make religion a matter of *personality*, a turn to the subject not as transient feeling, idiosyncratic taste, or some persistent sensation that I can discount. Personality is of course subjective, but in a very different relation to truth and reality. Being religious in Anacostas' sense is in the category with paranoia, *a total personality structure*. Whether religion in general or Christianity in particular is a personality *disorder* (like paranoia) or a sane, realistic *persona* is the proper question to ask of faith and its truth.

Serious religious belief—an intense attitude and no time off—invades the total subject, it defines his or her personality in the same manner that paranoia colors the entire life of the beleagured sufferer. Unlike subjective states such as pain or taste, paranoia is a subjective condition *which can only be defined in terms of truth and reality*. As Murdoch's "Plato" says, "it's beyond us, more real than us . . . what can't not be there." Religion in this construction can only be defined in terms of truth and reality. "It's not retiring from the world, it's knowing the world, the real world, the world as it really is, in all its details . . . everybody knows this." The paranoid believes that he is being pursued everywhere by hostile forces, that belief is at the core of his person. Presumably the rest of us do not believe that is how the world is in general or for his world in particular, so we decide that he has a personality disorder. He is "out of contact with reality." Unlike the phantom pain of the amputee we do not take his views as an understandable illusion that, distressing as it may be, is of no great harm. We point out to the amputee that it is only phantom pain and that he should place it in such a perspective. Presumably the amputee is able to make that judgment and while he continues to have the pain he does not engage in unrealistic activities, such as getting treatment for the missing limb. If the amputee comes to believe that his leg is really there he would be like the paranoid, seriously deluded. The strategy that works on phantom pain does not, unfortunately, work with the paranoid. Assuring him that in fact there are no enemies in no way alleviates the disorder. The amputee may be momentarily deceived, the paranoid is sick; the latter needs a cure that goes to the core of his whole personal project.

The issue for Christian faith when it is taken in the manner suggested by Anacostas is whether or not it is a personality disorder. Is living a Christian life out of touch with reality in a manner analogous to that of the paranoid personality? Christian personality as characterized by critics like Nietzsche or Freud would be classified as a personality disorder. Drenched in impossible guilt, the Christian penitential person turns away from the exuberance of life (Nietzsche) or suffers from the paralyzing neuroses of false consciousness (Freud). Any proper reply of Christians must rest on the claim that it is the Christian persona which is *in* order, the only truly sane, healthy persona. The Christian persona fits final reality and does so more properly than the Nietzschean hero or the Freudian stoic.

The Christian persona presumably defines a particular personality structure and as such excludes many alternative personality types. From the standpoint of the Christian persona, the paranoid is out of touch with reality because reality is the gift of a loving God. The World-Play is a work of love. To live a life dedicated to combating hostile enemies is living a life of delusion. Of course there are other contexts from which one would judge paranoia disordered and go on to dismiss the Christian critique as yet another sort of madness. Nevertheless, the argument to be joined between Christianity and its critics is on the issue of the human person in its relation to reality. What is a personality disorder? When is the personality *in* order? Franz Rosenzweig gets it right when he places religion within the categories expressed in the title of his book, *Understanding the Sick and the Healthy: A View of the World, Man, and God.*[2]

## Objectivity vs. Sanity

The fatal mistake that can be made if one categorizes faith as a personality (dis)order, out of touch or in touch with reality, is that one will jump to the conclusion that one must first tidy up one's view of reality and *then* decide on the (dis)ordered personality. Unhappily it is impossible to find reality without *first* finding sanity. The notion of deciding reality first is borrowed from the scientific approach to objectivity: an assessment of reality such as a neutral or detached observer might obtain—Descartes' empty subject. We are back with the initial distinction of subjective/objective. Reality is not to be colored by "subjective" interests. But the issue is not subjective opinion vs. detached objective truth, it is detached objective truth vs. the sane subject. Reality is not how the objective (scientific) observer sees "the world," reality is how a *sane persona* would see it. Detached objective observer and sane persona are not at all the same notion.

Is the detached observer a model of sanity? Sanity and insanity, personality order and disorder are decided by one's whole "take" on the world. One can, and should, in scientific discourse *play the role* of detached neutrality as much as possible. Adopting the detached role has immense value, but *living* as a detached persona is quite another matter altogether. If one says that one must first decide on reality and that this can only be done from the position of the detached persona, one should ask whether the detached persona has full access to reality. Put another way: should the scientific, detached observer become the life position, "an intense attitude and no time off"?

The idea of the detached persona is odd straightway because it seems to contradict what we ordinarily regard as a person. I think of my person as something with history, sex, passion, and desire, all of which I must fundamentally attempt to deny to reach the status of a detached persona. The detached person is the transcendent "person" of the Cartesian "I think," the "I" of scientific observation, which is rigorously neutral to personal characteristics. Of course I can *play the role* of the detached one as I might play the role of Hamlet, but I would not *be* Hamlet. I would always be conscious of role playing. If the theater caught fire, it would be me not Hamlet that looked for the exit. (Legend has it that Archimedes was so caught up in pure scientific contemplation that he gave no thought to escaping from his assassins.) There is a strong prima facie argument, then, that the detached persona is not at all in contact with something importantly real, with reality as a whole, with a world containing flesh and blood persons.

The question about the sanity/insanity of the detached persona hinges on just how an actual human being would see the world. What is the real world for the human, a world where historical persons—myself included—are real? The fictional "mad scientist" is mad because he *lives* as a detached person, it is his "intense attitude and no time off." It is not absurd to argue that someone who *lives* as a detached persona is either deeply perverse or insane: a sociopathic personality out of touch with reality. Bertrand Russell was an exponent of scientific detachment as the mental condition necessary for appropriating reality. The following comment by D. H. Lawrence who collaborated briefly with Russell in opposing World War I is illuminating:

> What ails Russell is, in matters of life and emotion, the inexperience of youth. He is vitally, emotionally, much too inexperienced in personal contact and conflict, for a man of his age and caliber. It isn't that life has been too much for him, but too little.[3]

From the standpoint of Lawrence's passionate engagement with life, what *ails* the detached Russell is unreality—life has been "too little" for him.

If one rejects the detached persona as structurally disordered for life and therefore unable to understand reality, this leaves wide open the issue of how proper personality order or disorder should be determined. How can we decide from within the inescapable structure of our persona which sort of persona is "in order" relative to reality and truth? An obvious key to this impossible task is the role of a moral sense in assessing reality. The detached observer fails to contact reality because he fails to accept any ethical dimension, which is part of the *reality* of a world with human beings. It is not so much a question of this or that morality but whether moral issues are raised in regard to human persons (and by extension to the world beyond the strictly human, such as the ethical treatment of animals and the environment). The detached observer can, of course, discriminate humans from nonhumans, but the medical doctor is discriminated from the veterinarian by a particular moral reality. The pediatrician does not regard her patients in the manner in which a veterinarian treats cats.

In deciding whether a particular persona is in contact with reality, we cannot avoid moral reality. Failure to place morality into the assessment of person and reality is a sure sign of insanity and the disordered personality. I want to emphasize this point since there is a strange but pervasive view that moral judgments *distort* reality. The root of this belief is again the notion that morality is "subjective" in the manner earlier discussed in connection with religious belief: a strict scientific objectvist may deny that anything beyond science is "real." Pierre Changeux, director of the Molecular Neurobiology Laboratory of the Pasteur Institute is at least forthright in expressing just such a scientific view. The moralities of the world, he claims "make up a virtual symphony of blindness and intolerance." They are, he opines, a species of "infection."[4] One must rise above morality to reach objectivity and truth. On the contrary, I think that Changeux expresses a view that is sociopathic, the stance of the detached persona who fails to contact *human* reality and the moral responsibilities inherent in that world.

Incorporating morality into sanity should be sufficient to exorcize our fascination with scientific detachment as the key to reality. In the long run, I want to go beyond moral reality to religious reality and its connection to sanity. There is a connection between moral perception and religious perception if for no other reason than that they both emerge within an engaged life in contrast to the life of the detached observer. My argument is that personality (dis)order can only be assessed by considering the fit between one's actions and the real world where "real world" includes recognition of moral and religious reality. Hegel says that to him who looks at the world rationally the world looks rationally back. However that may be, to one who looks at the world morally and religiously the world looks morally and religiously back. This can sound like a retreat into dismissive subjectivity, but for all that perception and reality arise together the just man does not believe that he *projects* justice or injustice onto the world, he thinks that he *discovers* justice in the world and the ways of humankind. One must, however, first *learn* to be just, to have the "skill" of justice to "observe" justice. That the art of justice is learned does not mean that it is negatively subjective. An art connoisseur learns her skill, perfects her taste, so that she can discover the world of aesthetic value. So with morality and religion.

If one lacks the "skill" of morality, fails to be trained in moral action and perception, we would regard such a person as sociopathic, out of touch with reality. Failure of aesthetic perception is not so immediately regarded as insane. We would be inclined, however, to regard such a person as suffering a human diminishment. We might pity his blindness as we would pity the man literally blind. Finally, however, there is something disturbing and ultimately frightening about someone who is "blind to beauty."

A similar pattern follows for religion. One must, as it were, acquire the "skills" of religion in order to discover the truths of religion. Morality, aesthetic sensibility, and religious perception are natural for humans in the sense that these are skills we can acquire and that are regarded as valuable and even essential ways of living and perceiving reality. Unlike some skills— for example, learning to play chess—the skills of art, morality, and religion seem to be ways in which we *discover* fundamental (human) reality. These are skills for "the game of life" to use a well worn cliché. If people do not learn the religious skill, a theologian like Rosenzweig will label them "sick." The Church exists to form and sustain Christian "skills"; the Church is the school of Christian perception.

A first-level claim that a religious person might make about the areligious person is that he suffers from personality diminishment, similar to the case of aesthetic blindness. One can, however, go on from there to allege that there is something deeply troubling about a profound lack of religious perception. It is important not to confuse religious perception with Church adherence or even a stated belief in God. Buddhism makes no claims about God but it would be quite wrong to deny the Buddha deep religious perception. Declared atheists like Sartre and Camus are deeply disturbed by the absence of God and thus I regard them as having important religious perceptions. For both the committed religious person and the dedicated atheist like Sartre, failure to see the religious dimension of life—for Sartre the death of God, which haunts humanity—is a failure to understand truth and reality. Anacostas would say that the areligious person is one who did not seek "an intense attitude with no time off." As such he lives the unreal and neurotic life of a dismembered self. Sartre was a religious atheist by Anacostas' definition.

We should not believe that sanity is easy to come by, something that happens to most folks as a matter of course. It is even more plausible to believe that most humans at most times have been somewhere on the neurotic-psychotic scale. As sober a scientific thinker as the modern philosopher Karl Popper regarded human history in general as a record of "international crime and mass murder."[5] If humans have spent their historical time as criminals and mass murderers, one could conclude that sociopathology is the rule not the exception. The Christology of the previous chapter would not disagree with Popper's characterization of human history. Absent a sense of the Author, the World-Play runs its destructive course of self-aggrandizement and assaulting the enemy. The nature of sanity may not be that easy to discover given what has passed as sanity in our history: war, vendetta, faddishness, and torpor.

## Concluding Philosophical Postscripts

In this chapter I have attempted to explicate the critical notions of "objective" and "subjective." The aim of that discussion has been to focus on the notion of "personality," the sane persona, as the central issue in the appraisal of religious belief. I now want to elaborate on the notion of "persona" or "self" since *teaching* the Christian persona is, in my judgement, the Church's essential task. It is important, therefore, to clarify the complex meanings that can be attached to "person" or "self." Having done so, I will turn to a philosophical challenge to the sort of intense persona that I claim characterizes the religious persona. Finally, as a postscript to these postscripts, I want to say something about the relation of faith and reason in the Catholic tradition. Failure to deal adequately with the subjective/objective distinction often misleads Church apologists into a false view of the rationality or irrationality of faith.

*Persona.*    The crucial issue for religion is sanity. Is the Christian persona sane? Before answering that question one needs to have some sense of what we mean when we refer to a "person." "Person" can be equated with "self," but the latter concept has a broader use. Paul Ricouer has delineated two quite different senses of self: *idem* and *ipse.*[6] Self as *idem* is roughly my natural, biological identity. I am the same (*idem*) self who was born in 1931, and there are straightforward scientific tests for confirming that identity, such as DNA sampling. Only in science fiction fancies about transporting my brain into someone else's body are there problems about the *idem,* biological self. If my brain were transplanted into Charles (or Charlene's) body would that entity still be me? In contrast to the *idem*-self, there is what Ricouer labels the *ipse*-self. This is what I am in my habits and behavior: my moral or spiritual self. If there is a problem of self-identity in the fiction of brain transfer, there is a differing identity problem about the spiritual self. After a life of dissipation, I have a religious conversion and join the Catholic Worker. I am a different person. Though I am the same *idem*-biological self, my friends can hardly recognize this new *ipse,* spiritual self.

The "self" at issue in religion is obviously my *ipse,* spiritual self, my persona. The biological self is set and, absent science fiction, remains. It is the spiritual self created by personal transfer from parents and culture that is our moral and spiritual concern. While my biological *idem*-self is fixed and permanent, *how I live* that biological self is variable according to my historical culture and particular circumstance. The spiritual self can be so overriding that I may even seek to alter my biological self in the light of my persona. Though I am a biological male, I might see myself as a feminine persona. I could then undertake a sex-change operation in order to make my biology conform to my persona. The resultant "femaleness" would be, however, only an artifice, more radical but no different in essence from dressing in female clothes. I would remain for the autopsy table a biological male.

Sex change is an extreme example in which one attempts to change the natural *idem*-self to conform to *ipse*-self, the persona. More common is the reverse: the attempt to conform the persona to nature, the *ipse*-self to the *idem*-self. Various "back to nature" philosophies seek to reconstruct or deconstruct the persona according to some presumed natural categories and structures. "Back to nature" as a spiritual strategy may even be urged on by scientific reductionisms that assert that personal behavior is nothing more than general animal instinct. "Back to nature" advice seems eminently more plausible than trying to make nature conform to my persona. We are, after all, a species of animal nature. But "back to nature" seems as impossible as the reverse strategy of taking a surgical knife to my biology. The result in either strategy depends on artifice. Nature religions engage in elaborate rituals or stringent asceticism to return the person to a presumed natural state. Biological determinists write solemn tracts commending animal urges as the "really real" of personal choice. Humans go "back to nature" only through ritual or argument. We are at best or worst prosthetic animals. Humanity is fatally and finally defined in history and culture. Once out of the Garden of Eden there is no return.

Even though "back to nature" depends on artifice, it may be the right artifice, the right life-strategy. Having wandered out of Eden we can act *as if* we were still there. The persona is, after all, a construct of history and culture that, from the standpoint of nature, may be regarded as "illusion." The temptation to regard the historical constructs of culture and person as illusions at best, delusions at worst, arises from the manifest clash of cultures and personal values that constitutes the human story. From tribal war to domestic abuse, the plot is marked by misunderstanding, distrust, antagonism, and destruction. Compared to the uniformity of the *idem*-self, biological nature, the *ipse*-self of culture seems irresolvably diverse and antagonistic.

In the previous chapters, I talked about how humans live as self-authoring fictions. Perhaps if we would realize that persona is a "fiction" of culture, we would be more tolerant of difference. Something like that urge lies behind the deconstructionist's celebration of difference. The personal self is a cultural style somewhat analogous to fashion in dress. What we need to attain peace is deconstruction of the self, the persona. The problem with that strategy is that humans do not regard their cultural persona as a fiction; they invest person and culture with the weight and fixity that would normally be assigned only to the fixity we find in *nature*. It is not by accident that we refer to a person's character as "second nature." If nature is not appealed to directly, various cultures and religions claim that their version of the spiritual self was decreed by a god. A god-established culture and persona can take on the transcendent fixity that we would otherwise apply only to biological nature.

Whether or not one rises to the level of self-consciously grounding culture in some god, human history writ large and small has been played out with humans acting as gods. Put less flamboyantly, we are tempted to act as characters in a novel. Characters in fiction are attractive because, as Henry James notes, their personae are "washed clean of awkward accretions." Like the individuals in *Six Characters in Search of an Author,* I want to live *in* a story; it would clarify my character and reveal the plot hidden beneath the messiness of my daily existence. If I am unable to locate the author of my life, I wander in bewilderment like Pirandello's characters. Failing, however, to find an author, I choose to master my life. I become my own author. Madame Arkadina is a splendid example of self-authoring. She acts the self-authoring goddess, the "star turn" to disastrous effect on the mere mortals who surround her. As self-authoring, her character (her second nature) has all the heedless destructive force of first nature's wind and storm.

The Christian story outlined in the previous chapters assumed that history, the world of human personae, is caught in inherent conflict. There is something fundamentally deranged in the formation of the human persona; as self-authoring it is self-enclosing, positing self against an other who is at best a stranger, at worst the enemy. The creedal formulation of this human flaw is the doctrine of "original sin." Is this account of the formation of the persona just too pessimistic? Is the essential structure of persona self-enclosing over and against the other, ultimately an enemy? Surely humans can create a persona that is not self-enclosing illusion? After all, the point of the Christian story is that humans should imitate the *persona Christi,* a persona that is not self-enclosing and that has no enemies. True enough, but the Christian answer is that we can only "create" that persona if we give over self-creating. The authentic human persona is shaped by God's grace through the action of Jesus Christ.

Deep arguments suggest that the human persona in its essence is founded on self-enclosure and antagonism. Freud's Oedipus complex founds the sense of ego on nothing less than patricide. Hegel projects the self as a seesaw conflict between master and slave. The theology of original sin offers its own account of the inherent flaw in the human person. If one examines a variety of strategies for avoiding the conflictual essence of the human persona, they all seem to rest on some deconstruction of self and persona. It is true of "back to nature" movements that would deconstruct individual personae into the great patterns of nature. It is certainly true of the Buddhist goal to achieve *anatta:* no-self. The peculiarity of Biblical religion is that it does not deconstruct the self to attain peace. Persona and history are not deconstructed, transcended, or subverted, they are "saved." Whatever else one might say about Biblical religion, it is unique in its hopes for persona as persona.

*The Religious Persona.*    If the issue for Christianity is the sanity of the Christian persona, there is a *formal* issue that can be raised even before one attends to specific acts and beliefs. I have accepted the definition of religion as "an intense attitude and no time off." "Intense attitude," as noted, is compatible with paranoia. Perhaps it is not only the content of paranoia that is the problem, but the intensity that is the root of insanity. If so, then any intense attitude would qualify as deranged. Is the religious *form* of life sane whatever its content?

Isaiah Berlin in a brilliant essay on the philosophy of history divided great thinkers into "hedgehogs" and "foxes."[7] Hedgehogs when under attack curl themselves into a protective ball, whereas foxes scamper, fight, or elude. The hedgehog knows one big thing, the fox knows many little things. There are great thinkers who know one big thing—Plato, Spinoza, Hegel—and there are those who know many things here and there—Aristotle, Hume, J. S. Mill. Hedgehoggery would seem to be the natural bent of religious thinkers: saints refer all things to God. St. Bonaventure, for example, writes *The Reduction of All the Arts to Theology*. Berlin opts for the foxes of life. In his judgment, life and the world just do not sum up in some grand overview or synthesis. Life is too diverse to seek the big fix. Murdoch's "Plato" sounds like the real Plato in offering a very hedgehoggery view: as for religion "[if] it is anything it must be everything."

Valuable as Berlin's distinction may be, there is a sense in which even "foxiness" is a totalizing view. If I resolve to be foxy, well, that is my synoptic philosophy. No one could accuse Aristotle or Hume of having helter-skelter philosophies. The problem is not so much "totalizing," it is the temptation of hedgehogs to construct an appearance/reality view of life and the world. This world of many foxy moments is ultimately only an illusion that dissolves into the One or the Absolute, into God, into the slide of the atoms or urges of the genes. It is refusal of a single dissolving reality above the multiple differing realities of the day that distinguishes philosophical foxes.

In that light, I would characterize Judaism and Christianity as "foxy" religions. Unlike the powerful transcending teaching of the Buddha or a grand "hedeghog" philosopher like Spinoza, Christianity and Judaism are particularist and, one might say, "down to earth." Walker Percy's claim that Judaism and Christianity are *not* members in good standing of the great world religions is meant to distinguish them from the flight to some wisdom above, which Berlin identifies with the great hedgehogs. In the particularity of Jewish history, in the notion of salvation through one, single, historical individual, Jesus of Nazareth, one aligns these "religious" views with all the utter particularity and differentiation that makes up the world of the fox. In the Christology of the previous chapter, the World-Play, with its vast cast of characters, its turmoil and passions, is not reduced to illusion by the revelation of the author.

*Faith and Reason.*   A philosophical discussion of objective and subjective is an appropriate point to offer a final postscript on the grand topic of faith and reason. Catholic apologists are almost universally insistent on the compatibility of faith and reason. They often view Protestantism as so concerned with the radical character of faith that reason is disparaged as a source of truth. Evidently Luther did say that "reason is a whore." I am equally concerned to maintain the role of reason in theology and I hope that this book is an example of rational argument. But the problem with applauding "faith and reason" is that neither term has a fixed meaning.

The root derivation of the term "rationality" is from the Latin *ratio*. While *ratio* is correctly translated as "reason," the term also lives a life as the mathematical notion of ratio. We ask in mathematics whether there is a ratio between one entity and another. In a right isoceles triangle, the hypotenuse of the triangle has no ratio with the two sides. The three sides are measured as 1, 1, and the square root of 2. The square root of 2 is an *ir*rational number or a *surd*. For all that the hypotenuse is a surd "measured" by an irrational number, the hypotenuse is not *ab*surd, it has a definite length—just that! The problem is that if you start with the sides as a definite, measurable length, you won't fit that measure exactly to the hypotenuse. (The reverse is also the case: if you start with the hypotenuse as the measured entity, then the sides cannot be measured exactly, they are surds.) When it comes to Christian "faith and reason," the question is whether there is a common ratio between reason—in its ordinary pursuits like science or philosophy—and faith. My contention is that there is no common ratio between science or mainline philosophy and faith. From the standpoint of rational science or rational philosophy, faith is a surd. Religion is therefore often regarded both positively and negatively as *ab*surd. *Credo quia absurdum* may be intoned by a Church father in a tone of piety, but rational absurdity will be rejected as unworthy by the careful philosopher. The fact that faith is a surd/absurd from the standpoint of scientific rationality does not in any way say that faith is without its own ratio or reason. Faith is no more an illusion than the irrational length of the hypotenuse in my mathematical example. The issue for faith is not whether it has a ratio or not, it is *which* ratio.

I have characterized the task of this book as one of uncovering "the logic of faith," "the language game of faith," or "the voice of faith." I could also ask for the *ratio* of faith: what sort of performance is faith? J. L. Austin's classic discussion of "I promise" is concerned to discover the proper logic/language game/ratio of promising.[8] Promising is a performative utterance; it is *doing* something with words, that is, *making* a promise. If I say "I will meet you tomorrow at 10:30 a.m.," you should be interested in knowing what language game I am playing here. Am I predicting that I will see tomorrow or am I promising? Given the ambiguity of the statement, I want to know against what circumstances and conditions the statement should be measured. If I do not show up at the time stated, how have I failed? Did I fail to keep a promise or did I make a false prediction? I want to know the proper *ratio* of the statement.

Faith in statement and performance must locate its proper *ratio,* the language game in which one understands Christian claims and commitments. I have concentrated the special *ratio* of Christianity in Jesus' statement "I am . . . the truth." It is my contention that this statement cannot be understood under the *ratio* "I am telling you the truth." No doubt Jesus does tell the truth, but if that were the basic *ratio* of "I am . . . the truth," he would be a prophet who delivered a message, not a savior. It would be blasphemous to proclaim even the best prophet as "Christ," "Son of God," and all the rest of the high Christological titles of the traditional Church. The elision from "I am . . . the truth" to "I am telling you the truth" seems simple, direct, and obvious, but it is, in my judgment, a fatal mistake. It is like mistaking the language game of "I promise" with the language game of "I predict."

In the next chapter, I will turn directly to the pope as *the* voice of the Church, the voice of faith. If the pope is the supreme teacher of faith, what is the task of that teaching? In this chapter I have suggested that the task for the Church is to shape the human person toward sanity. Sanity is measured by contact with the "truth" about reality. Since the Creator God is *the* reality and Jesus is the Word of the Creator God, what is said and done by the Church is "ratioed" to Christ. If the task of the Church is forming the sane, saintly person, the proper *ratio* for the sane person is a person: the *persona Christi.*

# Part 2

# The Voice of the Church

# CHAPTER SIX

# Pope: Professor, Judge, or Patriarch

*Io sono la tradizione; io sono la Chiesa.*

Pius IX

Since the theme of this book is the *voice* of the Catholic Church, it would seem simple enough to identify that voice: it is the papal voice. Any discussion of Catholicism flirts with the temptation to focus on the pope. Like all temptations I think it should be resisted. Concentration on the pope is the barely disguised opinion of many conservative Catholics for whom the pope *is* the Church. Pius IX actually claimed as much: *La traditio se io; io sono la Chiesa* (I am the tradition, I am the Church). As the presumed chief teacher and communicator for the Catholic faith the voice of papal discourse would appear to be central to my theme of "the medium is the message." If the Pope as *the* voice of the Church is the ultimate or unique vehicle for the Catholic message, the mode of papal speech and how that speech is to be received is crucial. Thus, though I think Pius IX was gravely wrong in how he understood what he said, public perception of the role of the papacy leads me to succumb to temptation by discussing the limitations and possibilities of "the papal voice." Concentrating on the pope is not an aberration of Pio Nono and conservative Catholics. In the long run the papal voice is in some sense integral to Catholicism— and perhaps to Christianity despite the strong opposition to the papal office in various Protestant traditions and demurral from Anglicans and Orthodox. In the end I will say some positive words about *io sono la Chiesa,* but in a sense quite different than Pius' intent.

## The Office of Pope

Positively or negatively one must realize not only that the papacy is unique among the Christian Churches and sects, but that it is difficult to discover a comparable position in any of the other world religions. Buddhism hardly pretends to be a doctrinal or a legalistic religion. The Buddha teaches Four Noble Truths as a way to serenity, but there is no God out there or *roshi* down here to rein in the errant. A Muslim *imam* may pronounce on the meaning of the Holy Qur'an, but no matter how revered his word, he may well be challenged by other high clerics. Rabbinical Judaism is rife with dispute, from the days of Shammai and Hillel to the present splits between Orthodox, Conservative, and Reformed branches of the great biblical faith. It is clear enough that Protestant communities split apart or divide internally on proper interpretation of the Bible. And no Orthodox patriarch can claim to sum the sense of the Church. That rabbis, ayatollahs, patriarchs, and the presiding bishop of the Episcopal Church may believe that they have stated *the* definitive religious truth is not to the point. What differentiates Catholicism from its religious confreres is the claim to have an infallible *office* of unchanging truth. The president of the Church of Latter Day Saints (Mormon) approximates papal authority but, unlike the popes, the president has been known to reverse previous doctrine through direct divine inspiration, such as the alteration of the status of blacks in the Mormon communion. I cite the "open texture" of religious interpretation almost everywhere save in Catholicism to emphasize how striking is the Catholic claim, but also to raise suspicion that there is something quite distinct—or odd or wrong or radically correct!—in the Catholic take on the nature of Christianity.

Having noticed the extraordinary role of the papacy in present day Catholicism, it is important to note that it has not always been so. For most of the history of the Church, the papacy has been a distant office called on more in emergency than as the ready purveyor of doctrine. The doctrine of papal infallibility was discussed during the middle ages but roundly rejected by a number of distinguished theologians. The declaration of papal infallibility did not occur until the nineteenth century, and strong voices were raised at the time against the doctrine as such or about the wisdom of making a formal declaration. A necessary qualification, therefore, in any analysis of the papal voice is that it has been a variable voice in the history of the Church — not always one with infallible inflection. There is no question but that the role of the pope has grown in the period since Vatican I. Twentieth-century Catholicism can be characterized by increasing concentration of authority in the papal office, by "papalization" of the Church. Such centralization may be a by-product of the declaration of papal infallibility, but it is at least as much the result of modern communication techniques, which have allowed Roman authorities to respond instantaneously to issues and events worldwide. Not an heretical aside shall fall but what your Holy Father shall know of it.

The Vatican's trigger-happy response to heresy may be understandable — heresy and schism are tragic events for the Church. The issue is about what sort of disagreement constitutes heresy. Too often heretical deviation has been interpreted as disagreement over the wrong "truth." The Galileo case is illustrative. Galileo held that the earth moved about the sun. Church officials disagreed because the Bible stated that the sun moved in the heavens. Joshua stopped the sun at the battle of Gibeon, he did not stop the earth ( Jo 10:13). The quarrel is a straightforward contestation about the truth of the assertion: the earth moves. This sort of disagreement about "truth" is often put forward as if the issue was a problem of faith. Can one hold to the truth of evolution and Genesis at the same time, for example — as if these were competing claims on the same sense of reality. The Galileo or Darwin controversies suggest that the Church possesses some super science that ordinary science cannot provide. The pervasive temptation to regard faith as supernatural *knowledge* leads me to begin analysis of the papal voice by asking what would be the case if the issue for the Church was supernatural knowledge and the Pope was a sort of superprofessor, someone who never got it wrong, who was infallible.

## Pope as Professor

Given the deep secular suspicions that there can be any truth at all in religion — not to mention infallible truth — a preliminary look at the papal claim to truth seems wholly in order. The Christian gospel purports to be "true," and the Pope is designated as the infallible spokesperson for that "truth." John Paul II was keen to defend the importance of truth in general and in Catholic discourse in particular. Benedict XVI has been no less emphatic about the importance of truth in the face of rampant relativism. John Paul's encyclical *Fides et Ratio* was an extended critique of the denial of truth in a range from philosophical relativism to scepticism to cynicism. University defenders of truth against the relativistic implications of such fashionable trends as deconstructionism have applauded the pope's defense of the academic domain but are likely to remain wary of Church-truth. The problem is that the truth about truth is highly complicated. The philosopher Richard Bernstein noted the complexity of "truth" in a commentary on *Fides et Ratio*:

> The word that is used with perhaps the greatest frequency . . . is *truth*. But it is used in a bewildering variety of ways: "ultimate Truth," "absolute truth," "universal truth," "the fullness of truth," "the different faces of human truth," "the truth attained by philosophy," "the truth of Revelation," "Jesus Christ as the truth," "the unity of truth," "different modes of truth," an "ulterior truth that would explain the meaning of life," "the truth of the person" are phrases repeated throughout the letter. Although it is clearly asserted that there are "different modes of truth," and that ultimately there is a harmony and *unity* of these truths, there is virtually no attempt to stand back and reflect upon the different *meanings* of "truth" and to show us precisely how they are compatible. Nor is any attempt made to show us how we are to reconcile conflicting claims to truth. But this is the issue which must be confronted if one is to *justify* the claim that the truths of reason and faith form a harmonious unity.[1]

Given the complexities pointed to by Prof. Bernstein, one can throw some light on the tangle of "truth" by considering the actual career of Karol Wojtyla, who moved from philosophy professor Wojtyla to Pope John Paul II, and theology professor Ratzinger, who became Benedict XVI. Both popes are surely among the most learned popes in the history of the Church. As former university professors, both are capable of complex and penetrating argument. All this is to the good, but there is a radical change of voice from a pope writing an encyclical to a professor writing a scholarly book.

What is the voice of truth in the professorial game? How does the papal game of truth, differ? Professorial scholarship, even the very best, speaks in a voice that invites comment and correction; papal encyclicals claim to settle issues. When professors Wojtyla or Ratzinger published their thoughts they entered into a complex dialogue. The scholarly medium of discourse demands debate; the voice is tentative *de lege* even if in academic polemic it is often not so *de facto*. The Church medium of proclamation seems to close debate; the tone is not at all tentative *de lege* or *de facto*. When the pope declares on some moral dispute, the dialogue is presumably concluded, the issue settled, the conversation brought to an end. *Pope* John Paul II says that ordination of women is not even to be discussed; *Professor* Wojtyla could never pronounce such a dictum.

The distinguished New Testament theologian N. T. Wright speaks in a typical professor-theologian's voice in the preface to his monumental, multivolume study of the origins of Christianity:

> . . . a final word of warning. I frequently tell my students that quite a high proportion of what I say is probably wrong, or at least flawed or skewed in some way which I do not at the moment realize. The only problem is that I do not know which bits are wrong; if I did I might do something about it. . . . [S]ince I am aware of the virtual certainty of error in some of what I write, I hope I will pay proper attention to the comment of those—and no doubt there will be many—who wish to draw my attention to the places where they find my statement of the evidence inadequate, my arguments weak, or conclusions unwarranted. Serious debate and confrontation is the stuff of academic life.[2]

That is definitely *not* pope-talk. As a Church hierarch, *the* Church hierarch, the Pope transcends (or abandons) discussion in the interests of doctrine. No wonder theologians, biblical scholars, and the laity in the pews feel left out; they simply have no place in a possible dialogue because *dialogue is not the medium of exchange,* not the language game being played. The papal *voice* appears authoritative and final.

The transition from professor to pope exemplifies one of those crucial transitions of language game that must be understood in order to position the voice of the Church. The pope is presumed to be a *teacher* of truth, but as such he seems quite unlike ordinary professorial teachers of truth. The latter hope that their conjectures and theories are true, but that is a conclusion only arrived at after extended testing and discussion, as Wright's remarks illustrate. The academic medium of exchange was summed up by the great American philosopher Charles Sanders Pierce. He placed academic, professorial discourse under the sign of "fallibilism": the notion that truth will only emerge as fallible (possibly false) statements are criticized over time and found to be acceptable. Popes, on the contrary, operate under the sign of "infallibilism": Church truths are apparently not open to fundamental testing, refutation or reconstruction. A professor who becomes a pope abandons the academic game. Is he then in any position to convey anything that might be construed as "truth"? Professors will think not. Academic apprehensions about Church-truth are not merely about content but more directly about the notion that truth can be *proclaimed* by an office. From the academic standpoint, the Church should just give up on papal proclamations of "truth." Christian claims are subject to the ordinary methods of testing in history and experience recognized in the academic trade, or they are mere conjecture: one pope's opinion.

The only way to avoid a fatal clash between professor and pope, is to make it clear that there are two radically different language games at play. What can be "known" by playing one game is just impossible in the other. There is no checkmate in checkers; therefore I cannot *know* the moment of checkmate in a game of checkers. Academic and Church language games are not always (or usually and unfortunately) clearly differentiated. Catholic apologists claiming infallibility often construe the pope as a super-professor who somehow transcends the fallibility rules of the academic game. Normal professors rely on mere human colleagues to critique and verify their theories; the pope has a divine colleague who gives him *the* right answer! The proper understanding is that fallibility (academic) and infallibility (Church), despite superficial linguistic identity, function in different language games and, as such, are not contradictory claims. Fallibilism is a rule in the academic game; infallibilism is a rule in the Church game.

Fundamentalism is a professor-like "solution" to Christian truth. Fundamentalism comes in different forms; the most common form is biblical fundamentalism, the notion that the Bible contains infallible facts and moral commands. Papal fundamentalism is somewhat more complex but in the long run rests on the same formal mistake as biblical fundamentalism. The biblical fundamentalist reads the Gospels as normal historical documents that are true in the same manner as Thucydides' history of the Peleponnesian War. Utter relativists to the side, Thucydides offers us a generally reliable account of what actually happened. Fundamentalism accepts the language game of traditional historians in so far as it views Gospel accounts as "straight history." The Gospels are "the simple truth" of what happened. Fundamentalist straight history strays from normal history only by the small step of recording unusual events (miracles) as on a par with more ordinary occurrences. Jesus was crucified under Pontius Pilate (firmly attested history) and rose from the dead (the reliable witness of the Gospel writers).

There are multiple problems with any professor-like view of Christian truth. In the first place it would seem to leave faith at the mercy of professors. Whatever else faith may be, it is not the consensus of historical scholarship. Fundamentalists, of course, move beyond the Gospels as the consensus of scholars because of the issue of authorship. Thucydides is a more or less reliable author when writing about the Peloponnesian War, the author of the Bible is wholly reliable: God Himself. Modern scholars may question the reliability of any secular source, but there is no quibbling with a divine author. Fundamentalism plays the academic language game of straight history but holds a trump card that is quite unavailable to the ordinary historian. Biblical history is "infallible truth" because the source is unimpeachable. Papal teaching can be construed on a similar fundamentalist structure, though instead of literal biblical reading it relies upon the unimpeachable guidance of the Holy Spirit in the tradition of the Church. Christian infallibility cannot be playing the professor's game with a trump card up your sleeve because Christian truth is not professorial truth, for example, historical or scientific truth. As suggested earlier and as will be developed more positively below, the truth of Christianity relates to the truth of sanity, to the true persona.

"Factual truth" cannot be "religious truth." Putting aside the question of the moral infallibility of the Bible, statements of religious belief are not simple factual attestations however well verified. One might affirm a creator as one of the odd facts of the cosmos like quasars and black holes, but worshiping such a god would be like worshiping a black hole. Not every "creator" is worthy of human trust. I neither trust nor mistrust the Big Bang. The Christian creed exists in the mode of worship, not in the mode of fact with a worshipful tag end. The biblical God can only be spoken about within the world of praise and prayer. In ordinary life we think that one can only talk about the king *with respect* (not the person, but the kingship). The biblical God, His God-ship, must be spoken to with praise and worship, otherwise you have the wrong object in mind.

In sum, the professorial game is played according to the rules of fallibilism. The religious game does not play a professorial game because it holds a trump (reporter, author, or document) that by definition cannot be doubted. If there is infallibility anywhere in popes or the Bible, it must exist in a different game of "truth."

## Pope as Judge

There is an alternative game to the professorial game that, since it is played with very different rules, has often been offered as a construction for the papal office. Popes must stop playing like professors, they must be judges. The papacy is an *office of decision* because popes play a *practical* game. The professor who becomes pope no longer enjoys the luxury of offering a learned hypothesis for discussion, he must *decide* for this or that moral issue. Because the practical world demands closure and decision, one sees the function of the pope as *the* judge, the Supreme Court in person. In the world of the practical, one cannot dither forever on the meaning of the law, so the judgment of the court is "the last word." (Biblical fundamentalists follow the same formal logic: it is not papal pronouncements that settle moral problems, it is the Ten Commandments or whatever other favored moral prescription is cited.)

The problem with the analogy to legal practice for traditional assertions about the papacy is that Supreme Courts are not "infallible" either in the wisdom of their decisions or the truths which support them. When the United States Supreme Court declared in the Dred Scott decision that runaway slaves must be returned to their owners, Abraham Lincoln commented that the Court did not "issue Holy Writ." Supreme Courts reverse themselves; consider, for example, the United States Supreme Court on the issue of "separate but equal" facilities for Negroes. Popes do not reverse themselves. (They actually do, but they don't say so.[3])

In order for pope to be infallible on matters of moral law, he would again have to hold a trump card. Using the Constitution as the fundamental analogy, one would note that humans made and can amend the United States Constitution, but God made the Ten Commandments and He shows no inclination to amend them. There is a continuing need, however, to interpret the Ten Commandments. What is the exact extent of, for example, "Thou shalt not commit adultery"? A recent U.S. court case ruled that an extramarital lesbian liaison could not be legally regarded as "adultery," though most Christians *would* consider this adultery. How do we know how to interpret the Ten Commandments? The common Catholic answer presumes that God has not only provided the Law, he has also provided an infallible interpreter of the Law. Unlike Judaism in which interpretation of the Law is a matter of on-going complex argument among many learned rabbis, in Catholicism the argument can be definitively settled in *official* teaching.

There would be some practical justification for the papal office if one interpreted the Bible in a law-and-obedience game. One might even grant infallibility on the supposition that God would not demand that we obey certain commands without also assuring that there was a methodology for interpreting the scope of the commands. The fundamental problem is that again one is playing the wrong game. To carry through a "Supreme Court" analogy for Church governance and the role of the pope, one would have to recast the relation between God and humanity wholly within a framework of morality, and that is almost as great a mistake as regarding the faith as part of the theoretical, albeit super-true. Recasting Christianity in the language game of practical morality falsifies the sense of faith.

There is an obvious temptation to accept a thoroughly practical construction of Christianity. Christianity is supposed to change my life. I am called upon to perform the works of mercy, to *live* a special sort of life. All that talk apparently exists in the realm of "the practical." It is the call to Christian life that leads many to reject a Church of dogma in favor of a Church of practice, fostering the works of peace, love and justice. I have tried to show that while Christian living presses toward peace, love, and justice, these practical ends are understood in a uniquely Christian way, a way expressed in the liturgy of baptism, scripture, and Eucharist. The Christian praxis that emerges from liturgy is not directly moral as if humans had the task of creating peace, love, and justice. The liturgy says that the real peace, love, and justice have already been created. Our task is to live according to what is already there. It is the difference between striving to make your fortune and undertaking the responsibilities of your munificent inheritance. There are ways of life that stem from striving on the one hand and being a responsible steward on the other, but the relation between my effort and the goal is radically changed. In the latter case I am *already* rich!

## Pope as Patriarch

Having rejected two plausible papal models, I want to suggest a quite different logic for the voice of the Church and the papal office.[4] In the encyclical *Ut Unum Sint,* "That they may be one," John Paul II invited Christian theologians, regardless of denomination, to join with him in understanding his ministry as "successor to Peter." In the encyclical, John Paul avoided many of the imperial titles that have so often given offense. Paul VI had rightly noted that "the pope . . . is undoubtedly the gravest obstacle in the path of ecumenism,"[5] so John Paul's invitation to a "patient and fraternal dialogue," if genuinely pursued, offered a remarkable opportunity. The opportunity is as important for Roman Catholics as it is for Protestants and the Orthodox. The importance for Catholics of a study of "the primacy of Peter" is crucial for developing a theology of Church, and it is clearly an unfinished historical task. Vatican I was artificially truncated by the arrival of Italian troops in Rome. As a result, the full schema of the Council was never accomplished. What had been intended as a broad study of the Church from the pope through bishops, priests, and people became only a statement about the pope with no counterbalancing understandings. From the standpoint of Vatican I, one might believe that the pope *is* the Church, as Pius IX stated. In a sense, Vatican II "completed" Vatican I by moving on from the status of the pope to the place of "the people of God" (Vatican II characterized the "Church" as encompassing all the baptized.) Vatican III (or Geneva I) should have the task of relating Vatican II back to the discussion of primacy in Vatican I. *Ut Unum Sint* was an implicit invitation for such a recursive dialogue. Without Vatican III or its logical equivalent, one is left with the present quarrel between popocracy and democracy as the proper structure for the Church. Both models fail to understand the reality of the Christian community.

The crucial text for papal claims has always been Matthew 16:15–19.

He said to them, "But who do you say that I am?" Simon Peter answered, "You are the Messiah, the Son of the Living God." And Jesus answered him, "Blessed are you, Simon son of Jonah! For flesh and blood has not revealed this to you, but my Father in heaven. And I tell you, you are Peter, and on this rock I will build my Church, and the gates of Hades will not prevail against it. I will give to you the keys to the kingdom of heaven, and whatever you bind on earth will be bound in heaven, and whatever you loose on earth will be loosed in heaven."

Since John Paul rests the issue of papal primacy on "successor of Peter," I suggest one begin a positive account of the papacy by asking "To whom is Peter the successor?" Asking that question is intended to place the pope, the "successor to Peter," within a deep biblical background. Four verses from Matthew extracted, isolated, and sanitized from biblical sensibility prove nothing. Using biblical parallels is commonplace in Christian understandings—a tale told of Miriam becomes a story for Mary, a prophecy for David becomes a sign for Jesus—and "Thou art Peter," the fundamental text of the Roman pontiffs, has striking biblical predecessors. I chose one from the Hebrew Bible: a similar story of a recognition, blessing, designation of a "new" name, and a "founding" of the people of God. If we are to understand "successor of Peter," the Hebrew precursor is highly significant.

The biblical patriarch Jacob wrestles through a long night with an unknown stranger (Gen: 32). At the breaking of the day, the unknown one has not prevailed; he touches the hollow of Jacob's thigh, and Jacob is lamed. Yet Jacob struggles on and will not release the dark stranger unless he blesses him. The stranger asks, "What is thy name?" "Jacob." "Thy name shall be called no more Jacob, but Israel, for as a prince hast thou power with God." And the stranger departs, refusing to give his name in return. Jacob called the place Peniel: "For I have seen God face to face and my life is preserved."

This brief tale presents the subject and substance of Jewish history—a history that the Bible asserts to be fundamental for humankind. The substance of Jewish history—one can say of *all* history—can be envisioned as a long night struggle with a dark stranger. Is he friend or enemy? Crippled, Jacob will not release the unknown one unless he is blessed. And so it is. Without learning his name, without seeing his face in the clear dawn, Jacob accepts a blessing. The stranger vanishes leaving Jacob only with the memory of an indecisive battle in the night, the name of Israel, and the conviction that he has seen God face to face. That generations of Jews who summon themselves as "Israel" should regard their long dark struggle in history as wrestling with *an unknown who blesses* is no more mysterious, puzzling, and daring than Jacob's conclusion that he has seen God face to face and been preserved.

In the night struggle of human history, do we confront an unknown who blesses? How outrageous, how doubtful to the modern mind! The turmoil of the ages seems a dark struggle with unknown forces which, far from leaving us with blessing, simply ignore us, scorning all meaning for the human struggle. Do we strive toward dawn and blessing, or is the human story merely thrashing in the indifferent cosmic dust? The story of Jacob declares for dawn.

The dark stranger asks his name. "Jacob." "Thy name shall be called no more Jacob, but Israel; for as a prince hast thou power with God." When one has wrestled with God through the darkness and emerged into dawn and blessing, one emerges not as mortal Jacob but as undying Israel. Since then, generations of Jews have called themselves to prayer with the cry, "*Shema Israel . . .*" "Hear, O Israel . . ." Eternal Israel is the *subject* of a history-with-God. What is the religious faith attested to by those who heed the call, "Hear, O Israel"? The great twentieth-century Jewish theologian Franz Rosenzweig makes the following startling statement:

> The belief [of the Jew] is not the content of a testimony, but rather the product of reproduction. The Jew, engendered a Jew, attests his belief by continuing to procreate the Jewish people. His belief is not in something; he is himself the belief.[6]

A child's birth shows that God has not given up hope. So it is with Eternal Israel. Every child attests to a fundamental hope—a hope not carried in philosophical argument but deep in the heart and soul. If one were to consider the tragedies of Jewish history—exile, diaspora, pogrom, annihilation—surely one could abandon hope. History is the nightmare of James Joyce's fiction and Jewish experience. Bringing forth children into the nightmare of this history witnesses to a hope beyond rational calculation. The belief of the Jew, as Rosenzweig says, "is not the content of some testimony . . . he is himself the belief."

With the story of Eternal Israel in mind, turn to the designation of another "people of God": the Church. Jesus asks, "Who do you say that I am?" What should we say? Jacob proclaims that he wrestles in the long night with a stranger who blesses. "I have seen God face to face." Simon Barjonah proclaims, "Thou art the Christ, the Son of the Living God." "Blessed art thou . . . henceforth art thou Peter and upon this rock I will build my Church."

How can we understand the extraordinary claims put forth in these two stories? Can one see God face to face? Could this man Jesus somehow be the Son of the Living God? Jacob/Israel and Simon/Peter say in variant ways, "I have seen God face to face and my life has been preserved." Imagine Jacob/Israel as the prefigurement of Simon/Peter. Simon believes that he has seen the Christ of God. For this recognition he is blessed by "the dark stranger," Jesus of the Gospels. ("He comes to us as One unknown, without a name, as of old, by the lakeside. . . . [T]o those who obey him . . . He will reveal himself in the toils, the conflicts, the sufferings which they shall pass through. . . . [T]hey shall learn in their own experience Who He is" [the concluding paragraph in Schweitzer's *The Quest of the Historical Jesus*].) He who sees in Jesus "the Son of the Living God" is transmuted from mortal Simon to eternal Peter, and on that rock the people of God are summoned from generation to generation without fail: the gates of hell shall not prevail against them. Name change as one is transformed by contact with God is also the case with the first patriarch, Abraham. After heeding God's call to leave his ancestral home, Abram becomes Abraham, "the father of faith." Religious patriarchy as "father of faith" follows from God's patriarchy, which is signaled by the fact that one now acts under a name given by God: Abraham, Israel, Peter.

The parallelism is far from fanciful. As Jews are summoned to prayer by invoking an immortal destiny in the name of Israel, Christians are summoned under the proclamation of Simon that this Jesus is the Christ of God. Peter's claim is the eternal faith of the Church as "the people of God." The parallelism of Jacob/Israel and Simon/Peter is compelling. But the problem is not parallelism; it is the sense of the community, the people of God, derived from comparing unfailing Church to Eternal Israel, considering Peter as successor to Jacob, and pope as successor of Peter.

To draw a general lesson about Church, let me expand the "pro-creational" view of Rosenzweig, taking seriously the notion of father of faith and thus father of the *eternal family,* which was, after all, God's great promise first to Abraham and then to Jacob/Israel. Rosenzweig sees Jewish faith carried forward not in dogma or moral deeds, but in procreation: the Jewish child brought forth is himself the belief. The center of the Jewish inspiration is that God is realized in the procreation of blood and bone. If the fundamental Hebrew belief is carried "bodily," then it is altogether appropriate that the Jew Jesus would say, "*I* am the way and the truth and the life." Jesus is not *delivering* a message, his life and death is the message. Rosenzweig says that in carrying forward the Jewish people from generation unto generation, the Jew in his very existence is the message of hope. Jesus in his very existence is the message of salvation. "*I* am the way . . . and the life."

Israel shows forth salvation in the body, in procreation of the people. In the synoptic account of his final meal, Jesus blesses bread and wine, offering them as his very body and blood, which will be witness to salvation and be the marker for his ongoing community. It is at the Last Supper as recorded by John that Jesus says "I am the way and the truth." The hope of Israel and the faith of the Church are carried not in creed and deed, but in the carrying forward of bodily presence—a continuation that is without fail. Jewish faith (as Eternal Israel) recreates the body of the people; Christian faith (as Church) "recreates" the body of Jesus and thus "procreates" the people of God in every generation.

Israel is a literal people, the Church is a sacramental people. Christianity spiritualizes the story of the eternal family. From a Jewish perspective, Christianity may seem to evaporate family by removing its palpable reality. Holy Fathers do not procreate; Jewish patriarchs surely do! On the other hand, Eternal Israel is more than a matter of blood lines. Judaism is not tribalism because this is a holy people, a priestly people. Israel is not self-enclosing, it exists as a holy witness for the world. Great rabbis have argued that all nations were present at Sinai and that all humanity is enfolded in Eternal Israel. It is not at all clear that one can regard the Christian Church as superseding that great Jewish inspiration. Rosenzweig regarded Christianity as missionary Judaism.

Is there a lesson in the succession from father Abram/Abraham and Jacob/Israel to Simon/Peter and on to Joseph Ratzinger/Benedict XVI? The function of the successor of both Simon/Peter and Jacob/Israel should be understood according to the circumstance of the original claim: "I have seen God face to face." The pope as the figure of Peter/Israel functions to assert Peter's original proclamation that God (the dark stranger, the unknown One by the lakeside) is *in our history,* and this nightmare tale moves toward dawn and blessing. There are three deep lessons corollary to this central and overriding proclamation.

First there is the claim that our palpable history is not all illusion and sin. God wrestles with us in history; this crucified man is the Christ of God. Humanity cannot turn aside from the agonies of history because God does not reside "above." Despair over history is not allowed because the one who wrestles with us on the ground in history leaves a blessing. Second lesson: Jacob is lamed, and Peter is certainly "lamed" repeatedly in his understanding of Jesus. Immediately after his crucial proclamation of the Christ, Jesus calls Peter "Satan" because he, Peter, cannot understand a suffering Messiah. In God's hands we are lamed. If we cannot despair over history, neither are we lords of history. And the third lesson is that Jacob never learns the name of the dark stranger. Not only are we not lords of history, lacking a name we cannot summon the God who is. For all that we believe that we wrestle with God, that here is the Christ, we cannot comprehend the ways of God as they lead through powerlessness and loss. If Israel/Peter/pope proclaim that God is with us in history, if they disallow despair and rebuke our pride, if they forbid us to summon the incomprehensible God, they have set out a broad agenda.

Underlying Judaism and Christianity is that God is real in history and that history is therefore real. In the earlier discussion of the Supreme Shakespeare, it was crucial that the World-Play remain real. Whatever the sins of Israel so stringently set forth by the prophets, they all affirm that God has not abandoned his covenant. Resurrection in Christianity repeats this Jewish theme for humankind: however you may reject me, I do not reject you. Christianity is by no means Jewish belief recycled. The dark stranger of Jacob/Israel's mythic story may be an easier figure for belief than an historical Nazarene carpenter who broke bread with the likes of Simon Barjonah. An historical Jesus may appear to move too far forward into daylight and dogma. On the analogy of Jacob/Israel, Peter is a "patriarch," but a sacramental patriarch, not literal father of a family but a Holy Father of the people of God. Literal patriarchs bear a bodily relation to their extended family (the procreational element in Rosenzweig's claim), whereas Peter is not patriarch of a biological family into which one is physically born but patriarch of a sacramental family into which one is spiritually born. The question of the papacy is how one understands the relation of sacramental father to the sacramental family (Church).

The pope as symbol of the sacramental family (in that sense a "holy father" and "patriarch") is not exactly the pope that Pius IX and Vatican I seemed to have had in mind. A familial/patriarchal interpretation shifts away from the didactic view of the pope as infallible professor in matters of faith and morals. Eternal Israel and Christian Church rest on revelations deeper than professorial, even super-professorial, teaching. An earthly father may "teach" his children various lessons about life, but if it is just teaching, the child might be well advised to read Plato or any other available sage. The authority and power of the relation is not the father's philosophical acuity, it is the spiritual relation of father-child. I will discuss the issue of "patriarchal teaching" in detail in subsequent chapters. For now, let me just note that fathers can have false teachings, but still be loving fathers. It is loving that is the ongoing lesson.

## Saving Patriarchy

Attempting to reconceive the papal voice as "patriarchal" rather than professorial or judicative may seem a classic case of "out of the frying pan into the fire." Feminist critics, such as Elizabeth Johnson, within and without the Church have bitterly condemned the culture of patriarchy as deeply and fundamentally demeaning to women. Patriarchy as understood by feminists is a pervasive social structure that privileges traditional "male" virtues while casting female ways as lesser and subservient. Given the feminist critique of patriarchy with which I am in full sympathy, one should be hesitant about using patriarchal language anywhere from Father Chuck in the local parish to the Holy Father on up to God "the Father" *Him*self. Nevertheless, I think it is worth trying to transvalue the term "patriarchy" not only because of the extensive use of patriarchal terminology in the tradition but because there may be an essential reality buried under falsely gendered authority. I tend to agree with Raymond Brown that in translating biblical terminology the principle should be precision rather than political correctness. Changing literal terms to avoid offense gives a false impression about the Bible. It suggests that it does *not* have to be interpreted and "corrected" according to our better understandings—the text was always politically correct!

Transvaluing "patriarchy" would be consistent with the general transvaluation of values in the New Testament. It is the meek who inherit the kingdom, it is enemies that are to be loved. Transvaluing "patriarchy" can be justified by considering how "slavery" is subverted in the New Testament and the history of Christian spirituality. Historical slavery can be regarded as a more generalized form of the oppression that marks patriarchy: a pervasive social structure that falsely positions everyone. A society that institutionalizes slavery positions everyone as either master or slave, free or bound; neither condition of the human is spiritually sound. The obvious personal diminishment of the slave—the fact that the slave can be sold like a piece of furniture—is matched by the personal diminishment of the master who blinds himself to the human reality of the slave-person before his eyes. Slavery is a pervasive evil that corrupts society root and branch. In a later chapter, I will discuss slave society as the very figure of a kingdom of sin.

Given the corruption of the culture of slavery, it is striking that the Bible throughout transvalues slavery when it comes to our relations with God. This is generally masked in English translations where the word "servant" has traditionally been used instead of the literal Greek of slave, slave girl, or slave boy. In the Magnificat, Mary refers to herself as the "handmaid" of the Lord. The word translated "handmaid" or "servant" is the Greek *doulos* which means slave and nothing other. Reading the Bible literally, we are urged to be "slaves" of the Lord. In contrast, the use of "slavery" as marking a proper relation *to other humans* is countered in the New Testament by Paul's admonition that in Christ there is neither slave nor free, in other words, the human relation of master and slave is dissolved in the relation to Christ since both are to be "slaves of God." What may be utterly corrupting for human-human relations—slavery (or patriarchy)—is demanded in the divine-human relation. God is master and "patriarch," Author and Creator.

The danger in retaining the language of patriarchy in the Church is that the destructive structures of the human institution, particularly the gender designation, will be carried over to the divine-human relation as well as the ecclesiastical structures of the Church. In the human structures of slavery and patriarchy the subservient one is necessarily diminished. Slaves in Roman law were referred to as *instrumentum vocale:* talking tools. This is precisely what is not supposed to be the case in the structures of divine-human slavery and patriarchy. In our previous analysis of the role of Christ in the World-Play, his role is not to diminish the human persona in all its shades and tempers, but to enhance it, make it more real. The Supreme Shakespeare does not create puppets, *instrumentum vocale,* to speak His lines. If there is slavery in the World-Play, it is a slavery that we impose on ourselves, the self-authoring restricting image that we project as a defensive measure against all others.

I cannot leave the matter of patriarchy without noting how the Church has misapplied the notion historically and up to the present day. The distortion is twofold. First there is the misleading identification of God with the male gender. Clearly the monotheistic God of the Hebrews is without gender, and in many ways his relation to humanity is better imaged by feminine characteristics, as Elizabeth Johnson has demonstrated in *She Who Is.*[7] The diminution of women continues in the Roman Catholic Church under the aegis of unreconstructed, gendered patriarchy. The second danger in retaining patriarchal (or matriarchal) language is a false sense of *hierarchical* (master/slave) domination buried in the notions. All too many of the ascetic practices of traditional Christianity have had the clear effect of destroying personal worth. But being a "slave" of the biblical Creator is meant to expand human vitality, not crimp it in self-loathing.

My attempt to save the notion of patriarchy is based in the fundamental need to retain *family logic* as the basic framework for understanding the traditional claims of the Catholic Church to be an institution of infallible hierarchic teaching. I happen to agree that hierarchy, infallibility, and teaching are essential characteristics of the Church, but I believe that they have been inserted into the wrong language game. One may, for instance, regard patriarchy as a fault because it is an instance of the fundamental distortion caused by political hierarchy. One can then say that hierarchy is fundamentally unacceptable because it is distant, impersonal, and didactic. If you believe that, you would opt for a democratic model of the Church. Deborah Tannen has pointed out, however, that there are different sorts of hierarchy.[8] Not all hierarchies are distant and impersonal. A "familial" hierarchy that can be close and intimate is the relation of grandparent to grandchild. (Maybe what the Church needs is a Holy Grandfather!)

According to the language game being played: academy, law court, or Church as sacramental family, infallible, hierarchy, and teaching will play quite different roles or no role at all. As the earlier sections of this chapter attempted to show, a notion like "infallibility" has no legitimate role to play in the logic of academic or scientific discourse or in the ruling of judges and courts. Attempts to insert infallible pronouncements into those language games is playing with a trump card up your sleeve. If there is to be any rescue of infallibility it will come within a very different language game, one that I designate as the logic of the *sacramental family*. The next chapters will explore this logic of family as it applies to the natural family and the Church as sacramental family.

# The Voice of the *Persona Christi*

> *[The Church's] inner obligation [is] to send all peoples to*
> *the school of Jesus, because he is the truth in person*
> *and, thereby, the way to be human.*
>
> Cardinal Ratzinger, *Truth and Tolerance*

Defending a "patriarchal," authorial God is one thing, translating patriarchal structure to the institution of the Church is quite another matter. I should be humble before God who is in the business of enriching my life and saving me from death, but humbling myself before a Borgia pope or even the saintly John XXIII is nowhere near as obvious. This chapter explores the possible rationale and the significant qualifications of the *official*—ultimately the papal—patriarchal voice of Catholicism

Patriarchy is the gendered expression of a special hierarchy of relation with its attendant claim for authority. There are those who on spiritual or political grounds regard hierarchal structure for the Church as fundamentally objectionable. One can appeal to the egalitarian spirit of the early Christian community or to the dangers of latter-day ecclesiastical power structures to reject hierarchy. Both appeals have clear validity, but I would argue that there is a proper and necessary sense of hierarchy for the Church that rests on the fundamental teaching function of the Church. If A teaches B, then in some sense one assumes—or hopes—that A possesses some superior authority on the issue at hand. Classroom teachers will sometimes say that they "learn from their students," which, while certainly true in many cases, cannot be a justification for the basic relation of teacher and student. It is a constant theme of this book that Church teaching is *not* classroom teaching, but teaching in some sense is an essential activity and obligation of the Church. The Catholic Church certainly claims hierarchal teaching—and *infallible* hierarchal teaching at that! The problem is to explicate the sort of teaching that could justify such an extravagant claim.

Let me recall the discussion of teaching in the previous chapter. The crucial qualification made about Church teaching was that it is *patriarchal* teaching—teaching uniquely defined as "fatherly." (Once again: "fatherly" is not intended as sexist but to repeat father/mother/parental is awkward. It makes the text read like a legal document with all the universality and dullness characteristic of such prose. Christian language is not addressed "to whom it may concern.") Christian teaching differs radically from our common sense of teaching, in other words, professorial teaching. The difference between patriarchal teaching and professorial teaching rests on the radical difference between *teaching Jesus* and *teaching the teachings of Jesus*. Church patriarchal teaching has, as the quotation from Benedict XVI at the head of this chapter indicates, the strange logic of "teaching a person." Papal teaching must conform to that strangeness.

A statement by Kierkegaard is helpful in understanding the special logic of patriarchal teaching.

> When the question of truth is raised subjectively, reflection is directed subjectively to the nature of the individual's relationship; if only the mode of this relationship is in the truth, the individual is in the truth even if he should happen to be . . . related to what is not true.[1]

Kierkegaard's use of "subjectively" is not to be confused with the "merely subjective" construal of religious belief favored by critics and enthusiasts of religion discussed earlier. For Kierkegaard "subjectively" points to the *subject,* the persona engaged. When I engage religiously in religion it is my *person* that speaks and listens. My person is not a subjective *opinion,* it is my full reality, it is my *self*. As Iris Murdoch's "Plato" says, "[Religion] has got to be the magnetic center of everything. . . . If it is not everywhere . . . it isn't what I mean. . . . It's to do with life as a whole."

Kierkegaard says that when and if my persona is engaged in a "true" relation, I am in the truth, even if what I say happens to be false to fact. There is a further (meta)truth for Kierkegaard's comment itself: there is the truth of fact/doctrine, there is the truth of relationship, and there is the metatruth that relates fact/doctrine and relationship. All three truths can be displayed in a single statement: "It is a fact that Moses wrote the first five books of the Bible, I tell you this as your father, and as father I always say what is true." The first clause is false, the second truthfully notes an existential relation, the third is a false claim about what follows from being father. Using Kierkegaard's distinction, the pope might then make a false statement and still speak within the truth as patriarch of the sacramental family. (Well into the twentieth century, papal teaching did claim that Moses wrote the first five books of the Bible.) The patriarch of the sacramental family does not exercise his patriarchal function primarily by making true statements but in carrying forward the truth of relationship: the truth of fathering the sacramental family.

There is a sense in which the claim "Moses wrote the first five books of the Bible" could be true to the modality of a truly fatherly voice. Though false to fact, it could be used to express the father's loving concern that the child give special respect to the biblical text. He bases this respect on a mistaken claim of authorship, but the real issue is respect for the text. I am not suggesting that one should be fast and loose with fact and doctrine — say anything as long as it is "fatherly." Doctrinal pronouncements lead a double life as fatherly and factual. One can fatally undermine the fatherly relation by loosely promulgating factual falsehoods. Indeed, being father *obligates* one to offer truths in the conventional sense. It was a considerable advance of the fatherly obligation to speak the factual truth when Catholic biblical scholarship was allowed to abandon the pious myth of Mosaic authorship of the first five books of the Bible. Not only does being factually correct about the authorship of the Bible prevent falsity on facts and the potential deterioration of trust, it also corrects a false view of how one assigns "sacredness" to texts, that is, they are not sacred because authored by revered patriarchs.

One can apply the truth of relationship to critical doctrinal issues. Various Christologies that characterize Jesus as Messiah, Lord, Son of God, and so on need to be tested not so much against some theological argument, biblical text, or traditional language, but on whether the person advocating a particular Christology sees herself in the *true existential relation* to Jesus as the Christ. One can characterize the relationship for lack of a better term as "worshipful." One might, therefore, say that Jesus is the *adopted* son of God but if you *worship* Jesus, your prayer and actions speak within the true existential relation: you have placed yourself *within* the truth of Christianity. When the language of adoption is rejected by the Church, it is because it seems insufficient to ground worship. Worship seems to demand a "substantial" relation ("of one substance with the Father") to justify calling Jesus Son of God and thus worthy of worship with the Father. If we worship, we must ask what sort of $X$ would be worthy of worship. Lots of "gods" are unworthy of worship, and in many interpretations of the biblical God that "god" is unworthy of worship. Faith is not just getting the language right as if we had to assent to some metaphysical characterization of God and Christ, it is that *worship* of Jesus demands certain linguistic turns.[2]

The basic function of a patriarch in the Church or a father in a natural family is not to be the fount of true statements or even moral surety, it is to continue to be *father* however he may falter on factual or philosophic, truth and be mistaken on moral insight. A father in the natural family who insists that he will only act as father if his children agree with his historical, philosophic or moral pronouncements misunderstands the nature of fathering. The usual Catholic view that the Holy Father announces infallible doctrine is a false reflection on the "truth" of relationship: the assumption that fathering infallibly produces true doctrine and moral judgment. Infallibility is a mark of *true fathering* not of the truths and tales that may issue from true fathering. If I tell my children an animal fable that illustrates the importance of courage in adversity, my intent is to encourage them toward a worthy life. The fact that the fable involves talking animals does not make me a liar who deceives his children. We are not, however, always talking to children, and there are times when my fatherly obligation demands that I replace fables with fact. One could say that a root problem with much Christian teaching is that it all too often stays in the land of pious fable and is thus rejected out of hand by adults and by cultures grown to maturity.

Genuine papal teaching rests within the right relation of father in the sacramental family. He is infallible when his voice is the *father's* voice: when what is said is carried within the structure of the existential relation. In

Wittgenstein's terms, the Christian teacher—the pope as primary teacher—must play the *sacramental-family* language game. Difference in doctrine—the fact that the child and parent may *not* agree that Moses wrote the first five books of the Bible or that Jesus is the adopted Son of God—cannot as such constitute a breaking of the parent-child relation. There are situations in which relation is based upon agreement on stated doctrine. In a voluntary organization like the Rotary Club or the Republican party, disagreement on doctrine constitutes separation from the cause. The family is clearly not such a voluntary organization nor is the Church. God is not the Ultimate Rotarian (not to mention the Supreme Republican!) with whom I can sever relations because I don't agree with his doctrines. As Iris Murdoch says, in religion we are not volunteers but conscripts. In the natural family we are also conscripts; I did not volunteer to be born into my family. Thus I have argued *extra ecclesia nullus,* there is no one really outside the Church because everyone is conscripted into God's grace.

The natural family is constituted by parentage, not doctrinal unity. If the Church is properly understood as a sacramental family, then there is no Church doctrine that can be understood outside the existential family relation. "Dogma" is a legitimate move only within the sacramental-family game; dogma is a possible play within the "parental" relation. Wittgenstein says "Only love could believe in the Resurrection." Only if one is playing the person to person game of life, death, and love can Resurrection be a possible play. Resurrection is not a move in the game of ordinary history or science. Those austere observations on fact and theory legitimately abstract from love and hence cannot make the move which is Resurrection.

Genuine Church teaching follows, then, from the existence of the sacramental family. The sacramental family will in some manner be structured like the natural family with "parents" who "teach." The pope as patriarch of the sacramental family fits that logic. When the Holy Father speaks in the *voice* of a holy father according to the logic of the sacramental family, there is a truth expressed even if the specific statement is factually false or morally misdirected. The fatherly voice is the voice of the sacramental family; the fatherly voice is the voice of the Church. In this way the Church through the Holy Father replicates the point made repeatedly: Jesus does not bring a message nor teach a doctrine, he *is* the doctrine: "*I* am . . . the truth."

## The Logic of "Family"

When the Holy Father speaks with the voice of a holy father he speaks "in the truth." Claiming that doctrine flows in some sense from the existential relation to a holy father, that true doctrine dwells in the existential relation expressed in the voice of a holy father, sounds ominously like Pius IX's *io sono la Chiesa*. To explicate this strange turn and to avoid its imperialistic overtones, I want to examine certain assumptions about the natural family. If the Church's deep structure is sacramental *family*, there are aspects of the *natural* family that can be transferred as a guide for understanding. Although I realize that there are all sorts of modern extensions of the notion of "family," for the sake of simplicity and clarity I use "family" in the paradigm case: biological parent-child.

What are some essential assumptions for the natural family? Family has at least three general interlinked characteristics: (1) family is a community with differing levels of personal maturity, (2) family constitutes an unbreakable bond based on given relation (biology) not choice, and (3) there is a deep obligation for the mature to create conditions that will allow the immature to develop in such manner that they live enriched, fulfilled lives. The three characteristics may be described in terms familiar to Church language: the family is hierarchic (mature to immature), infallible (unbreakably bonded), and teaches (the moral demand of parenting).

*Hierarchic.*   Personal maturity of the experienced over the inexperienced establishes the family as hierarchal. The hierarchy of mature competence may be rudimentary, for example, being able to transfer competencies to the child on how to eat, talk, control bodily functions, and so on, but it is an embedded assumption of parenting. How parents succeed or fail in passing on higher competencies (morality, psychological maturity) is the stuff of literary drama, psychoanalysis, and the sociology of families. Lack of parental maturity in the higher competencies is a sure recipe for family disaster.

*Infallibility.*   The family bond never "fails." It cannot be definitively broken whatever the failings of parent and child. The combination of hierarchy and infallibility differentiates the family from other intimate communities. Marriage and friendship may have sharp differentials of maturity (personal resource and enrichment) but they differ because they can be broken. One may divorce a spouse or break with a friend; one cannot divorce one's children or parents, and breaking these relations is always a self-wounding disaster. Modern extensions of "family" are often mere sentiment, as when a company refers to the work force as family or when a hip commune calls itself a family. These "families" are eminently breakable and thus fail the root notion of ancestral descent. In the ancestral family the fault line between parental wisdom or folly and infallible/unbreakable family bond is the perennial source of tragedy in literature and life.

*Teaching.* Teaching carries a special parental inflection not present in schoolroom teaching. As father, I do not take on the studied distance that marks my classroom teaching. When the angels appeared to the shepherds over Bethlehem they did not say, "Behold, we bring you a topic for discussion!" When I seek to educate my children I am not bringing up a topic for discussion. There are no deconstructionist parents who maintain a delightful indifference to the ways of their children. My responsibility as father is to bring to bear on my children whatever lessons of life I have eked out by trial and error, cogitation, or inspiration. It is a commonplace of modern "liberal" families to say that they are not going to instruct their children in religion (even the parent's own) usually with the proviso that the children can decide on religion when they become adults. Surely this is either an illusion or a downright evasion of parenting. If the parents are truly religious, in other words, believe that some faith offers the deepest and most important lessons of life, nothing could be a greater imperative than conveying the lesson of religion to children. One suspects that the "liberal" attitude is the lesson: like stamp collecting, religion is a hobby.

The combination of hierarchy, infallibility, and parental responsibility to teach the lessons-of-life constitutes a unique process. The goal of family teaching lies in the formation of the persona. What I seek to bring forth in my child is a *person,* a self who can live a fulfilled life—however I may rightly or wrongly conceive fulfilment. Forming the person of the other engages the person of the teacher-parent in a manner that is absent from classroom teaching. The cliché is right when it says that example is the best teacher. A father who teaches "lessons of life" that are radically other than his life fails to teach the lessons-of-life except the lesson that one need not pay any attention to teachers of the lessons-of-life. Holden Caulfield speaks for every adolescent building a self under the tutelage of imperfect tutors: adults are all phonies.

The importance of "good example" is properly noted, but the basic relation of parent to child in the formation of the self is deeper than example. "Example" may suggest that the child has some sort of independence of self from which to choose examples. The child has no such independence. The parent's persona *is* the message because the child has not yet attained an independent persona. For the child, the only persona he or she has is developed as a reflection of the parent's persona. The child starts off, at least, as a "mirror" of the parent. Instantiating the flawed persona of the parent can continue the cycle of family dysfuntion so often chronicled in psychoanalytic case studies.

## Hierarchy, Infallibility, and Teaching in the Sacramental Family

Hierarchy, infallibility, and teaching are central claims of the Catholic Church. If these marks are to be validated for the Church it is because something akin to the natural family assumptions are legitimately translated into the sacramental family. (At the deepest theological level, the situation is actually reversed: the patriarchy of God is the ideal for the natural family. For purposes of exposition it is clearer to start with the natural family. I discuss the theological reversal in due course.) The problem with "hierarchy, infallibility, and teaching" in the conventional apologetics for the Roman Catholic Church is that these terms are shifted out of the deep structures of *family* hierarchy, infallibility, and teaching. This distortion is most easily detected when "teaching" is misconstrued as some sort of "philosophical" teaching.[3] If one confuses *Church* teaching with anything that shades toward "philosophy," the other two components—hierarchy and infallibility—become fatally distorted. Infallibility is not a part of the philosophic (academic, scientific) game. No one has a vested, hierarchic authority in regard to philosophic truth. If the Church confuses creed with even such a lofty notion as a Christian philosophy, it may violate the essential logic of faith. I agree with Wittgenstein: "If Christianity is the truth then all the philosophy that is written about it is false."[4] Philosophy speaks Christianity in a false voice and so Christian truth is not conveyed.

Hierarchy, infallibility, and teaching are necessary marks of the Church, but they have legitimacy only if inserted in "family logic," not in the philosophy game.

To recapitulate: infallibility in family is not some miraculous guarantee of factual or philosophical wisdom. If I speak to my child from the depth of my fatherhood and she responds within the deep bond of childhood, there is an authenticity and truth in the interchange. When in the deep interchange of parent and child, parental love and filial piety are engaged, the conversation is, as Kierkegaard says, "in the truth" even if what is said is not true. Within family structure there is a place for infallibility, but it is not the place from which true statements necessarily flow. In family logic the truth of statements is tested by the truth of the parent-child relation. In the guiding term of this book, what is crucial is the parental *voice*. Assuming that the parental voice is the voice of the loving one seeking to form a child's life toward fulfilment, then *what* is said is guided by that voice.

The voice of the parent is the fundamental teaching of family. Primary family teaching is not smarting up the kids on algebra, it is the *formation of the person*. The formation of the person is carried in the voice of the parent and only secondarily and derivatively in the philosophical or factual teachings of the parent. The parent, presumably an already formed person, is the necessary means for the child to develop as a person. If the parent is deformed, the formation of the child is at risk. If the parental voice is distant, didactic, or dictatorial, one can predict unhappy results in the person of the child. And, of course, all too often the parental voice is distant, didactic, and dictatorial. Finding the true parental voice is not by any means easy or obvious because voice is nothing less than the persona of the parent expressed in word and gesture. I may say this or that, utter factual and philosophical truths without end to my child. But if these words are pronounced in a flawed personal voice, my *parental* teaching fails because I am forming the other from a false persona. The aim of the natural family is that the parent should form the person of the child toward a life of fulfilment. This is a "spiritual" obligation upon the parents, which they cannot avoid. This parental obligation is no easy task given the frequent, perhaps inevitable personal deformations of the parent. If the task of the parent is forming the child's persona from the resources of his or her persona, the fundamental question for parenting should be: *what is the true parental persona? Who is the true parent?*

## Forming the Christian Persona

It is the duty of the parent to form the persona of the child in a manner fitting the historical world in which he or she will live. For Christians, Cross and Resurrection are *the* markers for history, and so the true parental voice reflects the persona appropriate to that history. The Christian persona is the self capable of fulfilment in that history. Forming that persona is the aim of parental teaching. For Christians, then, the natural family depends on Christian formation to realize its proper aim. "Whoever loves father or mother more than me is not worthy of me" (Mt 10:37) is not a criticism of the natural family, it is a way of noting that even the natural family will find fulfilment only in Christ. The ideal parental persona conforms to the *persona Christi.*

The claim that the *persona Christi* is *the* well-formed authentic persona and thus the persona of the ideal parent for forming the persons of his or her children sounds arrogant and outrageous. Before justifying such a large claim, I remind the reader of the discussion of faith in the chapter on subjectivity. I argued there that Christian faith is a total personality structure; faith is in the same category as paranoia. The overriding issue about Christian faith is whether it is sane. Sanity involves a judgment about reality, but with the paradoxical twist that reality emerges from the standpoint of sanity. We do not, as it were, step back from the issue of sanity, survey reality, and *then* decide on the shape of sanity. The attitude of the detached observer of reality, while it may yield something we would regard as "objective truth," will, if taken as the living human persona, yield not sanity but the madness of the mad scientist.

There is general agreement that paranoia is insane, out of touch with "moral" reality. There are strong arguments by Freud, Nietzsche, and much lesser minds that Christianity is its own brand of insanity. For Nietzsche, Jewish-Christian belief is understood as something close to paranoia: the world-hating attitude of resentful slaves. If Nietzsche and Freud were correct, parental teaching from and toward the *persona Christi* would be deeply destructive of human fulfilment, which of course they both thought it was. The only successful Christian reply to a charge of faith-as-insanity must be to show that Christian faith is, far from being insane, the very essence of sanity. Saints are the truly sane.

Parents are charged to form "sane" children. The person-forming task of a natural father or mother should be a function of knowing reality and living accordingly. Parents often boast of a certain realism in their life lessons. "Don't trust anybody!" is claimed as realism in a world judged hostile and aggressive. (Isaiah Berlin once remarked that when someone says, "Let's be realistic!" you know he is about to announce a piece of "very shoddy policy.") What then is "realism," the *really* real, in the formation of the persona? If we cannot assess the real from what would seem the preferred stance of objective science, how do we know sanity and the real?

Christians believe that the real is given in the revelation of God in Christ. What is revealed is the truth about humans. Jesus is the model of sanity, the true *persona* of humanity, and thus the measure for reality. For Jesus, human sanity is knowing reality as God's creation. Human *in*sanity is regarding myself as *self*-created. As discussed, humans are deeply tempted to self-create themselves as fictions because the density of life is too threatening. Much better to cast myself as a character in a mythic-drama, partisan of a cause or an everlasting victim. In each of these disguises I define my self over and against some other. I locate an enemy, whether it be an opposing cause, an opaque person, or biological decay. ("She died after a valiant *battle* against cancer.") By defining self against the enemy, the obtuse, and natural necessity, I rise above the shocks and challenges of others and life itself. I attain "immortality."

Jesus shatters the delusion (insanity) of human self-creation, relocating human existence in reality with all its danger and chance. In our persistent belief in our self-created self, we sin against the reality of creation. Revelation about creation is not a piece of cosmic information like being told that our bodies are made of star dust; that sort of revelation might properly humble humanity in its pride, and it is, in fact, the moral message conveyed by various prophets of evolution or the unconscious. For Christianity, "demoting" humans from self-created to "mere" creations certainly has a humbling aspect, but the full revelation of Jesus has an effect opposite that of various genetic or psychic reductions of self-importance. To be *God's* creation has the ultimate effect of elevating and liberating the human persona, rather than humbling us to the machinations of the genes or the outbursts of the unconscious. We are liberated from our own self-fiction into the real, which, being the real of God, is supremely alive and loving.

Jesus reveals the sickness of self-creation, and in his life and death reveals and heals the sickness and insanity of the fictional self. In contrast to the normal human course, the flight from the real, Jesus descends into life, this "splendid waste," with all its joys and chanciness, pain and destruction. He says in effect, "I go down into the abyss of ignominy and death, yet God, the living God, is still there." In the real there is always life. In the kingdom of the creator God there are no enemies—not even death! By repositioning humanity as God's creation, Jesus dissolves the enmity inherent in self-and-other; he brings the peace that the world cannot give. By undermining the fictional self that grants me a spurious immortality as I rise above the mere accident of my existence, Jesus offers true victory over death, eternal life or, one might say, "life-ever-present." To be formed on the model of the *persona Christi* is to be formed into *life,* into reality, not fiction.

## Teaching the *persona Christi*

If Christianity claims that the sane person is the Christian persona, the teaching task of the Church is the formation of the *persona Christi*. The Church exists in the parental role of conveying sane personhood in a human world caught up in self-creating fiction and delusion. When the Church takes on the parental role of forming the *persona Christi,* following the logic of natural family formation, it must already instantiate in some fashion the *persona Christi.* The assumption that the parental Church is already sane and is forming the unformed becomes the basis for the Church claim for *hierarchal* teaching, that is, teaching from sanity already attained. Real sanity is sanctity, so if the Church is sane, it must also incorporate sanctity. A necessary mark of Church is that it is in some way "holy."

From whence does the Christian teacher acquire the *persona Christi?* If we were tracing natural family history we would say that it is culturally "inherited" as the family reasserts its history. Being born into a family history of generals or musicians makes a claim upon my life for good or ill. It can be crushing to be the child of genius! I may be born into a family that celebrates its history or one that protests its tragic past. Blacks and whites in America continue to suffer from the inherited history of slavery. Inherited histories may be psychically overcome or negligently forgotten. In the example of the Holocaust, I suggested a history that should not be forgotten or overcome. The Christian family inherits Jesus' Cross and Resurrection, which define the *persona Christi* as the history to be remembered, celebrated, and passed on in each generation. The Christian teacher is an echo of the voice of Jesus as the one whose persona is revealed in his life. The technical doctrine of apostolic succession expresses this family inheritance of the *persona Christi*.

Jesus as the founder of the sacramental family of Church is *the* sane one and his sanity, his *persona,* is what is to be transmitted. Again one needs to emphasize that the passage from person-to-person is not the passage of an ideology; persona is deeper and more intimate than ideology. If Jesus was the teacher of an ideology, we could dispense with his *life* and hold to his teaching. But Jesus says "everyone who lives and believes in *me* will never die" (Jn 11:26). We are enjoined to imitate the *persona Christi,* to live our lives as God's creation. Jesus is the only one who lives life fully as God's creation, obedient in all things to the will of the Father—that is the ground of his sanity and what earns him the title "son of God." If there is a "deposit of faith" in the Church, it is the continuing impress of the *persona Christi* within the life of the sacramental family. Jesus' message is that in his person the Kingdom of God has been realized, that in his life there is a fulfilment of this kingdom of peace. As the peaceable parent of the sacramental family, his *persona* is the content of the tradition.

Catholic papal apologetics concentrate on Matthew 16 where Jesus proclaims Simon to be Peter, the rock on which he will build his Church. Authoritative as that passage may be, it tells us little about *how* Peter is to go about his task. It is a principal contention of this book that the *how* is essential to the *what* of the message. To understand the *how* (and, therefore, the derived *what*) of Petrine leadership one would do better to attend to John 21. The latter passage is a post-resurrection story when, one might hope and assume, the Apostles have finally begun to understand the meaning of Jesus—something that Peter spectacularly fails to understand in the chapter from Matthew. The exchange between the resurrected Jesus and Peter is, as it were, final instructions. Three times Jesus asks Peter whether he loves him—no doubt recalling the three times that Peter denied him after his arrest. Three times Peter avows his love of the Lord. After each avowal, Jesus describes Peter's role: "Feed my sheep."

If the function of the Church is the formation of the *persona Christi* down the generations, the passage from John is crucial. Peter is to "feed" Christ's sheep *by transmitting to others the love of the Lord* to which he attests in confrontation with the Resurrected. There is more to attestation of love than verbal declaration. In love we shape our self in relation to the other; in the loving relation we become a new person. I am no longer my self alone, my person is deeply and wholly bound to the other. Peter redefined as "the one who loves the Lord"exists within the transforming reality of the *persona Christi*.

Peter, conformed by love to the Resurrected, becomes the exemplary medium for passing on binding love toward Jesus, toward the *persona Christi*. "Feeding the sheep" means forming the *persona Christi* in others. The doctrine of real presence in the Catholic interpretation of the Eucharist recognizes that the point of Christianity is transmitting the presence/ *persona* of Jesus. The *persona Christi* is the thread of Church life and formation. The sacramental family is defined by the continued presence of the *persona Christi*. As Abraham's seed can be said to give genetic continuity to the Hebrew family, so the *persona Christi* is the spiritual seed carried over generations in the sacramental family. The sacramental echo of the physical passing on of the patriarchal seeds is expressed in the ceremony of apostolic succession (the consecration of a bishop) by the physical sign of laying on of hands.

The structure of passing on "personhood" in family or Church is *essentially hierarchic* in so far as one must pass on from some level of fulfillment already attained. It is not surprising, therefore, that the Church adopts a parental model for the task of passing on the *persona Christi*. Without a notion of hierarchy, "family" becomes a discussion group or a voting democracy. There are "liberal" models of family that would recast the traditional family on that model. Similarly, some would recast the Church as a theological discussion group or a political democracy. While there is much to recommend both views of the Church as remedies for specific lacks and abuses of hierarchy, as synoptic theories they distort the fundamental truth of Church as sacramental family. A right understanding of the family model corrects the abuses singled out by those who espouse discussion or democracy.

## Institutional Father

Born into the natural family, we are formed as persons for well or ill by those who have "gone before," by parents. Born (again) in baptism into the sacramental family we are to be formed by holy parents according to the *persona Christi*. In the Catholic Church, teaching rests on a hierarchy culminating in the Holy *Father* who at least symbolically takes the privileged position accorded to the parent in the natural family. Unfortunately, setting down strict demands for formation by a holy parent as the condition for Church teaching disqualifies most popes. Holiness has not been a notable mark of the successors of St. Peter, and all too often the voice has not even been "fatherly" but a version of the super-professor or super-judge lecturing on some theological formula or laying down moral law. One can legitimately doubt that Christianity has been transmitted by popes and bishops; saints and martyrs have been the effective teachers of faith. As has been often remarked, if one were to look at the most influential Catholic figures of the past two centuries, they would not be popes and bishops but individuals like the Curé of Ars, Therese of Lisieux, or Dorothy Day.

The problem with the papal *office* is whether it makes sense to have an *institutional* father who may, alas, be anything but a holy father. One might think that an institutional father as impossible as a designated friend. The idea of the Pope as institutional father can easily lead toward the false constructions of the papacy discussed earlier. If election to the papacy were like promotion to professor of theology, one would review the scholarly works and academic reputation. Judges are reviewed on the basis of legal education, and experience in court and on the bench. Election to papal office rests on no such obvious certification of theological competency or moral probity. The cardinals in conclave are not necessarily trained theologians or deep moral philosophers. One can, of course, appeal to the Holy Spirit who infuses the Holy Father with just the right sense of theology and moral sense, but that answer is beside the point because the fundamental function of the pope as Christian teacher is neither philosophic truth nor judicial decision. The proper certification for a Holy Father as *the* transmitter of the *persona Christi* should be that he be *holy*. Papal election is not beatification.

Is there, then, any justification for the hierarchic function of the papal office? One reasonable justification for the designation "Holy Father" is that it expresses the proper *symbolism* for the essential teaching structure of Christian faith. The function of the Church is to fulfill the parental role and responsibility to shape the persona toward holiness. It is well, then, to signify the responsibility for the office even if—and perhaps especially—if the Holy Father at hand should fail in parental voice and sanctity. Using the title "father" designates the directions of fatherly success and failure, fatherly ways of speaking and acting. When the actual papal voice is neither holy nor fatherly, we may fault the incumbent for failing his station and duties.

I believe that there are two ways to go beyond the symbolic in justifying the role of hierarchal teaching and the role of the Pope as *the* hierarchal teacher. The first and more direct way is to examine in more detail just how one goes about *forming a person*. There are aspects of this common practice in the natural family that are directly applicable to Christian formation, to Church teaching. The second justification goes to the heart of "holiness": what exactly is the *persona Christi* to which Peter affirms his love in the crucial passage from John? If the aim of the Church is creation of holiness, it behooves us to understand the lesson of holiness presented in the story of Jesus. The holiness passed down to the person of Peter determines certain formal actions of the papal office which by-pass the issue of a particular pope's personal sanctity.

## Cosmos and Creed

In order to justify the role of institutional father, one can offer further explication of the pedagogy for forming a person and the *persona Christi* in particular. Christian faith constitutes a total personality structure. Faith is to be evaluated under the categories of sanity and insanity. Sanity, in turn, is defined as the proper relation of personality and reality: "inner" and "outer" properly matched. Sanity is a "subjective" state that can only be defined relative to truth and reality. The sane person's psychic attitude is attuned to the real world. The sane person's account of the world is the "real" world; the paranoid's description of an environing hostility is "unreal." The formula sounds right, but actual situations in life are not so clear. A person may be judged psychically quite healthy according to his or her emotions, attitudes, and actions, but have quite bizarre ideas about "reality." Freud thought sanity was defined by the psychic capacity to love and to work. It seems obvious that many people have those inner capacities combined with wild ideas—or no ideas—about social or cosmic reality. I may state my belief that the world is going to hell and yet arise day after day to cheerfully embrace my children before happily taking up my daily work. In reverse, it is obvious that Christians espouse high beliefs about a loving God who proclaims no enemies while they go about dourly denouncing sinners and slaying the heathen.

When faced with such discrepancy between psychic states and descriptions of external reality we may or may not wish to seek *proper* alignment. Proper alignment will be determined, however, according to inner standards of sanity. One may have no motive for persuading the cheerful worker to align his attitude to the gloom attendant on his expressed beliefs about cosmic disaster. The faith of the "simple peasant" is often lauded despite the mix of miracle and superstition that constitutes his beliefs about the world. Christian saints have often had very eccentric theologies up to and including mystical revelations which would be judged to be insane in a clinical setting. For all that, the true saint demonstrates sanity through the works of love.

Having noted that inner sanity and external belief may diverge, there is no doubt that getting the right cosmic setting for personal sanity can be important. Maybe my cheerful worker should come to understand that the capitalists are exploiting her good nature. Certainly my Christian crusader should amend his triumphalist ways according to the God who loves one and all. Cosmic beliefs can and often do constrain conduct and so must be carefully considered. If the Holy Father or anyone engaged in Christian formation is not holy, holiness is not likely to be passed on. On the other hand, the Holy Father or Christian teacher at any level has an obligation to offer a description of the world in which holiness, Christian sanity, is the proper persona to cultivate. In this sense, the Pope may function as *a teacher of cosmic belief* that justifies holiness regardless of the teacher's attained holiness.

The Church has the task of being holy and of describing a world in which holiness is sanity. When Peter three times declares his love of the Lord, he is conforming himself to the *persona Christi*. As one so conformed, he is positioned to form the personae of others accordingly. As the paranoid parent is the best transmitter of paranoia, the person defined as lover-of-the-Lord is the best transmitter of that persona. In teaching the *persona Christi* the apostle may go on to say: "This is how the world is!" The creed is *how the world is* as seen from the sanity of the *persona Christi*. By describing such a world one may hope to induce sanity. Teaching the creed is, therefore, a legitimate, if limited, pedagogy for sanity and sainthood. Like the paranoid parent who projects a world of enemies, the Christian teacher, the pope in this instance, is charged to preach a world with no enemies. Who knows, peace may emerge! If, however, in his teaching the official parent speaks in a voice which is dismissive or disdainful, the "no enemies" message will not be received because the existence of enemies is built into the dismissive voice.

The problem for the Church and for the papal office as the custodian of creed is how one truthfully characterizes the world from the standpoint of sanity and sanctity. As noted, sane and saintly people often have very bizarre views about the world. One might even argue that some fabulist views of the world are more conducive to good conduct, love, and work than sheer "realism." Belief in heavenly reward may offer a deep ground for morality and love. On the other hand, it may deflect attention from the cares of the earth to "pie in the sky by and by." In reverse, those who reject heaven as fantasy may judge that our fragile span of life gives special edge and poignancy to duty and love. Contrariwise, the realist's view of the finality of death may sap the commitments of the day. In his short story "The Wall," Jean-Paul Sartre presents a partisan who faces execution; for him, "death disenchants everything." Projections and rejections of heaven can be compatible with radically different attitudes toward life, radically different visions of the sane life. A "factual" belief in heaven or a denial of afterlife may have radically different spiritual outcomes. It is the spiritual outcome, the character of the persona, that is the goal of cosmic teaching.

There are two serious qualifications to explicating the papal office as the guardian of creed as "cosmic belief." The first and most salient is my basic thesis that the function of Christian teaching is not inculcating some set of cosmic beliefs to which one assents. The aim of Christian teaching is forming saints, some of whom may have and have had very strange articulated positions on reality. The second qualification is derived from this split between sane persona and strange dogma. The relation between the sane/saintly persona and dogmatic statement is far from deductive. The relation is tenuous, but this does not mean that one can play fast and loose with dogma. Quite the contrary, it is because it can be so difficult to get dogma to fit sanctity that we should take the efforts to state dogma so seriously. The traditional motto "faith seeking understanding" can be read as "sanctity seeking dogma" where dogma is, or should be, the cautiously derived, fragile "description" of a world where sainthood makes sense. Given that it took three centuries before Nicea and Chalcedon formulated a basic language for Christology, one can understand why the Church holds to that language with special tenacity. Both of these qualifications on Christian teaching—the formation of saints and the derivation of dogma—are stringent restrictions on the capacity of the papal office. The papal teacher may fail as holy and as father, and the papal teacher may defend a dogmatic statement that, despite its longevity, may have lost connection with the dimensions of sanctity it was intended to inscribe.

## Creed and Christ

The relation of holy fatherly voice and world description arises in acute form when it comes to describing Jesus. This cosmic/creedal Christological problem was obsessive in the early centuries of Christianity. It was not, however, a philosophical or technical theological problem as such. It was strictly akin to that of a sensitive biographer trying to fit words to the complex character being chronicled. What is the proper characterization of Lincoln? Was he a clinical depressive or were his black periods proper expressions of the tragedy of an unfolding war of brothers? The aim of creedal pedagogy is forming the *persona Christi,* and thus how one describes Jesus, his relation to reality, and our relation to him are crucial. Who is he and into what world would he fit? Why does who he is affect my life?

Take the last question first. I might be fascinated by the persona of Napoleon, but I may not want to be a general on horseback, nor do I have reason to think that I ought to have any such aspiration. With a parent it is different; I *must* relate to the persona of the parent. The family bond creates a relation to the parent with which I have to deal in wooden imitation, loving creativity, liberating rejection, or tragic denial. If the *persona Christi* is any concern of mine it is not simply that Jesus offers a model of morality, it is because I have a "family" bond to Christ and his Father God. *Describing* Jesus in divine attributes is a means of establishing a family connection beyond moral emulation. In Christian baptism I am born into a holy people established in the story of Jesus. Baptism consciously places the Christian in a continuous history determined by Christ. Christians believe that Jesus' history *defines* history: all humans are placed within the family bond to God whether they recognize it or not. Nietzsche's proclamation that God is dead demonstrates his clear recognition of a bond that must be consciously destroyed to liberate human life. The Church controverts Nietzsche by holding that loving fidelity to Christ is the true liberation of human life. For Nietzsche as for Christians what we cannot do is ignore the bond to God anymore than we can avoid the persona of parents in the natural family.

Because of the inescapable relation to God, Christians borrow words of family bonding: Jesus is our *brother,* the Son of God our *Father.* Christ becomes the governing persona in our lives. Familial terms place me in relation to Jesus in such a way that I must either accept the impress of his persona or consciously reject it as I might that of an abusive parent. What then, is the *persona Christi* impressed on Peter from which he was commanded to feed Christ's sheep? When Peter conforms his persona to the Resurrected in his triple protestation of love, just what is the *persona Christi* that is revealed?

## The *Persona* of Forgiveness

If Peter and his successors somehow convey the holy, we should ask what sort of person is Peter after his triple avowal of love. The contrast between the "rock" passage in Matthew and the triple avowal in John is critical. In the earlier passage the persona that Peter identifies in Jesus is a triumphant messianic persona. He cannot understand a Lord who will be crucified. This earns him a stern rebuke from Jesus. In Matthew, for all his verbal proclamation, Peter does *not* understand the *persona Christi.* If he were to conform himself to a triumphalist Jesus, he would fail to understand who Jesus is and what it means to be his follower. When we turn to the passage in John, much history has intervened. It is a different Peter who now meets a different Jesus. This Jesus is one crucified and resurrected. Who, then, does the Resurrected confront? He confronts one who has denied him three times. The earlier impetuous Peter who is eager to proclaim the triumphalist Lord is now the Peter who failed Jesus even to the point of denying he even knew the man. What would one normally expect from such a confrontation of the betrayed and his betrayer? In the ordinary course of human history, we would expect denunciation and dismissal. *Now* would be the time for Jesus to say to Peter, "Get behind me, Satan! You are a stumbling block to me." But of course this is just what Jesus does *not* say. On the contrary, he offers Peter the opportunity to restore fellowship. As he denied Jesus three times, now Peter is offered the opportunity to attest his love thrice over.

What is the *persona* presented by Jesus in this surprising turn of events? What is the *persona* to which Peter conforms himself in his triple affirmation of love and that becomes the "food" with which he will feed Christ's sheep? It seems clear that the *persona Christi* exemplified is the persona of *forgiveness*. When Peter loves the Lord he conforms his person to the *persona Christi* as one-who-returns-and-forgives. Peter then becomes the persona who forgives, the one empowered to forgive sins as the Resurrected expresses in this confrontation.

The connection between *persona Christi,* forgiveness, and sanctity is critical for defining the holiness of the Church and the true voice of Peter and his successors. In the terms of our earlier discussion: when Peter and his successors as Pope and Holy Father speak in the voice of forgiveness they are *in* the truth. One can illustrate the special meaning of holiness-as-forgiveness by considering the early heresy of Donatism. The Donatists who flourished in the fourth century of the common era insisted that the true Church can only exist in realized holiness. Donatism was an instance of the demand for perfectionism which has emerged periodically in the history of Christianity. Perfectionism would seem to express the basic demand for conforming my person to the *persona Christi*. The *persona Christi* is without sin and so I must be sinless to be truly Christian. "Be perfect, therefore, as your heavenly Father is perfect" (Mt 5:48). But the *persona Christi* to which Peter conforms himself and from which he is to feed the community is the persona of the forgiving one. It is in forgiving that the *persona Christi* is expressed. A proof text could be cited from Matthew 18:21–23. Again it is Peter who is the one in question; he asks Jesus how many times he is to forgive his brother. Jesus tells the parable of the master who forgives his servant a great debt only to have the servant turn round and throw his debtors into prison because they cannot pay up. The persona of the master (God, Jesus) is merciful; that is both the lesson of the parable to Peter and the meaning of Peter's meeting with the Resurrected. If the persona of Peter is not the persona of the merciful and forgiving one, then he becomes like the wicked servant in the parable: his "punishing" persona would be the very contradiction of the merciful persona of his Lord.

In reply to the perfectionism of the Donatists and their spiritual compatriots down the ages, one need only point out that the *perfection of holiness* as taught in the parable and in the meeting with the Resurrected is *forgiveness.* The Church does not become holy by casting forth sinners but by forgiving sinners. The Church is not the Church of essential saints; saints are sinners but sinners who know that they are forgiven. One becomes saintly because one has been forgiven, not because of spiritual athleticism.

Return then to the question of the pope as *Holy* Father. When does Holy Father speak with the voice of holiness? When he speaks with the voice of forgiveness, not the voice of punishment. One needs to choose *which* Peter conforms to the *persona Christi*: the Peter of Matthew 16 or John 21. The Peter who is "rock" quite misunderstands the *persona Christi;* the Peter who falls grievously, denying his Lord in the face of death only to be forgiven, understands how to be a disciple. The *holy* voice of Peter then and now is a *forgiving* voice. Such a voice would seem a far cry from the condemnations, anathemas, and persecutions that have characterized Christian history and the pronouncement of popes over the centuries.

The problem with demanding a forgiving voice is that it may appear to condone all sorts of conduct that is clearly evil. Such a conclusion does not follow, of course, from the meaning of "forgiveness" since if there were nothing really wrong, there would be nothing to forgive. My guest bumps into a vase and breaks it. She apologizes. "Forgive me!" "No need to apologize, it was a cheap imitation. Forget it!" Forgiveness only gets off the ground as a possibility when there is serious harm. The forgiving voice only arises when one can point to harm. Before the voice of forgiveness can be heard, the Church and the popes must recognize some evil at hand. What evil? The situation here has a curious reflexivity: the fundamental evil to which the Church points is the evil of rejecting forgiveness. The principle evil of humanity is that it does not recognize the need for the forgiving voice transmitted in Jesus. Our fundamental sin is the belief that we are self-creating. Self-creating is self-justifying. If there is something amiss with this self, I will repair it. No need for outside help! I will have more to say about the complex relation of a forgiving voice and the voice that denounces sin in the last chapters.

## The Official Father

I would sum up the legitimacy of the papal office under three headings: (1) centering the idea of Church in a "Holy Father"; (2) keeper of the creed, describing, as best one can, how the Church has delineated a cosmos in which sanctity is sanity; and (3) as "successor of Peter" transmitting the *persona Christi* as the voice of forgiveness—the voice that Peter comes to understand in his triple attestation of love of the Resurrected.

*Centering in the "Holy Father."* The task of the Church is, as the quotation at the head of this chapter from Cardinal Ratzinger indicates, "to send all peoples to the school of Jesus, because he is . . . the way to be human." One can state that task as the formation of the *persona Christi*: "the way to be human." As "teacher," the Church is to be a Holy Father, a Holy Mother, a Sane and Saintly Parent to the world. I am not enthusiastic about Pius IX's, "I am the Church," but there is a sense in which the Church is a Holy Father, Holy Mother, the great holy parent teaching us how to be human. When the individual holding the office of Holy Father fails to be holy and fatherly, he fails the office (duty) of the Church, which is to form the *persona Christi*.

*Keeper of the creed.* While authentic teaching is transmittal of the persona of Christ to the present moment through a chain of holiness, there is a legitimate role for constructing a creed—a cosmic picture, a description of humanity, history, and the world—in which the holiness of the *persona Christi* is sanity itself. A sane world is one in which Jesus is not a failed prophet, and Dorothy Day is not a fanatic. Describing a world fit for Jesus and holiness is not easy. A world of sinners—even forgiven sinners—has a hard time describing a world for holiness. Nevertheless, in the advancement of sanity, there is a role for attempting such descriptions. It would be foolish to discard the tradition. As we compare and contrast the present with the tradition we may come to understand what is required for holiness in our day and how to describe a world fit for holiness. The present-day musician understands music from its historic tradition. She can place her own composition and performance within that tradition as a key to excellence. At the same time, tradition is not repetition; rather, one uses tradition to create new forms which speak from and to the tradition. New works do not destroy the tradition, but they may well reorder and reevaluate the tradition. Tradition is the living faith of the dead, living in a continual creation beyond reiteration. I would not be offended by a description of the pope as the curator of the museum of Christian descriptions with the proviso that like any good curator he understands that it is a living museum.

*The "Voice of Forgiveness."*   The saintly persona speaks with the voice of forgiveness as Jesus speaks so often in his life and in his words from the Cross. Fortunately for the *office* of Holy Father, there is also something like "official" forgiveness. "I forgive" is a performative utterance, that is, it has an "official" function beyond the *persona* of the one who utters the words. If I say, "I forgive you," I have done the deed, I have forgiven you, whatever the bitterness and reservation I may hold in my heart. The office of pope can be the office of forgiveness however the individual pontiff may lack the holiness and fatherliness that would make such forgiveness "heartfelt."

In the last chapters of this book, I want to turn to how the Church might carry forward forgiveness in an official mode. The model that I will use is that of the psychotherapist. In psychotherapy there is a *pro forma* "forgiveness" of the patient. The classification of aberrant behavior as "sick" transfers it to the medical model of psychotherapy and thereby brackets any moral evaluation of the patient's actions. The psychotherapist acts officially in a mode of forgiveness whatever her actual feelings. I want to move from forgiveness in medical psychotherapy, to forgiveness in Christian soul-therapy. Before doing so, however, I need to be clear about the nature of the sickness. The sickness is "sin." Just as secular psychotherapy brackets morality as a necessity of therapy, so it is necessary to separate off morality from sin in the interest of Christian soul-therapy. The next chapter attempts that task.

# CHAPTER EIGHT

# Saving Morality

*Nietzsche was not crazy when he blamed morality for the worst evils, though he may have become too crazy about the idea. This is also why goodness, in trying to be born, will sometimes look like the destruction of morality.*

Stanley Cavell, *Must We Mean What We Say*

The Catholic Church claims that the hierarchical magisterium through the office of the pope is a teacher not only of faith but also of morals—and an infallible teacher of both. I have already raised problems with the magisterium as the "voice of faith," so it should not be surprising that I raise problems about the Church as the "voice of morals." Strangely enough, I think I am on better ground questioning the Church as authoritative moralist than as the voice of faith. In the long run, I can give grudging acceptance to "teacher of faith and morals" but only in the sense of morals as a derivative of faith. *The* voice of the Church— provided it clears its throat—is the voice of faith. Whatever morals may be at issue follow from whatever faith is all about.

At the risk of sounding like a former United States president, whether the Church is a teacher of faith and morals depends on what you mean by "and." The Church might be regarded as a schoolmaster conversant with two quite separate topics, say, math and ancient history. There is a teaching about one and then there is a teaching about the other, but the connection between the two is nonexistent or tangential at best. The simplest way of noting what is wrong with regarding morals as a separate ecclesiastic expertise is to emphasize that the proper interest of the Church is *sin*—and sin is something beyond simple morality. Sin is a peculiarly religious notion for which a rigorous secular moralist will find no use. Although secular moralists are quite capable of noting "radical evil," they would find no need to add the rhetorical flourish of "sin." Sin is not ordinary moral misconduct, it is an offense against God. It is immoral to lie, cheat, or steal, but on the face of it one does not need to refer these actions to God to discover their inherent faults.

The Catholic Church seems confused on the relation of morality and sin. There is a valuable tradition of Catholic moral argument based in natural law. What is not clear is how natural law morality relates to the theological notion of sin. Sometimes natural law gets an extra endorsement from the fact that God created "nature," but the basic presumption of standard natural law theorists is that considering nature alone would be enough to prove the moral point. Conventional Catholic sexual morality is a clear example. The natural law for sex is procreation—that is the natural function of the mechanism. Since God created nature and our sex organs, they have his special blessing and direction, but just plain secular biology will show how sex is to be used. I don't think this is at all a good argument at the level of nature or God, but something like that seems to govern traditional Catholic natural law discussions of issues such as contraception or homosexual behavior.

There are sophisticated Catholic natural law ethicists like Germaine Grisez and John Finnis who reject the "biologism" of the argument just presented. Their notion of natural *law* is actually a theory of natural *goods* that are rational to pursue. Having children is a natural good in the sense that one would be baffled by someone who wondered why having children is at all a good thing. Immorality is deliberately thwarting a natural good— thus an argument against contraception. God may get into the argument at this point not because of biology but because He made humans rational; He does not add anything to the rationality of the argument.

Considering natural goods is a promising move in a rational, nontheological discussion of morality. The great problem with any theory of natural goods is deciding what to do when there is a conflict between the realization of different natural goods. Health is a natural good, but what if a pregnancy a threatens a woman's health? Now God gets into the argument in a big way. If I read Finnis correctly, there cannot be a real conflict in natural goods since in God they are all compatible. No doubt, but at that point "natural" morality seems to have lost some of its naturalness.

I am happy enough that Church authorities are willing to argue the strictly moral (natural) case against a variety of evils. Morality gets all too little rational play from any quarter these days. Finnis and Grisez's opting for natural good is a persuasive opening for a rational discussion of morality. Nevertheless, no matter which version of natural law one may adopt for morality, the Church's special province is *sin*. The opposite of sin for Christians is not morality, it is faith. It would be more accurate to characterize the Church as a teacher of faith and salvation from sin. "Salvation from sin" may have some relation to morality in its conventional sense, but sin and morality exist in different spiritual universes.

My earlier characterization of Church used the acronym SNAPF: the Survivors Network of those Accepting and Preaching Forgiveness [of sin]. The Church story is about sin and forgiveness, not moral aspiration and failure. Insisting on the special character of sin is essential for preserving the idea and role of *Church*. Those not well disposed to all the supernatural flummery of traditional Christianity often regard the Church as the purveyor of ethical instruction and a support group for the morally inclined. Many churchgoers if pressed would themselves agree that the important thing about being a Christian is leading a certain "moral" life. The problem with that view is that in the long run morality can pretty well take care of itself. Any survey of world cultures will suggest that morality has more or less flourished and been flaunted everywhere. (Flaunting morality shows that it exists; one cannot flaunt a nothing.) There are some fascinating cultural variations in morality—mostly in the area of sexual practices—but when it comes to lying, cheating, stealing, and murdering one's kin and neighbors, human beings are generally agreed that these things are not to be done. Regarding Christianity as a moral code reduces religion to morality and, in effect, eliminates religion as a useful category. If being a good moral person is the essence of being a Christian, then, since it is obvious that Muslims, Hindus, and atheists can be good moral persons, differences in "religion" are inconsequential.

One can attempt to rescue the category of sin from being swallowed in morality by adding on the claim that offending my human brother is also offending God. No doubt this is theologically correct in so far as human beings are defined as "in the image of God." I am inclined to be very literal here about "image of God"; one does show some disrespect for the Queen by defacing her portrait, for example. Helpful as such an analogy may be, it makes sin a rather timid affair. It is cheap shot at the Queen to just deface her portrait. Given the high denunciation of sin in the tradition, the disrespect of defacement seems rather limp. Sin should be understood as a direct and bold offense against God. I do not mean that the only worthy sinner is someone shaking his fist at the heavens. Most sins are much more banal. I only mean that one must not tack on offense to God as "collateral damage." If Augustine is correct that our fundamental desire is for God, then God is the direct object of sin while our hapless sister is a mere occasion of theological offense. Reversing the "image" language: sin is an offense against God imaged in harm to my brother.

Sin is root and branch a theological notion, and it is sin and forgiveness that are the business of the Church. The extent of the Church's interest in morality will be defined by whatever morals *follow* from faith. One might argue that some ordinary moral conduct or habits are necessary for faith, conducive to faith, or block the possibility of faith. To the extent that faith requires a certain courage to face life in all its chanciness and destruction, one might promote the ordinary virtue of courage as a precondition for faith. For all that, however, the courageous person is not necessarily a person of faith nor is the coward a sinner. Courage may not even be a necessary *pre*condition of faith. Cowards have often had radical conversions to faith that changed their life; faith may produce courage to face the lions, not the other way round. Wretches in the grip of manifest immoralities may in a moment of revelation seek and even find salvation. It is often the precariousness of the immoral life which is most attuned to the radicalness of sin and salvation. There may be more possibility for a lustful Augustine to become a saint than for the bourgeois pillar of society.

I hope that these remarks at least suggest that there is some sort of distinction between immorality and sin. I want eventually to examine the nature of sin in more detail, but, given the insistent claim that the pope is infallible in faith and morals, I think it necessary to look directly at Catholic moral teaching. My aim is to show that the Church cannot sustain a claim for infallibility on moral issues. Church moral pronouncements fail three tests: (1) the historic record—various past papal moral directions are now regarded as clearly mistaken, (2) the logic of moral argument—the nature of moral discussion precludes infallible closure, and (3) the doctrine of original sin—the true fault line of humanity is deeper than immorality and, as such, compromises the possibility of moral infallibility. Eventually, I want to offer a direct Christological critique of "infallible moral teaching," but I will lead up to that by at least glancing at the actual history of moral instruction in the Church.

Although I do not believe that Catholic moral thought can sustain a claim for infallibility, I believe that it constitutes a valuable and important tradition of moral argument. Rational or "natural law/good" moral theory makes sense in terms of deep Christian commitments to the reality of the natural world, so it is not anomalous that there is such a tradition within Catholicism. The Catholic moral tradition has three interconnected positives: it is (1) comprehensive, (2) rational, and (3) often correct.

*Comprehensive.* Instead of settling on a few spectacular moral moments, Catholic moralists have blanketed all human actions with moral concern. Aquinas was correct to regard *all* human acts as coming under moral scrutiny. Catholic moralists opine on everything from science to sex. Comprehensive moral concern is both a blessing and a problem. The blessing is that it alerts us to the moral resonance of every action; the problem is that in deciding on any specific course of action one cannot be a "single issue" moralist. A temptation to which the Church too often succumbs in its obsession with sexual morality.

*Rational.* Catholic moral teaching is to be applauded for its insistent rationality. Unlike certain species of fundamentalism that can only declaim on morality from select Biblical passages, Catholic moralists under the aegis of "natural law"—complex as that slogan may be—have been able and willing to enter into the general human discussion of morality.

*Correct.* Catholic moral teaching over the centuries has more often than not been correct. This is not surprising for two reasons. Christians may believe in "the peace that the world cannot give" but they are also for the peace that the world can give. Second, since morality is an achievement, however fragile, of human rationality, to the extent that Catholic moralists have entered the rational fray, they benefit from rational deliberation and contribute to it.

I would give the Catholic moral tradition at least a B+ when it comes to argument and judgment about the right and the good. The problem is that it can only be B+, even though it claims to be A+. *Infallible* teaching on moral matters would yield an A+ score, 100% correct.

## Infallible Morality as Historic Failure

Judge John Noonan has been a particularly sharp critic of the claim to consistent and unfailing papal moral pronouncement. Not only have positions changed, past pronouncements are now regarded as downright wrong! In his recent book, *A Church that Can and Cannot Change: The Development of Catholic Moral Teaching,*[1] Noonan takes up four moral issues upon which the Church's official position has changed: slavery, usury, religious freedom, and divorce. Slavery is the most compelling case since it is a practice and institution that would clearly be regarded in the present day as morally wrong. John Paul II in *Veritatis Splendor* cites slavery as one of those acts "which in the tradition of the Church have been termed intrinsically evil: they are such always and per se." As a matter of cold history, Catholic moralists up to and including the popes in official pronouncements never questioned the institution of slavery before Leo XIII's *In Plurimus* of 1885 (a document that in its historical claims exemplifies the Catholic resort to amnesia when it becomes necessary to change moral doctrine).

On each of the issues discussed, Noonan makes a conclusive case for the existence of radical change in Catholic moral thought. Usury violated natural law because money, being an inert artifice, could not breed. Religious freedom, which was an abomination for popes up to the twentieth century, becomes a recognition of the intrinsic dignity of the individual in Vatican II. Teaching on divorce has not changed notably in public pronouncements, but Noonan points out that current thinking about the indissolubility of marriage when one of the partners is a non-Catholic is so confused that some sort of change is inevitable.

A single strike-out ruins a perfect batting average. The claim to unfailing ability to spot intrinsic evil cannot be substantiated by the record. The danger of pointing to this less-than-perfect record is that one might then dismiss the whole effort embedded in the Catholic moral tradition. Moral insight is not easily come by, and the persistence and pervasiveness of moral argument within the Catholic Church is, as suggested above, a great contribution to culture in general, which is all too prone to snap judgments or dismissal of moral argument overall. Once one makes the hyper-claim of infallibility, however, then egregious mistakes like those in the history of pronouncements on slavery are likely to undermine that authority altogether. Claiming too much is as bad as claiming too little. By claiming infallibility on morals, the Church absents itself from the complex process of moral judgement—a process that should always be open to correction or enrichment not only about goods in the abstract but in the thick context of individual ethical choice.

The factors that seem to have influenced the changes in Catholic moral teaching that Noonan delineates are instructive. In each case it would seem that the Church changed its teaching because social conditions changed. The growth of capitalism and the role of merchant bankers bypassed the moral restrictions on usury. At first such evasion was accomplished by legalistic legerdemain which, as Noonan notes, would have done credit to an Enron accountant. Legal obfuscation was finally dropped and plain old lending money at interest emerged as morally permissible. Religious freedom seems to have emerged from the perceived success of the American experiment separating Church and state. Slavery was condemned by the pope well after most of the world had abandoned the practice. The fact that social conditions may guide moral thought need not result in the relativistic suspicions of the deconstructionists. In a more constructive guise, Alasdair MacIntyre has argued persuasively that morality is always a work in progress within some specific historical tradition. Transcendent morality is a fiction, a rhetorical excess.[2] Despite the necessary cultural embededness of moral insight, there can be sound moral judgments. I will offer a model for sound moral argument *within* an historic tradition after looking first at the logic of moral argument.

## Infallible Morality Violates the Logic of Moral Argument

It is not the purpose of this book to explicate in any detail the ways of moral argument. I offer a sketch of how such argument proceeds because understanding the *logic* of moral discussions rules out infallibility. John Noonan's acronym on moral argument, A.B.L.E., is a sensible characterization of the enterprise. A: analogy. Law and morality constantly search for ways in which a new situation is like some settled conviction. Stem cell research is like abortion—or is it? Analogies can often leave out vital differences. B: balance. Morality and law have a loose organic character. Single issue advocacy without considering broader effects is to be approached with caution. L: logic. Arguments must hold together, but there are many logical arguments for many differing ethical positions. Balance among arguments is not a matter settled by formal logic. The notion of "balance" suggests it is a matter of "weighing" arguments, which is not at all like making a logical deduction. E: experience. The lone voice of Bartolomé de Las Casas protested against Spanish colonial slavery because he came to understand that institution from the experience of the slaves. Noonan's acronymic guideline captures how moral argument proceeds. The great temptation of moralists in and out of the Church is to exalt logic above the other factors. Analogy, balance, and experience are legitimate tools of moral assessment, but they are not mechanical measures. A good analogy, a sense of balance, and learning the proper lesson from experience cannot be set forth in rules and formulae. Aristotle was correct when he said that in the long run it is the person of "practical wisdom" who gives the rule for ethical discernment. Practical wisdom is not a technique that can be learned like the rules of the syllogism.

The upshot of the above argument is that morality is inherently an activity that cannot be "infallible," and so the Church's claim to infallible moral teaching violates the very essence of moral insight. Murder and a host of other immoralities can, of course, be intrinsically and infallibly evil *by definition*. Murder is "wrongful" killing as opposed to "justifiable homicide." Having built immorality into the meaning of "murder," it is of course true that murder is always and everywhere self-evidently immoral. But the problem of moral discourse is not one of defining, it is a problem of deciding how to characterize an action or way of life. Moral judgments should be synthetic, not analytic. Proclaiming this or that activity as intrinsically evil can short circuit the labor of ethical assessment. It is a rhetorical flourish that, while it may move the hearer, damages the credibility of the speaker. Abandoning rhetorical overkill does not thereby leave matters of morality up in the air. Slavery is an evil and there are strong arguments that would justify that conclusion. One cannot say that slavery is self-evidently (intrinsically) evil in the sense in which we think that it is self-evident, analytically true by definition. If that were the case one would have to regard past slave cultures and their defenders as utterly irrational. It is as if they affirmed that there were round squares! No, they were not irrational in that sense, they were morally wrong and that is enough.

Moving away from "intrinsic evil" to morality-in-history is not abandoning rational or natural goods because it is these rational ends for human life that are brought to bear when we seek to understand the issue at hand (by analogy) and balance it against experience in a coherent (logical) assessment of what is to be done. I agree with Alasdair MacIntyre that rationality and natural goods arise within thick cultural practices. Not all cultures are alike in their notions of what is rational and what is naturally good. At first glance this may seem to be a direct line to the relativism so abhorred by the pontiffs. I believe that the conclusion of relativism is, however, the result of superficial appraisal of differing cultures. One can fixate on some spectacular difference — usually in sexual morals — and conclude for radical difference. If, however, one gains a thick description of the "alien" culture one will, I believe, find entry points of commonality that can be deeply enriching and even transforming to the cultures in question. The only really alien culture is a "thin" culture based on whim, slogan, and immediacy, in other words, a culture without its own thick rationality. A thin culture has a thin rationality and is to that extent an amoral culture beyond the pale of rational moral discussion.

I have frequently used analogies from the arts in presenting my arguments. I do so again as a model for moral discussion. Suppose someone were to say that there was an infallible guidebook, institution, or individual who could pronounce definitively on the beautiful and the trashy in art. I do not think we would believe this was possible. The history of art suggests that tastes have varied remarkably. Works once highly valued now seem trivial, while masterpieces by unknowns are rescued from the historical basement. On that basis one might abandon assessment of artistic value altogether: it is all relative, a succession of fashions — there is no disputing about taste! Yet, despite the obvious variability of artistic judgments and differing artistic cultures, for example, between Western and Eastern traditions of painting and music, utter relativism about artistic value seems quite unacceptable. Put most precisely: it is wholly unacceptable *to those who actually practice the arts*. Perhaps to the casual consumer what is "good" in art is whatever strikes her fancy at the record shop or the print gallery, but to the dedicated composer, performer, or painter, the distinctions ranging from masterpiece to kitsch are real. No one who lives deeply in the artistic tradition will accept facile relativism. This is not because there is some handy catechism of the beautiful or *Academie des Beaux Arts* that infallibly pronounces on artistic value. All such treatises and institutions exist only *ex post facto* after whatever the tradition produces in its on-going life. Not only is there no transcendent authority on artistic value, there is no use in the art world for the "intrinsically beautiful" or "intrinsically ugly." (What do you say about Duchamp's *Fountain*?) Even the greatest art does not exist as the *infallible* standard of value. For all that, anyone practicing the art of painting will recognize the genuine value of Rembrandt or Caravaggio; any musician will revere Mozart. There is a precipitate of value that emerges within the practice of the arts that guides the present artist without demanding that she imitate the past—in fact which demands that she *not* imitate the past but that she enrich the tradition by building upon achievements within the tradition.

I believe that the artistic analogy illuminates moral life and moral argument. The first demand for moral life and argument is that individuals *engage in the practice*. There are two ways in which one can disengage from moral practice. One obvious means of disengagement is the road of relativism. Morality is the local fashion, which I may or may not choose to follow. The other way of disengaging from the moral life appears as the antithesis of relativism: it is the way of dogmatic pronouncement. How can that be? Dogmatism about good and evil may seem the very essence of morality. I think not. Dogmatism disengages from the moral life when it claims a position above the ongoing moral practices and traditions of human society. Dogmatism claims to have a transcendent handbook of the intrinsically good and intrinsically bad such that all one has to do is fit the particular case to the rule. Dogmatism, in short, makes moral judgment too easy when, in fact and history, moral insight comes from hard-won wisdom and experience.

So much for why moral argument considered historically and in terms of its inner structure fails to reach infallibility. The fact that it fails absolute certainty, far from denigrating moral argument, makes it of the greatest importance. Being as it is complex, many sided, and vastly important, nothing short of the most extended and scrupulous attention to moral issues is demanded. The current problem with moral argument is not simple relativism, but that we live in an era of bumper sticker morality.


## Beginning with Sin

Even if a Christian moral philosopher were to disagree with an historically based and open-textured account of moral discussion, I think she should go on to consider the problem of sin and whether the doctrine of sin affects moral judgment. I believe that the doctrine of sin has profound effect on ordinary morality. To make that argument I turn to a direct look at the meaning of sin. If sin is not simple immorality, what is it and how does the Church have special authority over sin? I rely on an exceptionally useful account by Alistair McFayden, *Bound to Sin.*[3] McFayden focuses on that most unattractive Christian notion: original sin. For McFayden, our multiple "sins" are variations on the original sin. Original sin as a doctrine runs directly counter to deep moral convictions of the modern world because it seems to immerse everyone in sin regardless of their direct action. Traditional Christian doctrine even claims that infants come with original sin and need baptism to alleviate that unhappy condition. Such a picture of essential depravity is most offensive to the modern conviction that blame can only be attached to acts which the individual wills in his or her freedom. Imputing guilt for some deed in which I was not a direct actor is both logically indefensible and morally offensive.

McFayden's most accessible argument for the category of sin, and original sin at that, parallels the feminist critique of patriarchy that was discussed earlier in connection with the "patriarchal" voice of the pope. Feminist critics argue that patriarchy is our pervasive cultural condition. There is no escaping the structures of patriarchy since from the earliest moment male and female infants and children are schooled in the culture of patriarchy. There is rejoicing over the birth of a male child, grudging acceptance of daughters. One can broaden the distortions of patriarchy by regarding it as only one form of the power discrepancies that seem to mark all cultures. "Master and slave" is the law of human society, the power of the dominant over the subservient: plantation overseer over blacks, corporate executives over wage-slaves, males over females, and so on. In all societies one is born into the group with power or the one without power. To the extent that one assimilates the culture of master (male) or the culture of slave (female), the human personality is warped and diminished.

This depressing notion of original sin is not by any means a strange and perverse Christian idea. While not labeling the issue "sin", various contemporary theorists have agreed with the notion that society is always in a disequilibrium of power. Michel Foucault says that one *cannot* escape the distortions of power. Foucault's society is Hobbes' war of all against all with nothing but temporary truces and balances of power in prospect. There is no "just" or "moral" ideal that can be envisaged or attained. Foucault was a champion of homosexual causes, but he understood this effort not as a gesture of "true" morality but simply a way for the homosexual community to create a viable space within the continual power conflict that marks any society. Foucault's view of society approximates the traditional doctrine of original sin: the human world is fundamentally and irreparably distorted.

If society is fundamentally always and everywhere distorted under patriarchy, slavery, late capitalism, or sexism, this affects the type of person within that society. Societies create personality types that react positively or negatively to the social pattern. In the inevitable distortions of society one may either accept or avoid being a patriarchic or sexist person, but either way one's person is a product of the social structure. The contemporary rejection of original sin is based on the notion that individuals can transcend the social construction of personality. One acts freely when one makes decisions that are not implicated in the social structure within which one has been nurtured. It is this modern construction of the idea of "free will" that the doctrine of original sin rejects.

The notion of original sin and Foucault's philosophy of social disequilibrium reject any escape to a "free will" above social construction. As discussed earlier, in the practice and ideal of science the individual researcher transcends into a realm of pure thought. The scientist does not investigate and claim truth based on her sex or race, so the fact that she exists within a slave, patriarchal, democratic, or despotic culture is a matter of indifference. Great science has, in fact, been done in some of the least attractive political times. The modern view of free will, which rejects original sin, rests on a similar claim for attaining a transcendent *persona* above culture. The individual conscience can reach a transcendent morality above any particular moral culture. From such a purified stance the individual may judge the culture at hand and refuse to accommodate to its diminishing social conditions. This type of rational morality is characteristic of the Enlightenment and of its greatest philosopher, Immanuel Kant. The moral stance emulates the scientific stance: transcendent, universal morality grounded in free will.

It would be beyond the scope of this book to attempt any evaluation of the Kantian view of free will and the moral law. I am content to emphasize the profound difference between such rational morality and the direction of the doctrine of original sin. Suffice it to say that the Enlightenment view of human rationality and its attendant morality has come under profound criticism from contemporary deconstructionists and multiculturalists. The doctrine of original sin shares the deconstructive assumption. Humans are historically embedded: there is no freedom of reason *above* historical condition.


## No One Is Innocent: Victims and Infants

The view that destructive history dominates over free will is at the core of the doctrine of original sin. Everyone is born into this or that culture, which, whatever the particular contestations of power, inevitably sets forth a set of values that predetermine one's action and imagination. Reinhold Niebuhr quipped that original sin was the one Christian doctrine for which there was clear historical proof. True enough, but the problem is deeper than empirical generalization. History left to humanity alone is fatally determined to be Stephen Daedelus' "nightmare." Christians hold that human history left to itself is an area of unfreedom, of binding in false power relations, of sin. Baptism is the second birth and acts as the signature for history both in its sinfulness (Cross) and the possibility of salvation from that sinfulness (Resurrection). The core notion of original sin is that there is no escaping history — no *human* escape from history.

Admitting that discrepancy of power may make history a nightmare, why are the *victims* of history tainted with sin, as *original* sin seems to imply? The powerful in history (patriarchs, masters, elites) may be sinful but surely not their victims (women, slaves, the oppressed). In addition, there is the special Christian peculiarity of imputing original sin even to infants who in their biological innocence are below the distortions of history. It is necessary to explicate the universality of sin even to victims to establish the need for Christian universal salvation.

Surely some people are innocent of sin since they do not dominate; they suffer and so they avoid the guilt of the powerful. McFayden argues persuasively that the "victim" is not released from the grip of sin. Given the depth and pervasiveness of an alienating culture, the individual victim's responses and actions are distorted. There are obvious ways in which this is the case. Acting against the patriarchic structure may replicate its essential distortions. A false feminist revolution might view salvation from patriarchy as accomplished if women were to attain the sort of hierarchic power invested in males. But this "solution" would merely replicate the sin of false relationship with a switch in gender. What is needed is a feminist revolution that would establish right relations between men and women. But do we know what "right relations" would be? Foucault suggests that homosexuals should exert power to attain social space, but there is no right relation envisaged. Hegel thought that conflicts in cultures contained the implicit seeds of their eventual resolution, but that is a claim with its own considerable coefficient of incredibility. The victim may give up on the prospect of escaping the power distortions of society and withdraw, but that stance suggests complicity with the power distortions in place.

McFayden makes his case as difficult as possible by discussing the problem of sexual abuse of children. Clearly they are victims. Unless the child somehow enticed the adult, what guilt can attach to the child? McFayden argues that though the burden of guilt bears on the perpetrator, the result of abuse throws the victim into a disordered state in which his responses are warped. Silence is the primary way in which the victim "accepts" the abuse. Since the abuser is often a parent or trusted authority, the child's normal dependence on an adult world is radically disrupted. The child is thrown into accepting the abuse because she cannot reveal what is happening. To reveal the abuse would be to shatter her world, a world on which she is dependent and thus a world she cannot abandon despite its betrayal. She accepts being a victim and in that sense is complicit in the abuse. The pattern of victim dependence and complicity in abusive relations is well recognized in psychological studies of such situations. Indeed, it may be the inevitability of complicity that is the deepest damage of childhood sexual abuse.

The darkest part of the traditional doctrine of original sin goes beyond the complex problems of victimhood to the notion of infant depravity. The practice of infant baptism suggests that just being *biologically born* already puts the human infant in a guilty state. St. Augustine gave a particularly depressing twist to this doctrine by surmising that it is because infants are the inevitable product of sexual lust that they are damned. Augustine thought that in Paradise sex was without lust but, after the Fall, lust infected the infant as surely as AIDS is passed on from parent to fetus. In the traditional catechism, dying without baptism did not exactly consign the hapless babe to hell. Theologians invented Limbo as a proper destination: not heavenly bliss but some sort of natural bliss. I think that one might just as well forget Augustine's metaphysical biology of sin; the problem of birth-into-history is enough of a problematic to justify deploying the notion of original sin. So it has been, and so Limbo does not get a mention in the current *Catechism of the Catholic Church*. Nevertheless, I want to say a passing good word about Limbo and infant baptism.

The Peaceweavers might be said to seek a withdrawal from history by refusing the baptismal (twice born) option. If humans would only place themselves at the biological level, regarding themselves as part of the ecology of the planet, they would live in the peace of nature. Refusing baptism is refusing history, and in that sense the Peaceweavers bypass any "salvation in/of history." Their ideal state is similar to the theologian's Limbo: natural pleasure without God. There is a certain analytic truth to the claim that without baptism there is no salvation, that is, there is no life with God. Refusing history is refusing the individual *persona,* refusing the whole *dramatis personae* of the great World-Play with all its loves and catastrophes. Christianity claims that only in the emergence out of nature and species into history is there a sense of "person" and a personal God.

The objection to infant baptism in the Churches is, nevertheless, not without point. The argument is that since baptism initiates into faith, it should be something that is undertaken only when the individual is of age and has thoroughly considered what he believes. The only problem with that argument is that when parents name their infants—and even Peaceweavers indulge in this practice—they start down the track of forming an historical persona. When the Christian parents name children, they are affirming their existence in a special history. If we name infants, if we regard them from the moment of birth as persons, we should, as Christians, regard them as henceforth cast in the World-Play of salvation. Infant baptism is the moment of recognition for the parents that the child is placed into salvation history in terms of which his or her persona is to be formed.

Let this suffice for now about the notion of sin. The important point is that sin in the Christian tradition is something deeper than individual misconduct. Humans as humans are just not in a position to exercise the sort of free, consumer's choice that is envisaged in the doctrine of free will. In the Christian story persons are formed within the destructive social institutions that are the warp of human history. If there is to be freedom it must come through a radical reconstruction of history, which means immersion in a nondestructive society created by actions quite beyond the capacities of the human actors. This nondestructive society is the Church, the society created by the action of Jesus Christ in history. Christ's action? The forgiveness of sin.

## Is Morality Sinful?

If the Gospel message is forgiveness of sin, a divine rescue of history, what effect does such a message have on everyday morality? As usual in discussing the paradox that is Christianity, the effect is both trivial and profound—which may amount to the same thing. It can be trivial in the sense that realization of sin and salvation may quite bypass human moral good sense. As claimed earlier, morality can pretty well get along on its own. One who wants to learn about morality as such would be well advised to read Plato, Aristotle, Spinoza, Kant, and the other great moralists. Frankly, on morality they are much better guides than the Bible. They are not guides at all on sin.

On the other hand, the introduction of sin has profound effects on morality. From the standpoint of sin, one might be advised to be wary of morality and its teachers. In so far as great philosophers and lesser ethical pundits act within the circumference of strictly human interests and capacities, one may practice a hermeneutic of suspicion about the universality of their prescriptions. Can any *human* thinker no matter how learned and profound really rise above the social conditions of his time? Aristotle, who is about as good a moralist as one can conjure, regarded women as defective males and thought that there were "natural slaves."

Given original sin or the Foucaultian version thereof, all moralists are infected with distortions of power from which there is no escape. The fact that moral teachers often assume that they have discovered a species of transcendent, universal morality quite detached from the social conditions within which they live can be its own special sin of arrogance.

The deconstructionist suspicion of universal morality has been a cause of deep concern in official Catholic circles. The theme has been at the center of many of Benedict XVI's comments. The pope insists on "universal moral truths," on "intrinsically evil acts." A recent article in *The National Catholic Reporter* was headlined "Seminary Leaders Foresee Tightening up of Moral Teaching." In the article, Bishop John Nienstedt, one of the official visitors in the review of seminary training was quoted: "The big question is relativism. . . . [S]eminarians . . . have to have a sense of confidence in the objective truth of the faith."[4] It should be no surprise that I regard this demand for *objective* truth as dangerously misleading. There is a universality and truth to the Christian way of life, but it is not objective in the sense normally attached to that notion.

For Christians the doctrine of original sin should at least give initial pause about the *human* ability to reach the heights of objective moral insight. One suspects that papal declaration of "intrinsic evil" finally rests on extrarational, religious underpinnings. The pope could claim that although humans are always limited in their moral insight, the Bible as the Word of God or the promptings of the Holy Spirit escape human limitation and tells us what is truly good, really evil. The Bible or the Holy Spirit transcend the limitations that deconstructionists may point out in regard to this or that culture. But I believe that passing *morality* on to the Bible or the Holy Spirit is a bad move.

I am not certain that there is any moral law in the Bible. The whole point of this argument is that the Bible is interested in *sin,* not morality. The Word of God convicts the human world of sin and also forgives sin, but it is not the word that sets down a moral code for humanity. It would be a structural fault in papal moral reasoning to insinuate divine warrant into mere moral reasoning. (I have already touched on this issue in discussing the pope as *judge.*) Moral positions that are eminently sensible, persuasive, and even conclusive are given an extra added attraction as unimpeachable truths. There are quite good moral arguments, there are sound conclusions to be made about the moral life, but as Aristotle pointed out, ethics is not a precise science ending in demonstrations with the universality of Euclid's theorems.

## Christological Critique of Infallible Morality

It is bad enough that "infallible morality" fails the historical test and violates the logic of moral discussion, most damning for the Church should be that it fails the Christological test. There is something quite un-Christian in claiming infallibility in *moral* judgment. If there is something "infallible" in the Church's instructional portfolio it must be somewhere else than in the moral game. The text of the New Testament would suggest that the Church is authoritative on sin, not morals. Infallibility about sin requires less-than-infallibility about morality.

I have likened sin to pervasive social structures like patriarchy or slavery. The claim is made that any and all actions within such sinful structures are perverse. The universal perversity of the society infects individual action. Even the victim in the struggle for power acts perversely in envy, complicity, or withdrawal. Human morality and individual actions are always shaded with the original sin. Absolute moralists display a special danger since they seem to claim a transcendent, God's eye view of right and wrong. From the perspective of sin, a transcendent moral claim is a prideful offense against God.

The doctrine of original sin affects morality in three ways. (1) The doctrine of sin relativizes morality insofar as it sees all *human* moral structures and actions as compromised. Original sin, like the pervasive structures of patriarchy and slavery, positions everyone in the culture in false relations. In so far as the human persona is shaped by strictly human culture, we live in a Foucaultian sinful world of distorted power. (2) Faith that history has been rescued from the fatality of sin in the message and life of Christ allows the Christian to move beyond the sheer moral relativism and deconstructive rejection of history. (3) Recognition that we are saved from sin, that history is divine comedy, creates its own shape of life and action, "morals" that exist *as a consequence of faith*. Actions that are sanctioned by ordinary morality reappear, but the inner life of the action is radically changed. While peace is indeed a moral goal for Christians, the inner life and meaning of peace in Christianity is quite different than the peace that emerges from prudent moral calculation, for example, Hobbes' least worst bargain or retroversion to the Peaceweavers' realm of natural ecology.

*Sin makes absolute morality impossible.* This is the most obvious of the claims. The assumption of original sin is that humanly speaking no one is innocent. As disagreeable as original sin may be to the modern mind, it has the identical structure of current social critiques like Foucault's. Make the social construction of humanity deep enough and broad enough and morality is an illusion, the ideology of the strong. One need not be a French philosopher to deconstruct morality. Pressed ever so slightly, the man on the street becomes a deconstructionist in the sense that he regards alien moralities as the product of "bad" social conditioning. Happily, the man on the street also believes that he has been raised in the right society (the USA, the Catholic Church, the Southern Baptist Convention) so that his morality escapes the false perspective of other cultures. The Qur'an and the Vedas mislead, but the Bible teaches "true" morality. Pressed just a tad more—say in Philosophy 101 at State U.—our sturdy evangelical comes to wonder why his society and his sacred text escapes the deconstruction of morals applied to other cultures. Our student emerges as a paragon of tolerance. One should not criticize the beliefs and actions of others. If he retains a sense of morality as something more than taste, it is either because he has retained some moral habits despite his new sophistication or because it seems prudent to "go with the flow."

There is, then, a widespread suspicion that relativism via social construction is the unhappy secret of morality. The shrill denunciations of relativism by everyone from biblicists to recent popes may be taken as proof of the shakiness of morality. Fear that all will slip away into some chaos of fashion or desire simply ups the rhetoric. Morality must be absolute, there are intrinsic evils, the Bible or the magisterium has an infallible insight into the *really* moral. Morality should be defended, but this is the wrong epistemology, in other words, the wrong method for "knowing" moral good and evil.

*Sin makes morality necessary; salvation makes morality possible.* Original sin or its deconstructionist analogues should make us suspicious of infallible moralities based on absolute truths. There goes morality! Not at all. The outcome of the argument should not be the abandonment of moral thought and ethical training, it should be quite the opposite. It is because morality is complex and socially conditioned that we need continuous and careful reassessment, re-understanding, and recovery of the goods of human society. There is no shortcut to moral truth in the Bible, ecclesiastic pronouncements, or national ethos. Pervasive social distortion should make us wary of absolutes, but it does not alleviate the moral task—it makes the moral life more difficult and moral argument more imperative. Trying to shortcut morality by citing the Bible or the latest papal pronouncement is like trying to decide on the quality of a work of art without bothering to immerse yourself in art's history and practice.

If moral argument, complex as it is, is *necessary,* it must also be *possible.* It is the claim that moral argument is impossible that makes the deconstructionist claim so radical and so worrisome. The reason that deconstructionists reject moral argument is that they do not believe that there is some neutral, transcendent view point, the stance of a truly dispassionate *persona,* from which one could judge moral truth. Moral judgments are self-serving and subjective; never neutral and objective. Under the ban of original sin, Christians would take the same pessimistic attitude toward moral "truth." Christians hold that there is salvation from sin, but this salvation is not a transcendence or a retreat from history, but a deep understanding of history and God's relation to history. The Christian transcendence of sinful self is not accomplished by historical withdrawal. The Christian demand to "love your enemies" illustrates the peculiar character of Christian transcendence. Ancient Stoics withdraw from the world of enemies because the actual historical world is fiction and illusion. Deconstructionists relativize enemies. There are no "enemies" as such, opposition is just the way of the world. When everyone is an enemy, no one is an enemy! Unlike Stoics who disdain the real existence of enemies, and contrary to the perpetual oppositional stance of the deconstructionist war of all against all, the Christian actively loves enemies, turns the other cheek, and forgives the persecutor.

In contrast to those who reject and relativize history, the transcendence of the Christian self—the *persona Christi*—offers a comedic stance *within* history. The comedic stance in history is the analog to transcendent neutrality above history. From the standpoint of transcendent morality, human history is either tragedy or farce—probably both. Comedic perception is the functional equivalent of the presumption of a transcendent moral view. The difference—and it is profound—is that the comedic voice accepts history, acts in history. The comedic voice transcends the sinful world not by icy neutrality, but by love and forgiveness. Love and forgiveness engages the other. Love and forgiveness do not abandon the other to tragic and farcical passion. It is from the comedic stance that Christian "morality" emerges.

*Faith's comedic morality.* Christian faith would be empty if it did not affect the life of the believer. I have been relying throughout on Iris Murdoch's characterization of religion as "an intense attitude with no time off." Religious belief was placed in the same category as paranoia: a totalizing personality structure. Like paranoia, religious belief has a comprehensive effect on attitude and action. How, then, can one say that faith does not shape the moral life? Paranoia commands the attitudes and actions of the paranoid: he is fearful, suspicious, wary in every action and human interchange. The world is the world of enemies; from the inside of the personality life is total war! The genuine Christian persona is infused with what would seem to be the exact opposite of the paranoid: the world is one in which one loves one's enemies. The contrast is total war or total peace.

Comparing paranoia and religious faith illustrates how these states differ from the normal conditions of moral action and assessment. Just as there is no use trying to persuade the paranoid that my utterly benign gesture is not a mask for hostility, so there is no use trying to persuade the Christian believer that her malignant executioner is an enemy. Belief that the World-Play as a story of total war or a story of total peace is not an empirical conclusion from the current existence of hostilities or lack thereof. War or peace are grounded in an "intense attitude with no time off." Because paranoia and faith are deep, total personality structures they do not seem to be properly characterized as *moral* positions. This is clear with paranoia: we do not attach moral blame to the anger of the psychotic paranoid; his problems are deeper than moral action and beyond moral argument. It may be shocking to think of Christian faith as insane, but moderate reflection might suggest that there is something very odd in regarding our obviously hostile world as without enemies. Without quite saying that Christianity is insane, Freud regards the Christian command to love one's neighbor as oneself as thoroughly irrational, and when it comes to "Love thine enemies" he can only conclude that it is an instance of *Credo quia absurdum.*[5]

The *moral* defender of peace will cite self-interest or the moral right to life of the other and so on. But when asked to justify her personality-of-peace the Christian believer does something quite different: she asserts her faith in the story of Jesus, a story that reconstructs history as divine comedy. Her argument bypasses moral argument. Yes, there are good moral arguments for peace, but whether or not one accepts those arguments the Christian believer holds that peace is the fundamental structure of human history under God. Our task is not to argue ourselves into a state of peace but to recognize a peace already given in the lordship of Christ.

The moral outcome of Christian revelation is rooted in those attitudes and actions appropriate to a belief that one is acting in the World-Play as divine comedy. The actions that stem from that core belief are not to be confused with this or that moral rule, whether it be the Ten Commandments or the latest catechism from Rome. The Ten Commandments may be a by-product of a comedic vision, but keeping the commandments need have no relation whatsoever to such a vision. Forbidding adultery is a prudent rule for keeping families and societies together and need not be accompanied by any large view of human history, that is, the place of adultery in the World-Play. Sexual fidelity may even be accompanied by a grim view of the World-Play; it might be paradise to be sexually promiscuous, but given a human history of jealousy and strife, I bite my tongue and practice sexual discretion. (Such a grim scenario is sketched in Freud's *Civilization and its Discontents*.) On the whole it is better that humans practice sexual fidelity, but grim-faced fidelity misses the mark of *Christian* morality. If the commandment forbidding adultery is valid for Christians it must be understood as the proper stage direction for playing comedy.

Christians are charged to enact the divine comedy within the givens of a particular culture and their own personal capacities and desires. Like Brother Lawrence we are all in the kitchen of life and are asked to rejoice nevertheless. It would be a worthwhile task to develop a detailed exposition of those attitudes that are consonant with a Christian comedic vision. This exposition would be in some that the functional equivalent of the Ten Commandments, a species of distinctive Christian morality. The most obvious positive injunction is "Love your enemies," for in a comedy there are no final enemies. That would preclude a host of "ordinary" moral actions: murder, revenge, hatred, jealousy, and so on. In Dickens' comic version of *Romeo and Juliet* (the Crummles version of the play in *Nicholas Nickleby*)

Juliet wakes up in time, Romeo only suffers a flesh wound, the Montagues and Capulets rejoice, and everyone sings "Rule Britannia."

Beyond directly anticomedic actions and attitudes, there will have to be a certain fluidity and openness to what is "demanded" by the comedic vision because what is important is discovering the *spirit* of the action. Sometimes an action may be grounded in hostility, sometimes not. Lying can surely be hostile, treating the other as enemy, but sometimes it can be a loving gesture because the truth would be crushing. In Shakespearean comedy, lying is often a necessary subterfuge, which the character uses to unmask some deeper deception on the part of the other. In *All's Well That Ends Well,* Helena not only disguises herself to follow Bertram, the lover who spurned her, she pretends to be Bertram's Florentine girlfriend. Carrying forward this deception, Helena conceives a child by Bertram. It is then reported that Helena is dead (another lie on top of the lying disguises). Returning to France, Bertram discovers that Helena is alive and that she has borne his child. He finally comes to his senses and "all's well that ends well."

## Beyond Good and Evil

The Christology presented in this book offers the history of Jesus as a story beyond moral agency. It is not in his moral *action* that he is Savior but in his *passion*. He masters life not by moral mastery in the manner of, say, Aristotle's "great-souled" man who would have borne crucifixion with "nobility," but as one who is deeply troubled, who cries out in fear that he has been forsaken. Jesus can say "I am the *life*" because he suffers life in all its shocks even unto death on the Cross. But—the Christian paradox—by suffering life in all its pain and excess, Jesus is resurrected as the one who has mastered life, who is the Lord of life. Given the figure of Christ as one who engages life and death to the full, the passionate individual who plunges into the vital chaos of life, risking tragedy and loss, seems closer to the saint than the prudent moral agent. It is no wonder that a thief understands Christ on the Cross. There is a rich literary tradition starting at least with the Gospels themselves that finds the lost sheep, the sinner who repents, the prodigal son as the one closest to the Father's heart. The prudent moral man is the elder son who does his duty, but joy accompanies the one who knows sin and yet returns.

One has to be careful in setting forth the connection of passion and saintliness. One can overromanticize the connection, suggest that one plunge into sin so that grace may abound. Contemporary art which aims to shock morality has a point: life can be chaos and waste. The message of life's messiness is itself, however, messy. Is it a condemnation of humanity or a blessing? Does the chaos of life ridicule our orderly notions, or is there some deep truth to be learned within the fullness of life? No doubt there is chaotic vitality and we may need to be shocked from our illusions about mastery of life — even and perhaps especially *moral* mastery — by an art of disorder and disturbance. The erotic impinges, death intervenes. There is no bridge from death in Venice to death in Auschwitz. In much post-Duchampian art the message is often just chaos over creation. The message is cynicism and despair. Chaos is not, however, the message of the Bible. Jesus' life and message are the message of the Creator; the Creator is precisely the one who masters chaos, who masters suffering. This mastery of chaos and suffering is accomplished not by rising above suffering but by investing the fullness of life with ultimate meaning.

This chapter has been about sin and morality. Morality as a rational human practice is of the greatest importance to human flourishing. For that reason it requires scrupulous attention both in the training of moral habits and the assessment of human goods. Because it is a *human* practice, it should not be elevated above human capacities as if it were direct divine command. There is a divine demand, but it is beyond morality in creation, life, and history. From the standpoint of the Creator God, there are two avenues of sin. One is the sin of self-creation when we enclose ourselves in some self-concept creating a destructive split between self and other. The opposite direction of sin also denies creation but in terms of what one might call *self-chaos*. The individual lives life as mere chaos. In so far as accepting chaos shakes the complacency of the self-assured, there can be a profound spiritual lesson conveyed. The question that arises, however, is whether one comes to any meaning *through* chaos. Whether this is truly an alternative sin is problematic. I may, paradoxically, construct my persona as the chaotic one. I am the one you can never count on to be the same — which means I become encased in my own self creating chaos.

In Joseph Conrad's *Lord Jim,* the protagonist, Jim, has been morally scarred by an early act of apparent cowardice. How is he to reconstruct his life? A veteran in the ocean trade, the German merchant Stein, expresses the answer and the lesson of the book.

> There is only one remedy! One thing can us from being ourselves cure! . . . How to be! *Ach!* How to be. Yes! Very funny this terrible thing is. A man that is born falls into a dream, like a man who falls into the sea. If he tries to climb out into the air as inexperienced people endeavour to do, he drowns—*nicht wahr?* . . . No! I tell you! The way is to the destructive element submit yourself, and with the exertion of your hands and feet in the water make the deep, deep sea keep you up. So, if you ask me—how to be.[6]

"[T]o the destructive element submit yourself" echoes the Christian injunction that one must die and be born again. Only if you submit yourself to the destructive element that is life-and-death and keep yourself "afloat" do you discover "how to be." Otherwise, one is like the man who falls into the sea and tries to escape "into the air" of pure thought or self-willed action. In that way we "drown" because we pretend that we are not immersed in life-and-death. I live my life as if I, flesh and blood, were an example of an idea. The alternative way to drown is, of course, to fall into the sea and not exert onself. Instead of making "the deep, deep sea keep you up," you drown in despair.

Morality relates to right action; sin asks "how to be." The meaning of life is not, finally, found in morality but in what we make of life. Sin is an escape from life, an escape into the air of idea, or sin is drowning, life as chaos. Jesus is not the moral master, the moral teacher, he is "the way, the life, and the truth." If we immerse ourselves in the "chaos" of his death, we rise into the Creator of life.

Given this argument that the voice of Christianity is not and ought not to be the voice of moral instruction, in the next chapter I want to sum up the overall argument of the book by describing the voice of the Church beyond morality: the voice that forgives sin.

# CHAPTER NINE

# The Forgiving Voice

*The Lord God has given me a disciple's tongue,*
*that I may know how to speak to the weary.*
*Morning after morning, he opens my ear that I may listen.*

Isaiah 50:4

      The principal argument of this book has been that the *what* of faith cannot be isolated from the *how* of voice. Ultimately *what* and *how* coalesce. I have claimed that the *what* of Christian faith is history as *divina commedia* because of the action of Jesus Christ. In the order of reality *commedia* reigns. Being told "Tonight we are playing comedy!" alerts the actors to the *voice* of the performance. What is the comedic voice? We experience the voice of the *divina commedia* from masters of Christian comedic performance, from the *hilaritas* of the saints. To him who looks at the word with saintly *hilaritas,* the world looks back as divine comedy. There is no neutral, objective assessment that will reveal history as comedy, tragedy, or any sort of story at all. The *persona Christi,* realized in the *hilaritas* of the saints, reveals the comedic reality of the world. In this chapter I want to sum up the authentic Christian voice by contrasting it to some of the other commanding voices that have been outlined in the course of this book.

## Voices and History

For Michel Foucault, history is everywhere and always subject to the inevitable distortions of unequal power. The voice that speaks in such a world is essentially a voice of power—a voice that either asserts power or seeks power. Arguments are not based on some neutral access to "truth," they are instruments of power for overcoming the other. Psychological manipulation and *ad hominem* argument are legitimate since the aim of discourse is asserting or gaining power. In history there is neither truth nor morality, only a ceaseless struggle that compromises both the victor and the vanquished. Foucault's voice is *the voice of propaganda.*[1]

If one views history as a Foucaultian arena of the distortions of power, one may seek to withdraw from history, searching for truth above or beyond historical distortion. Truth above or beyond history takes many forms. One effective voice is the *scientific voice* of theoretical detachment. The scientific voice is marvelously suited to realities detached from human history, for example, the detached reality of the distant galaxies or the deep of fundamental particles. If scientific detachment turns toward the human world it can simply chronicle from above the causal determinism of historical behavior. One may, however, go beyond the theoretical structuring of natural or social science and adopt scientific detachment as a moral position: an *ethic of withdrawal.*

There are two dominant forms of ethical withdrawal from history: from "above" and from "below." One may withdraw from history to an eternal moral realm above, as in the case of classical Stoicism. Alternatively, one can retreat from history back to the simple pleasures of nature and the earth, as in classical Epicureanism. Ancient Stoics quite disregarded history: the two great Roman Stoics were an emperor, Marcus Aurelius, and a slave, Epictetus. Historical position made no difference in judging a life worthy because the moral world existed "above" in the eternal of the rational mind. The alternate direction of withdrawal, Epicureanism, has received bad press, but it was actually a doctrine of return to natural simplicity. The Peaceweavers and various New Age movements are modern "Epicureans" who withdraw from history in the direction of nature and its peace.

Withdrawal from history either "above" in reason or "below" in nature creates the *voice of the sage.* The sage *knows* some truth that goes beyond the fatal distortions of history. The scientist aspires to detachment from personal, historical limitation in order to attain the stance of universal truth, the sage gives ethical value to historical detachment. Whether the moral lesson of the cosmos is eternal order as with the Stoics or our fleeting life in nature as with the Epicureans, the result is a philosophical voice. I characterize these voices as "philosophic" because of the general notion that philosophy rests on some sort of universalism, a detachment from particularity, so that one may glimpse Truth, such as, eternal Forms (Plato), the nature of Being (Aristotle), the nature of Mind (Descartes, Kant), and so on. Because the voice of the philosophic sage knows some Truth, he is legitimated to teach what he knows. Follow the argument and one learns the lessons of the philosopher.[2] Moral philosophy seems to claim that if one can learn to think correctly or practice some appropriate method, reality and the good life can be known and pursued. The voice of the philosophic sage differs profoundly from the propaganda voice because the sage holds that truth is discoverable.

Having discovered a way to truth beyond history, the sage teaches and creates disciples and companions who share in the way to truth and peace. Both Stoics and Epicureans created communities of the enlightened to enjoy in mutuality the certainty of reason or the simplicity of nature. If one can educate the few, why not the many? Perhaps society at large could be reformed according to a truth discovered beyond history in reason or nature. Plato's *Republic* lays out a thoroughgoing reform of society on the basis of transcendent philosophic truth. It was only Plato's disillusionment trying to reform the kingdom of Syracuse that caused him to retreat to the "grove of Academus." Social reformers down the ages think that Plato gave up too easily. The *philosophes* of the Enlightenment projected a "heavenly city" spied through reason. Like Plato of the *Republic* they sought to apply this rational pattern as therapy to the social pathologies of the age. Marx was heir to the rational vision of an ideal state. Unlike the Enlightenment political philosophers, he believed that history was self-correcting and that he, Marx, understood history's causality. Both Enlightenment political theory and Marxism reject the Foucaultian struggle for power. Like sages of old these theorists believed that philosophy in a "scientific" mode can detach itself sufficiently from the distortions of history to discover truth and goodness. Philosophy trumps propaganda or "ideology" as Marx puts it. History can be saved through a political or moral science. These various political philosophies transmute the voice of the reclusive sage into the *voice of the social therapist* charged to reform history in the light of reason.

A final voice worth noting is the *aesthetic voice,* which seems to be the primary voice of deconstructionism. (It may be the reason why deconstruction has found its best home in departments of literature.) The aesthetic voice is not a voice with any positive program for the sinful world. Its moral agenda is tolerance. Unlike the edgy voice of Foucault who champions the underdog in the struggle for power, the stern voice of the Stoic sage who abandons history as inevitable tragedy, the placid voice of the Epicurean retreatant, or the revolutionary voice of a Marxist social therapist for history, the aesthetic voice adopts a bemused attitude toward the historical World-Play—it is *just* a play. Derrida's characterization of differing cultures as a "dance of myriad choreographies" expresses the tolerance of the aesthetic distance. Duchamp's aesthetic deconstruction of life is expressed in his pseudonym: Selavy, *c'est la vie.*

## Obsessive History

The array of voices set forth are *voices toward history.* One can—and perhaps most people do—adopt no settled voice toward history. Life is one damn thing after another, sometimes good, sometimes bad, tragic today, comic tomorrow. History as hurly-burly may be the most sensible attitude to take: play it as it lays! The common man's day-by-day attitude has some affinity with the aesthetic view of history: a variety show, except that he is *in* the mix of tragedy, comedy, farce, and sheer boredom that the aesthete views with literary composure. Christianity rejects history as hurly-burly and thus shares with the variety of voices outlined an obsessive view of history overall. One imagines the Jewish girl at Yad Vashem abandoning life as inconstant teenage fashion for an obsessive view of history as threat to the Jews.

A necessary formal requirement for understanding the Christian voice is accepting an "obsessive" and synoptic view of human history. Iris Murdoch's definition of religion notes its obsessive character: "[I]t's happening all the time. If it's not everywhere . . . it isn't what I mean. . . . It's to do with life as a whole and not a lot of random choices." The common man and Isaiah Berlin's sly philosophic fox may reject the religious voice simply because of its obsessive and synoptic view of history. History is just too messy, too diverse, too variegated to be summed in Christian salvation history or the Marxist struggle of the proletariat. I commented earlier about the "foxy" character of Jewish and Christian religion. The problem of hedgehoggery is not that it is synoptic and obsessive, but that it achieves overall synoptic order by separating historical appearance from transcendent reality, for example, the world as appearance and God as reality. Biblical faith does not divide world and God as appearance and reality. History is brutally real for Jewish and Christian faith. For that reason there remains something inherently fractured, fragmentary—messy—about the Christian view of history.

The Christian voice cannot be equated with any of the above obsessive views of history but it contains echoes of each. So compelling are these "echoes" that there has been a constant temptation in and out of the Church to identify Christianity with one or the other of the alternative voices. Early Christianity has been likened to the withdrawal to the eternal of the Stoics but also to the simplicity of the Epicureans. Retrojection of philosophic positions onto early Christianity has extended even to Jesus. John Dominic Crosson casts Jesus as an itinerant Cynic philosopher.[3]

What is the proper comparison of Christianity with the voices already outlined? Christianity takes as mordant a view of human history as Foucault: original sin is at our *origin* and is humanly incurable. Comparing the Christian voice with Foucault poses an immediate problem for faith. How can the Christian voice rise above propaganda, rise above the distortions of truth that are inevitable in history as the contestation of power? What is of critical importance is that Christianity does *not* solve the Foucaultian problem through one of the various strategies for overcoming history outlined above. In the long run, the voice of the sage, the moral or social therapist, and the Marxist revolutionary are all rejected because they are grounded on some human capacity: a science, spiritual wisdom, or manual of discipline by which one attains the truth. Christians reject the notion that one can be saved from history by human effort in reason, meditation, or the simple life. While there may be some steps in the right direction within these various strategies, they are all forms of the Pelagian heresy: salvation by works. Christianity asserts that salvation from original sin, from history as contestation of power, is a *gift* of God. Christians need a savior not a sage.

It is not just that the truth of Christianity comes as a gift, it is also *what* is revealed that leads to the rejection of the sage. Biblical fundamentalism replaces the authentic voice of Christianity with the voice of Jesus as sage. He knows something that we do not and is gracious enough to tell us. "Only the Son knows the Father." But Jesus is not telling us about God, Christians claim that he is "God with us." Christianity does not rest on the truth *from* Jesus, but on the truth *of* Jesus.

## A Therapeutic Voice

Rejection of the voice of the sage requires us to look with a critical eye on various ways in which the Church has presented its own Christian "therapy" for history, its cure for the sinfulness of the world. Monastic life and Christian contemplation have often seemed to be detachments from an historical world of sin akin to the inspiration of Stoicim or the simple life of the Epicurean cult. Yet even in their most negative attitudes toward the tawdriness of historical times, monks have prayed for the world. Prayer is thankful recognition that a cure has been effected in the life of the savior. Stoic and Epicurean philosophers did not pray for the world, being quite content to live in the rational company of the select or the bonds of natural affection.

If contemplation or withdrawal are not in themselves instruments of salvation, how should we evaluate the voice of the active Church offering moral or political therapy for history? It does seem that the Church is forever advocating specific ethical or social programs to cure a sinful world. This urge for reform has often gone beyond mere admonition to a thoroughgoing Christian reconstruction of society. Gregory VII and John Calvin, in their attempts to realize Christ's kingdom here and now, can seem as much social revolutionaries as Robespierre and Karl Marx. Christian attempts at social reconstruction rest on different grounds than that of secular revolutionaries. Secular revolutionaries hold that in some part or fashion morals and politics can be grasped as a rational reform, even as a "science." The moral "scientist" looks on society as "curable" according to human reason.

There are three interesting inflections in the voice of the thorough-going rational reformer of history. It is important to underline these aspects of the reformer's voice since they are also presumed to be characteristic of the voice of the Church. Given attained truth, the secular moral or social reconstructionist speaks with a *didactic voice*. He *knows* what constitutes the good for individuals and society. The voice of the moral scientist is, therefore, an *authoritarian voice,* a *nondemocratic voice*. "I *know* that this is the right course, whatever you may think to the contrary." But in fact the Marxist theoretician is no more democratic than your attending physician when he prescribes treatment. When history (the sick patient) does not cooperate, the secular revolutionary, if he has sufficient power and conviction about his goal, will seek to forcibly reeducate, cure, or annihilate the social laggards who fail to act in terms of the truth. The actual history of the French, Soviet, or Chinese communist revolutions offer clear examples of how a scientific cure of history can play out. In terms of the dramatic metaphor of the World-Play, the Enlightenment *philosophes* and their rationalist descendents solve the plot complications by a *deus ex machina,* the rational savant who, like Plato's philosopher-king, descends into the murk of history and cures its philosophic blindness.

If one comes to regard Christian Truth as the sort of truth claimed by transcendent moralists and secular political revolutionaries, then the voice of the Church will also display the characteristics of that voice: *didactic, nondemocratic moral/social therapy. And,* of course, that is exactly how the voice of the Church often sounds and how it just as often so regards itself. Didactic, authoritarian therapy may be quite acceptable from one's cardiologist because his dictates are straight from the latest issue of the *New England Journal of Medicine*: prestige science. But if one attempts to align Christian teaching, Christian therapy, and Christian "hierarchical" authority with the therapeutic language game of the scientist or sage, the Christian claim for truth will seem anywhere from implausible to impossible. When it comes to science vs. the Bible or Church authority, it is no contest.

Having denied Christian truth as contesting with science, I would assert that the voice of the Church is in its own way properly therapeutic, didactic, and nondemocratic. The Christian doctrine of original sin admittedly poses the Foucaultian problem of truth: is "truth" merely the propaganda of the power? The most direct way for Christianity to solve the problem of propaganda would be to stake out a claim to truth analogous to that of the scientist or sage. But I have argued throughout this presentation that escaping the subjectivism and relativism of the propaganda voice in objective truth akin to science or philosophic rationality is a fatal distortion for the Christian voice. Yet there is a Christian "therapy" that speaks with authority based in truth, though not at all in the sense of science and philosophy.

## Christian Soul-Therapy

To understand the special character of Christian therapy I turn to modern soul-therapy: secular psychotherapy. Aligning the Christian therapeutic voice with modern psychotherapy seems appropriate. I have consistently located religious belief in the formation of the persona. The question for faith is a question of sanity. Is Christian faith sane or is it its own form of mental disorder akin to paranoia, a psychic state that invests the core of personality? Using psychoanalysis as a model, I want to suggest how Christianity understands the "cure" for the *psyche:* soul.

Of what are we to be cured by faith? Of sin. That being so it is necessary to emphasize again the locus and nature of sin. In the previous chapter, I tried to disentangle morality and sin. There is, as indicated, no little confusion about sin and morality in traditional Church statements. Take the standard Church slogan for dealing with sinners: "love the sinner, not the sin." Amiable as it may be, the slogan is seriously misleading about the nature of sin. Sin is not some piece of bad conduct, the weed in the garden; it is the pervasive warping of the persona. Freud regarded the neuroses of his patients as their *Kern des Wesens:* the core of their being. Sin lies at *Kern des Wesens.* Paranoia is an obsession which colors my whole self. The therapist clearly wants to alleviate the patient's psychosis. The therapist does not love the paranoia any more than the Christian loves sin. But paranoia is not like pneumonia, a disease that can be cured *ab extra.* A good dose of penicillin will take care of the pneumonia whatever the persona of the patient: a grumpy and depressed patient may get rid of pneumonia as surely as the happy optimist. Not so with therapy for the paranoid. As a total personality structure, the patient can be cured—if cure is possible—only at the center of his paranoid persona. The role of the psychotherapist therefore differs radically from that of the medical practitioner because the therapist reaches for the persona of the patient.

Psychoanalysis casts itself on a medical model in order to bracket moral judgment. In biological medicine one does not blame the patient for the illness. Fundamentally, however, the medical model is misleading for psychotherapy because there is no patient, that is, someone who is *passive* to the ministrations of the doctor. Psychotherapy and the cure for sin only work at the personal core of the patient, who is therefore anything but passive. (Thus the cliché that the patient has to cure himself.) Achieving an appropriate relation to the person of the patient is thus the critical turn in the course of psychotherapy. It is called "transference," a complex process in which the patient becomes personally attached to the therapist. The patient is said to "fall in love with the therapist."[4] Later understandings of the psychoanalytic process have noted that transference is at some level a two-way process. There must be *counter*-transference: at least the patient must come to believe that the therapist is emotionally involved in the interchange. The therapist must in some sense be seen to enter the world of the paranoid, be perceived as personally *there* in order to restructure the sufferer's destructive core. He who is without paranoia must become paranoid (enter the paranoid's personal world) to rescue him from his malaise. ("He made him to be sin who knew no sin," 2 Cor 5:21.)

## Transference: Getting to the Patient

If transference and counter-transference constitute critical moments in psychoanalysis, analogous structures are crucial for Christian "therapy." I want, therefore, to sketch three models of secular psychotherapy insofar as they achieve or fail to achieve transference. Many years ago I saw the film *Three Approaches to Psychotherapy,* which demonstrated three methods as practiced by three different practitioners: Carl Rogers (client centered therapy), Frederick S. "Fritz" Perls (Gestalt therapy), and Albert Ellis (cognitive therapy). In the film each therapist was seen with the same patient for twenty minutes. The differences were striking. Rogers sat quietly, deeply absorbed in what the patient said. Perls attacked the patient for her evasions. Ellis lectured her on what she should do to improve her condition. Rogers and Perls both "got to the patient"; there was definite "transference." At the conclusion of Rogers' session the patient burst into tears, apparently overwhelmed by Rogers' concerned acceptance of what she was saying. With Perls, the patient achieved "negative" transference— she was very angry. As far as I could tell, with Ellis the ending mood was some mixture of boredom and annoyance. These three modalities offer interesting perspectives on what might count as the Christian therapeutic voice.

To call Albert Ellis' approach "cognitive" seems on the mark. Essentially he marshaled arguments for and against certain types of conduct. He made suggestions about how the patient should comport herself to alleviate her distress. The therapy exemplified the didactic voice, telling the patient from the standpoint of Ellis' grasp of the science of psychology what she must (practical or moral "must") do to be cured. The problem was that the patient's persona was "sick," and as such she was not susceptible to didactic instruction and rational argument. Presumably she already knew that her actions and feelings were wrong, but she had no idea how to eliminate them. Being lectured about what was rationally right was useless. Being told to follow this or that piece of practical advice was just what she could not do because her neurosis blocked such actions.

Rogers, in contrast to Ellis, did not lecture—he barely said a word— but his deep listening moved the woman into a situation of trust. He was with her in her distress, she did not need to keep up a brave face but could weep from the pain of her illness. Rogers' approach was certainly not "didactic" in the fashion of Ellis' practical advice. Perls also reached something at the core of the patient; she could give over a brave face and be angry with the therapist. Listening or "attacking" were, of course, only the first steps in the course of a cure, but they were necessary steps to move the therapist and the patient into a personal interchange. Only when the patient could weep with the therapist or attack him was she engaged at the level where the illness resided and where change could be effected.

How might these models fit the voice of the Church? I do not think I would be totally wrong to suggest that the model by which the Church is most often understood is that of cognitive therapy: didactic moral injunction and practical advice. Not only is that the way the Church so often seems to the public, I suspect that this model may be the unstated assumption of many Church pronouncements. Continual affirmation of objective moral standards as the mark of Christian faith fits the cognitive model. The problem with that model for Christian therapy should be obvious from my brief sketch of Albert Ellis' interchange with the patient. Finally, the world, like Ellis' patient, is somewhere between bored and annoyed with this moral demand to "shape up." Deep in its soul the world knows its sinful persona and recognizes that didactic moral advice is just what it cannot heed. The world's persona being irrational, neurotic, or sinful cannot follow rational, sane, or spiritual advice.

What could one adopt from the other psychotherapeutic models? One would be tempted to start with Perls. The Christian voice on the model of Old Testament prophetism seeks to "convict the world of sin." The neurotic/sinful soul lives a lie, pretending that aberrant behavior is sanity. The paranoid believes that the world is hostile but in reality the belief is a pretense thrown up to avoid facing his own troubled persona. He is not really at odds with the world but with himself. The paranoid projects self-hatred outward and creates a hateful world. There has been a long-running discussion in psychoanalytic circles about whether psychotics are, at some level of their persona, dissembling. They know, deep down, that their psychosis is a lie to themselves.[5]

Is mental illness a species of self-deception? Sartre noted that there is something odd about the Freudian structure of "repression."[6] In Freud's description it would seem that the aberration at the core of the persona is an unknown that must be "discovered" through the course of the analysis. Sartre questioned this notion of discovery because of the tendency of patients to become ever more agitated even to the point of breaking off therapy as the analysis comes close to naming the problem . It would seem that at some level the ego knows what is repressed and creates resistance to discovery. Unlike a strictly medical investigation where the patient is simply ignorant of the cause of his back pain and awaits with expectation the diagnosis of the physician, in the case of neurosis the patient in some sense knows the problem and resists the therapist's threatened uncovering of the repressed. However psychotherapeutic theory may answer the issue of mental illness as self-deception, the Christian claim is that sin is a form of self-deception. As outlined in the discussion of the World-Play, the fundamental sin of humanity is the self-deception of self-creation: the belief that we are the masters of our self and times. Once one starts down the path of humans as self-creating, the path that anoints humans as gods, lying and evasion become the coin of the realm. The Devil is the father of lies, and the biggest lie we tell is the lie to ourselves.

I am deeply sympathetic to the Church voice as prophetic in the Old Testament mode. The modern world and the persona that it exemplifies is rife with self-deception. Refusing the self-deception of the self-created persona, convicting the world of sin, would seem therefore to be an appropriate and available voice of Christianity. I am not hopeful. There are two problems with a voice of Christian prophetism. The first relates to the failure of the cognitive model. It is not easy to distinguish between moral critique and the prophetic revelation of self-deception. Both are judgmental over human conduct, but what is being judged in the two cases is fundamentally different. Moral critique is piecemeal; prophetic denunciation goes to *Kern des Wesens,* addressing the total personality structure. Moral criticism addresses a specific fault, for example, alcoholism, wheras psychotherapy or prophetic judgement address the addictive personality. The reason I am not hopeful about the Christian prophetic voice is that the world generally regards prophetism as morality with a loud voice. If I am correct that deep in the self or soul the world knows that it is sick and brokenhearted, prophetism-as-morality will be rejected out of hand as useless.

The second problem with attempting the prophetic voice rests on a simple fact of contemporary history. Perls was "the doctor"; he was an accepted authority. The woman in question recognized that she was in a therapeutic situation and that this doctor was somehow the instrument of cure. At one time the Church may have stood in an authoritative position somehow analogous to the modern soul-therapist, but that is simply not so today. Why does the contemporary world reject the voice of the Church as authoritative? One obvious reason would be psychotherapy itself. Instead of the strange ministrations of the priest we have the scientific ministrations of the medical practitioner. A second mode of rejection is more radical. It asserts that there are *no* authoritative voices for the human psyche, psychotherapy included. There is no "true" human society or persona, only a Foucaultian jostling for power or the deconstructionists' tolerant *c'est la vie.* Today the Christian prophetic voice is truly "crying in the wilderness." I want to see what can be done to meet these two challenges in order to locate authority for Christian soul-therapy.

## Constructing a Wise Myth

The challenge of modern, medical psychotherapy for Christian soul-therapy is important because as the voice of science it repeats in modern guise the teachings of the ancient sage discussed at the beginning of this chapter. Not only does science replace Christian ministration, in Freud's view religious faith is precisely what scientific therapy seeks to cure. Christian therapy is not only outmoded in the manner in which bleeding patients is outmoded physical medicine, Christian "therapy" is the disease itself. Given the prestige of psychoanalysis as soul-therapy and its claim to replace superstition with science, one way to open the way to Christian therapy is to look more closely at psychoanalysis as science.

The authority of modern psychotherapy is certainly based on its aura as medical science. Psychiatrists earn the MD degree and choose psychiatry as their specialty. There is, however, a serious question about whether psychotherapy is science based. Various empirical studies have failed to confirm the connections between early trauma and later mental illness. I am more interested, however, in whether the inner logic of the psychotherapeutic cure can be thought to be scientific. Wittgenstein was not alone in arguing that Freud's interpretations of behavior were not based on anything that could count as scientific evidence. "Freud is constantly claiming to be scientific. But what he gives is *speculation*."[7] Wittgenstein goes on to suggest that what happens in the therapeutic process is the construction of a "myth" that the patient comes to believe. By fitting current anxieties into the constructed story, the patient may, as it were, make sense out of what seemed senseless in his life. Psychoanalytic interpretation of erratic behavior is like the interpretation of an obscure poem. What seemed at first to be a jumble of disorganized, arbitrarily chosen words is revealed by the skillful interpreter to be put together in a coherent meaning.[8] Interpretation is radically different from discovering the "cause" of the incoherence, for example, the poet was drunk when he wrote the poem. Finding the cause is not at all finding the way to cure. I might discover that my neurosis was caused by a traumatic event but my life may could remain as disorganized as the drunkenly disorganized poem. Patients who suffer from post-traumatic stress know the cause of the distress; what they don't know is how to fit this distress into their present life.

Poetic interpretation is hardly a science, it is an art. When it comes to poetic interpretation there is no final, definitive reading. Johnson, Coleridge, A. C. Bradley, and Harold Bloom offer insightful interpretations of Shakespeare, but none has brought Shakespearian commentary to its definitive "scientific" conclusion. There are, however, better and worse interpretations of Shakespeare. So with the mythic interpretations of psychotherapy. Wittgenstein did not think that any old myth would do as long as it consoled the patient. He was, in fact, sharply critical of Freud's preferred myths. On one occasion he argued that while a certain piece of advice from Freud was "clever" it lacked "wisdom."[9] Wittgenstein found wisdom in his favorite novelists like Gottfried Keller and Dostoevsky. For Wittgenstein, one could say, sanity is fitting one's life into a "wise" story. Life in a wise story is the key to Christian therapy.

If psychotherapy is not science based, what is going on that eventuates in the "cure"? The clue is in transference and counter-transference between the therapist and the patient. The therapist is attempting to reconstruct the self-destructive persona of the patient. The persona of the therapist must be presumed sane lest the result of the transference should be the sort of interlocking neuroses often found in intimate relations. In our earlier discussion of the initial formation of the child's persona by a parent, we noted the crucial importance of the sane parent. Neurotic parents form neurotic children. A standard interpretation of the psychotherapeutic process is that the sane therapist takes on the role of parent in order to re-form the damaged persona of the patient. Psychotherapy as formation of the persona by transference from parent (therapist parental figure) to child (patient) raises our earlier question, "Who is the sane parent/therapist?" In what does sanity consist?

Focusing on the *process* of transference from parent or therapist underscores the fact that persona is constructed through some person-forming history. The child's persona is constructed within the history of a particular family. Psychotherapy is on the right track when it seeks to understand the patient's problem by looking at family history. Gathering family history may extend back to parents, grandparents, and beyond because it was these antecedents who formed the persona of the patient's parents. Go back far enough and one is not dealing with simple family history but social history: the history of the Jews, the history of Americans, the culture of women. We gather some idea about the persona of someone when we describe her in these broad historic categories, for example, a wealthy Jewish American teenager at Yad Vashem. Her persona was the construct of her specific history.

If persona is essentially historical, what about the persona and sanity of the psychotherapist? What is his or her history? Take Freud: what persona did his history create? Freud was acutely conscious of his Jewish history but rejected positive involvement in that history. Scientific rationality was attractive in part *because* it transcended such religious identity. In this regard, Freud shared the views of the Enlightenment that projected the "rights of man" beyond such historical accretions as race or religion.[10] (Given the ideology of universal humanity, the Enlightenment marks the period when Jews began to be assimilated into society after centuries of historical repression.) It was important for Freud that psychotherapy be regarded as a science because science could define the human person and sanity beyond historical deflection. Like the ancients, he faced the vagaries of history with a deep belief in scientific reason. Freud's well-noted stoicism revealed his personal sanity and a sense of resignation in the face of "civilization and its discontents."

One could argue, then, that Freudian psychoanalysis is itself a view toward history: a view that transcended mere history in the person of the scientist, sage, and stoic. But that is only one choice about history and not necessarily the sane choice. I would argue that each and every persona, including the persona of any individual psychotherapist, is deeply and essentially historical. Sanity is an artifact of history; sanity is not based in science but in sane history. One might, of course, disperse sanity across particular histories; this is in a sense the deconstructionist/relativist view of sanity. The teenager at Yad Vashem came face to face with the reality of Jewish history. The sane persona within Holocaust history should be "on guard." Freud, facing the persecution of Jewish history, chose sanity as above history in a science of the human self. I have argued, however, that the persona of science is an empty persona. It achieves universality at the price of the essential historicity of persona. A truly *universal* definition of sanity would have to rest on a universal history. It would not be implausible to take the Holocaust as a sign for human history as universal nightmare. Traditional Judaism would say that the Jewish history of Exodus and Covenant is the universal story of human history. Christians see Cross and Resurrection as the ultimate marker for history.

If persona is essentially historical, the problem of the authentic/ sane human persona may seem insolvable. Foucault and deconstructionists argue determinedly that there can be no universal sense of sanity because of the obvious diversity of human societies and the disparate personae that they construct. Against these relativistic conclusions, the biblical claim is that there is universal history, a history that is common to all humanity and in terms of which sanity should be defined. Biblical history is authoritative for humankind. The problem is how to assert biblical/Christian history as authoritative in the modern world. How can the Church speak authoritatively to the world without resorting to the trump card of biblical quotation or the adventitious intervention of the Holy Spirit?

## The Voice of Silence

Psychotherapy may fail on a scientific model akin to physical medicine yet work as a cure for personality deformation. Personality formation, deformation, and re-formation depend on an historical transfer of persona. Psychotherapy replays parental formation but without imposed trauma or neurosis. Does the cure, the sanity achieved, constitute more than social adjustment? The radical challenge to *any* soul-therapy is the claim that no voice is authoritative because there is no "true" model of the properly functioning human psyche. A Foucaultian sees psychotherapy not as a "science of the soul" but as an instrument of social control. Psychiatry, the Christian voice, or any other claimant to construct the authentic human person is to be rejected.

A deeper examination of the assumptions of soul-therapy as expressed in psychoanalysis can, I believe, establish a notion of sanity that is universal and authoritative. I take my clue for discovering sanity and authenticity from Carl Rogers' practice of deep listening. If we are searching for the voice of sanity, of authentic and universal sanity, it is "the listening voice" that is the key. In a paradoxical fashion, the silence of the listener becomes the "voice" of authority. The key to preaching the Gospel is not first defined by how one *speaks* but how one *listens*. Silence and listening are both preliminary and integral to the ultimate voice of the Church: the voice of forgiveness.

To make any sense out of the idea of a listening voice and why it can be a key to soul-therapy, one must realize that listening is an extraordinarily difficult art. Not only is it a hard won achievement for the listener, it is a high challenge for the one who speaks. Often as not, listening is not true listening at all, it is just waiting my turn so that I can dominate the argument. In turn, speaking can be outright self imposition or chatter that fills up the speaking space lest anyone else say something that could wound my *amour propre*. If one accepts the Foucaultian struggle for power or the Christian idea of original sin, it comes as no surprise that speaking and listening are compromised as self-projecting and self-protecting.

Given the inherent distortions of speaking and listening, Rogerian therapeutic listening is presumed to be *authentic* listening. The therapist receives what the patient says fully, transparently, and without a rush to judgement or the urge to intervene. Such deep listening is, therefore, also an exercise in forgiving. The therapist lets the patient's anxieties all tumble out in whatever incoherent form. There is no moral condemnation, only deep concern. The therapist receives the persona of the other fully as it manifests itself in speech, tone, and gesture To accomplish the ability to receive the patient, the therapist undergoes analysis so that his psyche is cleansed as far as possible from its own neurotic blockages that would hinder the ability to listen. Therapeutic "hearing," however, goes beyond passive reception. The therapist listens with "the third ear." She receives without reservation the patient's claim that he is "really very happy in his marriage," but the third ear catches a shrillness that reveals suppressed anxiety. Psychotherapeutic theory is based on the notion that the therapist grasps something in what is said that the patient does not understand or is unwilling to admit to consciousness. The *authority* of the analyst is based on what is heard with the third ear. He knows something that the patient does not, he is an authority about the persona of the patient.

Third ear dynamics are an everyday phenomena. We continuously interpret what the other says beyond the manifest meaning of the words. "She said she was sorry, but she didn't sound sorry!" The fact that the other *interprets* my speaking has the unhappy outcome that, despite my deepest desire to project my persona on the world, it is the *listener* who evaluates my success. I failed to convince her that I really was sorry! If one accepts the notion that humans seek to dominate their social space, then I succeed in that task only when the listener accepts my domination. I only know that my projected persona has mastered the situation if the other conforms to my self projection. Speaking and listening follows both the complex dialectic of Hegel's master and slave and the Sartrean analysis that leads him to conclude that "Hell is other people." Hell is other people because my self is finally subject to the view of the other. In Sartre's stage setting of Hell in *No Exit* there are no mirrors: I cannot see myself so I have to depend on the eminently undependable other for *self*-assurance. In short, as in the Hegelian analysis, it is the other, the presumed "passive" one, the "slave" who merely listens, that holds the upper hand. Paradoxically, the listening other is an authority over my persona. Some one else will be the author of my biography!

Psychotherapy obviously rests on the authority of the listener-therapist. The question is whether the listener who re-forms my persona gives me something "true" or whether I end up capitulating to the fact that the listener always has "the last word." Consider the dynamics of listening as it might apply to the situation of the Church. I have already noted that for better or for worse the Church does not enjoy the authoritative stature that it once enjoyed in earlier ages. I doubt that any amount of subtle theology or ecclesiastical huffing and puffing can recapture that previous eminence. When one admits that the Church has lost its authoritative voice, it would be most accurate to say that it has lost its assertive and didactic standing in the eyes of secular society. Assertion of authority cannot be from already accepted teaching or prophetic critique because in the public eye the Christian soul therapist does not enjoy the official status granted the doctor or psychotherapist. Given this reality, the Church should refrain from the didactic and even the prophetic role, falling back instead on the inescapable authority of the one who listens. Instead of rushing to comment and critique in the manner of Ellis' cognitive therapy, reaching for the prophetic voice *a la* Perls, adopting a listening voice would be a first step toward establishing authority.

The listening voice would be more than a tactical trick: it is deeply grounded in the Christian story itself. Recalling Wittgenstein's view of psychoanalysis, sanity is fitting my life into a wise story, a sane story. The wise story in which Christians are to live is committed to listening. The epigraph for this chapter from Isaiah is instructive. The prophet has been given "a disciple's tongue" that he "may know how to speak to the weary." And how does he initiate that task? "Morning after morning, he opens my ear that I may listen." The task of the Church is "to speak to the weary." (In secular society it speaks to the "wary.") Wary or weary, the Church should seek to manifest itself in the manner of Isaiah: as a deep *listener* to the postures and chatter of the world. In the dynamics of listening in which the listener has "the last word," a listening Church would be positioned to have the last word.

But is there a *last* word, the word that heals rather than continues the cycle of domination? As suggested, not every "listening" is open, transparent and receptive. There is a special characteristic of the therapeutic listening voice that is essential to the "cure" and that grounds the capacity to have the last word beyond the back and forth trading of speaking-listening. For Christians it is the word beyond the contestations of self and sin. The last word is the forgiving word. The listening voice for soul-therapy must be a *forgiving voice*. We have already noted that in the psychotherapeutic context the therapist is nonjudgmental. The aberrant conduct of the client is reclassified from moral to medical. The alcoholic is not wicked *simpliciter,* he is "sick"; alcoholism is a disease. Awkward as it may be theoretically, medical terminology accomplishes the necessary move out of condemnation toward cure. The rationale for the shift is not just a therapeutic strategy. If there is to be a change of behavior, it will have to come from the core of the person. In Christian terms one speaks with the voice of forgiveness not because one is ignorant or indifferent to the immorality of the aberrant behavior but because sin is at the core of the person. The language of core may be misleading. One has to understand that the soul is the whole persona, it is not some pure substrate that has, unfortunately, been encrusted with sin like a piece of clean paper scribbled on by an errant hand. This is why "condemn the sin, love the sinner" misstates the spiritual problem of sin. My quirky, sinful symptoms are the expressions of my troubled self, they run deep and make me to be the persona that I am.

Forgiving listening attains an authenticity that rises above the normal skirmish of speech and counter-speech. Forgiving listening bypasses the normal defense mechanisms of neurosis and sin. The fundamental fault of neurosis and sin is the fictional persona, it is the surface that I show to the world as a way of masking the anxiety at the heart of my self. Following Sartre's formulation that Hell is other people, the other is an everlasting threat to my projected self. I become a nothing in the eyes of the other. Ralph Ellison's depiction of the hell of racism was well expressed in the notion of the Negro as "the invisible man." The black man is invisible to the dominant white culture, a nothing. Hell is being invisible. It has been said that the deepest Hell is inhabited by those whom even God forgot.

Suppose one could change the speaking-listening assumption: suppose that the other is utterly forgiving, the one who listens to me, really sees me, the one to whom I am not in any way invisible. The listener is not just waiting his turn to dominate the social space, to tell me *who* I am for his own purposes. This other receives my hastily assembled, rather haphazard, fragile, and bristly defensive self. There is a forgiving acceptance because the other recognizes the false bravado of my defensive persona. The forgiving other understands the anxiety at the core of my persona which erects the rigid barricades of self protection. If we translate the structure of such ideal therapeutic listening into the voice of the Church, the first injunction would seem to be listening to the neurosis/sin of the world. Instead of rushing to condemnation, one would ask: what is the deep meaning of this behavior and belief? What fears have constructed this persona, creating this fragile and defensive way of life and thought?

The Christian listening voice must constantly ask whether it has really listened deeply to the sinful ways of the world because sin is *revealing*. Sin is the false projection of real need. Rushing to attack the false front bypasses the deep hurt and genuine cure in the manner in which Albert Ellis' haste to advise his patient left her merely bored. In *The Brothers Karamazov*, Ivan offers a devastating attack on a God who permits the suffering of children and follows it up with the rejection of the Church of the Grand Inquisitor. Dostoevsky's genius and deep insight into the Christian voice is displayed when Jesus says nothing to the Grand Inquisitor, he kisses the old man. The saintly Alyosha repeats that silent Christian reply at the end of Ivan's condemnations.

Deep and forgiving listening creates self-establishing authority because it relates to the fundamental reality of humanity beyond the everyday posturing that marks the world defined by power and sin. There would not be the everlasting jockeying for power, for the persistent masks of sin, or for the fictive defensive self, but instead for a deep desire at the core of the self that is unmet. What is the deep desire of the core persona? What drives humanity to create the crust of neurosis and sin as a guard against what is feared at the core? Philip Larkin in a poem—happily entitled in the terminology of this chapter—"Faith Healing" spells it out. The scene is an evangelical faith healing session in which the lame and the halt come forward for "some twenty seconds" to receive the touch and blessing of the white haired healer. After the exhortation and the placing of hands

the faithful move off "Like losing thoughts . . . not back into their lives /
Just yet; . . . To re-awake at kindness, thinking a voice / At last calls them
alone." What is the healing that the penitents are truly seeking? Larkin
sums it:

> In everyone there sleeps
> A sense of life lived according to love.
> To some it means the difference they could make
> By loving others, but across most it sweeps
> As all they might have done had they been loved.
> That nothing cures.[11]

The Christian message denies the last line of the poem. The Creator God
calls to each of us alone and says without qualification that we have been
fully loved. St. Augustine's famous opening statement in the *Confessions*
expresses the logic of soul-cure: "Thou hast made us for thyself, and our
hearts are restless until they rest in thee." The restless heart longs to be
"have been loved." Fearing that the other will not love enough, cannot love
enough, I create my defenses. If, however, my heart turns to a love that
knows me through and through, who establishes no defenses against me,
who is always listening, always forgiving, then I am "cured."

In the final chapter, I want to give the poetic conclusion of this chapter a pragmatic turn. One can read the above as mere poetry or mere piety.
I want to suggest that there are concrete ways in which the Church can act
out the Christian voice. Spelling out these structures will, I hope, suggest
that there is more than pious sentiment in the notion of a listening and
forgiving voice. Not only do I think that the listening and forgiving voice
is theologically correct—it might actually have some effect!

# CHAPTER TEN

# Practice and Structure

---

*Dialogue first comes into being when there is not only speech but listening. . . . To listen means to know and acknowledge another and to allow him to step into the realm of one's own "I." It is a readiness to assimilate his words, and therein his being, into one's reality as well as assimilate oneself to him in corresponding fashion. Thus, after the act of listening, I am another man, my own being is enriched and deepened because it is united with the being of the other and, through him, with the being of the world.*

Joseph Ratzinger,
*The Nature and Mission of Theology*

    The conclusion of this study has been that the voice of the Church should be a listening voice—listening as ground of the *forgiving voice*. Common experience and the uncommon doctrine of original sin should make it clear that listening, *real* listening, *deep* listening, is a rare accomplishment. The third ear of the psychiatrist is achieved only after extended analysis and training. For Christians, the third ear means listening with "the ear of Christ," listening in the *persona Christi*. The gift of Cross and Resurrection have so changed the normal course of human history that Christian listening becomes a possible direction even if such perfect listening may never be fully attained in any given instance. Cross and Resurrection show that our efforts at listening are not exercises in illusion. In a Foucaultian world or an unredeemed world, deep listening is futile since history is nothing but a contestation of power. Listening in the mode of the *persona Christi* is listening grounded in forgiveness. There is the forgiveness in the initial willingness to listen at all, and then there is the forgiveness that emerges when the authentic core of humanity is released from the falsity of sin into the true desire of the heart.

In this concluding chapter, I want to offer some suggestions about practices and structures for the Church that would enhance the listening essential to the voice of faith. As indicated in the introductory chapter, calls for listening have come not only from those on the "liberal" side of the Church who are opposed to various current practices, but from those on the "conservative" side like Germaine Grisez who criticize the bishops for failing to discuss straightforwardly and openly the arguments of dissenters. There is no lack of demand for dialogue nor specific suggestions on how this dialogue might be structured. My own suggestions will be brief, and I hold no claim to originality or finality on specific ways and means.

The value of this study, I hope, is not in discovering some definitive set of practices and structures for listening and dialogue, it is in the attempt to ground dialogue in Christological fundamentals. Whenever the issue of "dialogue" in the Church is raised, two immediate objections arise: the Church is not a democracy, and the Church is not a theological discussion group. I agree with both objections. Because the Church is founded in "truth," it cannot decide matters by vote. Truth is no more a matter of popularity in the Church than are astrophysics or evolution in science. At the same time, the Church is also not an academic discussion group or a form of ongoing scientific inquiry. The studied distance of academic discussion and the fallibilist assumptions of scientific inquiry are not modalities for faith. I fail my academic or scientific duty if I do not continually question my own theory; I fail my love if I continually question my commitment. The fact that democracy and discussion fail as models for the Church, does not mean that "open" dialogue is precluded. On the contrary, the basic argument of the whole book is that faith demands openness: the loving openness to the other that goes beyond academic discussion and political decision. No one has stated this more accurately or eloquently than Cardinal Ratzinger in the quotation that is the epigraph of this chapter.

## Listening as Common Sense and Uncommon Therapy

Common sense alone should indicate that careful listening is a sensible first step in presenting the faith of the Church to the world. There is no use stating a position unless I have some sense that the listener can understand it. "I heard what you said, but 'it is all Greek to me.'" Argument is not talking to yourself in a convincing tone. Christian deep listening is more than a common sense preliminary. If one construes the real task of the Church to be "soul therapy," deep listening is an ingredient of the cure. Deep listening exists within the emotional bond that both discovers the illness *and* offers the dynamic for cure. If listening moves to lecturing, the "cure" fails because the emotional structure necessary for shaping the persona is broken.

There is a crucial difference between deep listening in Freudian therapy and Christian soul-therapy: the relation between the analyst and patient, the Church and the world. The difference lies in the ultimate status of the one who listens. This difference has direct practical importance for specifying the practices of the Church. For Freud, the analyst uncovers what the patient truly desires, but what is desired is ultimately impossible. The core desires of the psyche are summed in the pleasure principle. Freud says, "[W]hat decides the purpose of life is simply the programme of the pleasure principle . . . yet its programme is at loggerheads with the whole world, with the macrocosm as much as with the microcosm."[1] The core desire of the person, the "programme of the pleasure principle" cannot be realized. Neurosis attempts to achieve the goal of the pleasure principle through unrealistic displacement. Freudian therapy seeks to make the patient aware of a fundamental striving that cannot be realized so that the individual can adjust to the more "modest reality principle."[2] For Freud, religion is mass neurosis because it seeks to achieve the pleasure principle in a fanciful heaven.

Freudian therapy reaches the truth of the psyche and then seeks to adjust the individual to modest reality, learning to live with "civilization and its discontents." Christian soul-therapy rests on a radically different assumption which is, of course, why Freud regards Christianity as mass neurosis. When in Christian "analysis" one uncovers the *Kern des Wesens,* one does not uncover the unreal goal of the pleasure principle, one uncovers the desire for God. The core of my being, according to Freud, is "at loggerheads with the whole world," the core of my being in Christian analysis is the desire for God, which God has set about making real. Christian soul-therapy searches for the restless heart so that it can be directed toward the reality that will satisfy its restlessness. What the other *really* desires at the core of the psyche needs no "realistic" deflection because life and history are at loggerheads. In Philip Larkin's poem, the brokenhearted lament is what "they might have done had they been loved." Larkin's comment on that desire: "That nothing cures." Freud would agree: nothing cures primal desire. As a Christian, what I truly desire is to have been loved, and that is realized in God's love in the action of Christ.

From a practical standpoint, the differing dynamics make Christian soul-therapy more hopeful. Christianity does not adopt a stoic resignation toward life and history. Christian activism is not a fluke. Freudian stoicism makes psychotherapy a two-step process. First one uncovers the core of being, points out that its goal is unrealistic, and then seeks to adjust the psyche to reality. The identification of what counts as realistic sets limits to transference. The patient must not *really* fall in love with the analyst, and even more so the analyst must maintain the distance of a realistic therapist from the patient. Failure to maintain realism about the psychodynamics of standard therapy corrupts the process. Christian therapy is not split in this fashion because it does not judge the core of being that is revealed as unrealistic. Because the core does not need deflection into reality, the affective relation (transference) between the Christian who listens and the "patient" is fundamentally altered. In Christian listening, if one reaches the core of the human persona, one reaches that which seeks to be loved. The Christian therapist offers that love by being *persona Christi* for the other. If the Christian therapist were a saint, she would in that measure express the *persona Christi,* the loving one who fulfills the patient's deepest need. True, the individual Christian teacher, confessor, therapist, or saint, being only human, cannot *be* Christ, but in so far as the saint lives in the story of Christ, she is inviting the patient to join her in that story. After the cure, analyst and patient share a common life of love in Christ. Put conventionally: one joins the Church. One of the problems with ordinary psychotherapy is that it not become "interminable." Realism demands that the patient give over dependence on the parental therapy. Christian soul-therapy on the other hand *is* interminable: one finds in the *persona Christi,* as expressed in the loving "analyst," the ever-loving God and lives in that love. One could say that the life and practices of the Church constitute an interminable therapy-and-cure for the brokenhearted.

With that understanding of Christian listening, I want to look at how the Church actually listens. I examine the Church-as-listener in two broad areas: listening *within* to the voices of believers and other Christians; listening *without* to the world. On neither score has the Church been a good listener. Paradoxically, since Vatican II, the popes have been better listeners outside the Church than inside. I offer some actual examples of non-listening, which, though far from comprehensive or the basis of a some statistical survey, will, I fear, be recognized as typical. I present these examples in a series starting from "below" with the failure to listen to the laity on up to failure to listen to bishops. Having indicated specific failures of listening, I will offer some modest suggestions for practice and structure that could enhance listening.

## Is Anybody Listening up There?

In 1985 the American bishops launched a project to write a pastoral letter on women in the Church. To prepare for this task, listening sessions were set up across the various dioceses. Women of all circumstances and conditions participated: vowed religious and the divorced, devotees of our Lady of Fatima and women who had had abortions, the fervent and the alienated. The first draft of the pastoral quoted at length the voices of the women who spoke. The draft was put aside. A second draft appeared absent the specific testimonies because, one might suppose, the voices of alienation were too critical of the Church. Generalities and suggested directions were substituted. The second draft was again put aside — presumably because of official objections to expressing even general concerns inconsistent with Church teaching. At this point, the whole project was dropped and no pastoral on women has appeared down to the present day.

The unhappy history of the planned pastoral is a prime example of the failure to listen. One could surmise that the suppression on the pastoral was motivated by fear. The concerns raised by the actual voices of the women could not be accommodated to official teachings and so the voices were suppressed rather than offering any change or enrichment of teachings. It may be too generous to suggest fear as the motivation for suppression; one might suggest intellectual laziness. Garry Wills has written an entire book, *Papal Sins,*[3] about ecclesiastical laziness expressed in routine, tired, and superficial argument. I am inclined to the darkest view: the failure to listen was a failure of faith. Faith holds that at the heart of those to whom one listens is the desire for God. The Christian "third ear" is always listening for the core of being which, in the case of the women contacted for the pastoral, may drive one to the desperation of abortion, another to praying for a miracle from Our Lady of Fatima. How did their varied life courses relate to the desire to have been loved? Unless one is prepared by either intellectual confidence or depth of faith to hear the direct expression of the brokenhearted, no soul-therapy is possible. It is as if a psychotherapist refused to hear the actual history of the patient, confining his "therapy" to directing her to change her behavior.

Maybe there is some hierarchic imperative to discount the voices of laity—women especially it would seem!—but what about the ordained? They are, after all, part of "the establishment." One of the saddest examples of failure to listen to priests is chronicled in David Gibson's *The Coming Catholic Church*. In 1987, Fr. Frank McNulty was chosen by fellow priests to address John Paul II about their concerns. His address was poignantly entitled "If Priests Could Open Up Their Hearts." McNulty expressed the desire of priests "to reconsider mandatory celibacy, allow theologians a 'free sense of inquiry', to give priests a say in the selection of bishops, and to provide greater roles for women in the Church." His address was "interrupted thirteen times by thunderous applause."[4] Thunderous applause notwithstanding, there were no actions in the papacy of John Paul II that spoke to these concerns. If anything, the concerns were dismissed by the reiteration of traditional positions and the graceless handling of dissent by the Congregation for the Doctrine of the Faith (CDF).

But, then, priests are not the *official* teachers of the Church—that is the role of bishops. How then are bishops selected and how are they listened to? I recently attended a conference at the Wharton School on the management practices of the Church.[5] One of the most telling anecdotes came from the head of a professional search firm, a "headhunter," who looked at the manner in which bishops are chosen. We know from Fr. McNulty's requests to the pope that the voices of the diocesan priests are not listened to. Other bishops may make suggestions, but the principal influence in selecting candidates for a *terna,* three names forwarded to the papal nuncio, are the various cardinals who, on the historical record, often use these recommendations to foster personal ecclesiastical agendas. Having received the *terna,* the nuncio offers his own recommendations to Rome. The headhunter asked the nuncio whether in making his recommendation he interviewed the potential candidates. The nuncio seemed taken back by the very idea. The search firm professional was appalled and said that he would *never* recommend a candidate for a leading position whom he had not personally interviewed.

Having started with failure to listen to the voices of women, failing to listen to the voices of priests, having the nuncio fail to meet face-to-face with a candidate for bishop, one can finish off this tale of non-dialogue with the failure of the synod of bishops that emerged from Vatican II. As noted in the first chapter, the notion behind a periodic gathering of bishops in Rome was to express in structure and practice collegiality in the governance of the Church. The voice of the Church was not to be the papal voice alone, but the collegial voice of the pope with the bishops of the world. The actual conduct of the synods held has been anything but collegial; it has certainly not been an exercise in *listening.* The assembled bishops have been presented with a preliminary schema drawn up by curial officials. Just such a precast curial schema was presented to the bishops assembled for Vatican II. Given the dynamics of the council and the benevolent acquiescence of John XXIII, the curial schema was scrapped. The reason for rejecting the schema was the perception that reiterating traditional formulae was pointless. One would have to judge from the reaction to the post–Vatican II synods that they have been just that: window dressing for the status quo. At the risk of more offense than I really intend, the synods have approximated meetings of the old Soviet parliament where some party *apparatchik* received acclamation for the latest Five Year Plan.

The Roman synods have been closed to public scrutiny. Each of the assembled bishops is given five minutes to make a statement. In the most recent synod held under the pontificate of Benedict XVI, there was some limited time offered for actual discussion and a few bishops brought up burning issues, such as the shortage of priests and mandatory celibacy. Whether it was the whiff of controversy or not, news briefs were sharply curtailed. Whatever dialogue on difficult issues may have occurred behind closed doors, the sense of the meeting was probably summed up best by Cardinal Pell from Sydney who noted the "massive unanimity" of the bishops on the issues, particularly on the "precious gift" of celibacy for priests.[6]

If you are a Catholic "conservative" you may well judge that non-dialogue is just as it should be. Truth resides at the top and is handed down from the papal curia to the synod of bishops to the priests to the laity in the pews. But failure to listen simply cannot be defended. I cite two primary faults: it is bad management and it is contrary to the meaning of faith.

The management failure should be obvious. The headhunter who was appalled at the failure of the nuncio to personally interview potential bishops could well have been an Opus Dei conservative as far as I know. But if you think that we should "leave it to mitres" and appoint truly "safe" bishops, it would be only good management to check out the candidate as a conduit of creedal orthodoxy. And so on down the line: maybe what Fr. McNulty was seeking was just all wrong, but it would behoove "management" to convince its "sales force" that the strategy from on top is truly sound. If convincing is not part of one's repertoire of managerial tricks, then obedience is the default position. George Weigel would be correct, then, in his allegation that destructive dissent within American Catholicism began when Paul VI failed to punish priests who protested *Humanae Vitae*.[7] Of course "obedience" is a form of "listening." *The Catechism of the Catholic Faith* defines "obedience of faith" by referring to the Latin root *ob-audire:* to hear or listen to. Obedience as "listening to" is like Ring Lardner's line: "Shut up!" he explained.

I have cited a few cases in which laity and lower orders of the Church have had serious disagreements with papal teachings, for example, mandatory celibacy for priests. The problem is not confined to a few isolated instances and some disgruntled individuals. Survey after survey of the broad Catholic population in even the most traditional Catholic countries like Ireland, Italy, and Spain show that the vast majority of Catholics share Fr. McNulty's concerns of 1987. Cardinal Pell may report "massive unanimity" among the bishops at the pre-scripted Roman synod, but there is no such unanimity between the positions taken there and the majority of Catholics in Europe and America. They are not convinced and they are not likely to obey. It would be possible to deflect a criticism about "bad management" by insisting again that the Church's "business" is to reiterate the truth come what may. As suggested earlier, there are enthusiasts of left and right who would be quite content with a remnant Church of true believers. If people are not convinced by the truth and will not obey, so much the worse for them. In a marvelous ironic twist, the pope could cast himself as Galileo, insisting in righteous isolation on the Truth. A censured Galileo muttered "It [the earth] moves!"; a censorious pope would proclaim "It [the Church] does not move!"

However one may decide on good management, the fundamental problem with not listening is that it is a failure of faith. Christian belief is grounded in the fundamental longing of all people toward God. God is the true desire of humanity's restless heart. That desire is, however, diverted and obscured by sin. In our haste to protect ourselves from the shocks of life, we create a shell of self into which we withdraw for solace or distraction. This sinful self does not realize its true desire. The Church's task is not to abandon humanity to its neurotic ways, withdrawing into a self-protective remnant from which it can lecture humanity on its faults. The task of the Church is to cure the soul, which is not effected by lecturing. To effect a cure, the Church must listen to the world, catch in the perverse and destructive voices of the world the true cry of the soul. If listening is a demand of faith and the cure of the soul, there is first of all a significant burden on the Church to examine itself in the manner of the secular psychotherapist. The psychotherapist must undergo the most stringent self-analysis to make sure as far as possible that he is not himself encumbered by unrecognized neurotic twists that block his ability to hear the patient. Scrupulous self-analysis is not a one-time accomplishment, it is an ongoing task. So with the Church as soul-therapist. It requires the most stringent and continuing self-scrutiny to assure as far as possible that self-satisfaction, ecclesial pride, theological torpor, simple fear—in short, sin—is not blocking the listening voice of the *persona Christi*.

Surely, one will say, listening is not enough. Later in this chapter, I want to deal with the silence of Pius XII on the Holocaust. There is a time when the pope must speak out, but for now, I want only to emphasize the need to listen. The Church may move to the prophetic voice but, as discussed in the previous chapter, the world has great difficulty hearing a genuinely *prophetic* voice. What it often hears is morality in a loud voice; moral absolutism about which it is wary on both historic and logical grounds. The Church may certainly engage in moral discourse and even denunciation, but it finally goes beyond the voice of morals—even and especially when the Church is correct in the moral position taken. What the Church soul-therapist must do is find the sin that drives the immorality. For the psychoanalyst the unacceptable behavior is only a symptom; for the Christian therapist, immorality is a symptom of sin, soul-sickness. One can only get to the level of fundamental sickness and sin by the deep listening that finally discovers the persona that brings the various immoralities into a *Gestalt*. In short: moral denunciation is just not enough. It short circuits the demands of faith.

## Listening to the People of God

If my account of the Church as a bad listener is at all correct, there are simple and obvious ways in which one can create structures and practices of listening. There is no guarantee that any of these structures will solve the problems that beset the Church, just as there is no guarantee that the structured therapeutic sessions of the psychoanalyst will result in a cure. There are, however, procedural rules for the Church's therapeutic listening that would be conducive to progress. I would suggest three *practices* which are essential: dialogue must be participatory, public, and patient.

*Participatory.* One could start with including the voices of the majority of Catholic believers: women. The failure of the proposed pastoral on women is only typical. Recently, new rules were promulgated by Rome to govern convents of enclosed women. Evidently no consultation with the communities concerned was undertaken before issuing the rules. Participants in any dialogue should be chosen according to the nature of the issue and the formal structure: council, synod, presbytery, and so on, but one general rule would be to seek out contrary voices. If a "devil's advocate" is judged appropriate in the process of beatification, counter opinions should be sought in directing the holiness of Church policies.

*Public.* I was surprised to learn at the Wharton conference that there is a lay advisory group to the United States Conference of Catholic Bishops. One of the functions of this group is to place items for discussion on the agenda of the bishops' meetings. Unfortunately, both what is suggested and whether or how it is discussed are never made public. Since the Wharton meeting was concerned with good management, it was strongly urged that the actions of the lay advisers be made public. The sessions of the Roman Synod or any other similar bodies should be made appropriately public. Anyone who lived through the period of Vatican II and read the reports in the *New Yorker* from the pseudonymous Xavier Rynne knows how exciting it was to hear about the thrust and counter thrust of argument and debate. Contrary to the fear that episcopal disagreement confuses the faithful, there is the perception that the faith is worthy of impassioned discussion.

*Patience.*   An assumption of psychotherapy is that there is no quick fix. If the problem is the structure of the persona, that structure has been formed either by deep trauma or long experience and probably both. One can neither form nor re-form the persona overnight. One expects extended listening as the therapist finds the core that addresses the fundamental problem. The caution of patience and extended listening should be applied to all Church deliberation. After all, it took three centuries to settle on Trinitarian doctrine.

Assuming the practices of participation, public information, and patience, I offer some brief comments on specific structures.

*Councils.*   At the time of the Great Western Schism in the fifteenth century, the fathers of the Councils of Constance and Basel who resolved the crisis decreed that there should be councils held every ten years. The voice of the Church was not to be the voice of the pope alone but the pope in council. This injunction was rapidly subverted by subsequent pontiffs to the point at which "conciliarism" came to be regarded as heresy.[8] A clear structural recommendation would be revival of conciliarism. The bishops' synods that resulted from Vatican II are a practical accommodation to the complexity and cost of a truly worldwide ecumenical council. It may be highly desirable, nevertheless, to mandate full-scale councils on a more extended time period, say, every thirty to forty years following the cycle of generational change.

The structure and practices of these gatherings are also important. First, the synods or councils must be publically reported on, not closed as has been the practice. Second, synods must be informed by *periti,* theologians chosen by the bishops and pope, to enrich and inform the discussions. The theological *periti* must not be only "house theologians"; it is imperative that critics and faithful "dissenters" be part of the discussion. To assure that the *periti* are no more pre-scripted than the curial schemas of present practice, it would be desirable to allow professional Catholic theological societies to nominate *periti*. This is by no means a radical break. In the middle ages, for example, Church issues were frequently referred to the theological faculty at Paris for recommendation. There have been councils at which the number of theologians actually voting on issues outnumbered the bishops in attendance. Third, synods and councils should give active voice to those charged with immediate pastoral care and to those for whom they minister. One needs not only the voices of bishops and theologians, but the voices of the Father McNultys, men and women religious, and lay persons. Every effort must be made at synods and definitely at ecumenical councils to actively incorporate the voices of other Christian communities and other faiths.

The subject matter of synods should not be preset from above. The synods must have the courage to head into the most troubling issues. This means that consultations that reach deeply into the concerns of laity and pastors must precede the synodal gathering. The most recent synod on the Eucharist may have been edifying, but it did not address issues that deeply concern most Catholic worshipers.[9] What should be the outcome of synods? Here is where listening and patience become paramount. There should be no urgency to settle matters, tidy up, and go home. Simple honesty would suggest that some matters are so novel or so complex that no cut and dry answer is possible—and may never be possible. The issue of homosexuality may be a prime example. It is well known that the notion of a "homosexual" is a recent invention. To be sure, homosexual behavior has been widespread and historically present for ages, both condemned and commended. What is novel is the notion of a homosexual life choice or destiny. Not only is the notion novel, it is unclear whether the homosexual persona is genetic, cultural, or some combination of both. Given novelty and complexity, patience in pronouncing on homosexuality would seem in order.

*Diocesan Synods.*　　The older Code of Canon Law decreed that there was to be a diocesan synod every ten years. Revisions in the 1980s dropped the idea of a fixed schedule in favor of "when needed," as the diocesan bishop might determine. In the diocese in which I currently live there has not been a synod for almost fifty years. While we were living in the Diocese of Rochester, New York, a truly broad scale, representative synod was held as the result of extensive consultation at all levels from the parishes on up. The "danger" of synods was realized in the Rochester process: you end up where the official Church does not wish to go. The synod recommended, among other controversial issues, the ordination of women. Rather than risk demonstrating that he presides over an unruly and rebellious diocese, a bishop may well avoid a synod. The result, of course, is the development of a Church with a split personality.

*Listening to theologians.*    Conciliar and synodal structures are vertical—there also needs to be more horizontal listening within the Church. One of the most acute splits in the contemporary Church in America is between Catholicism at Catholic colleges and universities and Catholicism at the parish church. As with all the tensions in the Church this split has been played differently by liberals and conservatives. Liberals find exciting and fresh ideas about all aspects of faith in the work of many university theologians and biblical scholars. Conservatives reject the educational trend in the major Catholic colleges in favor of such new institutions as Ave Maria in Naples, Florida, where fidelity to the *magisterium* is part of the college charter. Conservatives hold that the papal constitution on Catholic higher education, *Ex Corde Ecclesiae,* was a signal that something was wrong with the Catholicity of mainline Catholic universities. The decree in *Ex Corde* that theologians must obtain a *mandatum* from the diocesan bishop was thought to be a way of insuring faithful adherence to the *magisterium* in all Catholic institutions. Fortunately, as far as I am concerned, the *mandatum* has been so liberally administered that no coalescence toward "orthodoxy" has occurred. The split between university Catholicism and the parish in everything from theology to liturgy remains. At the Wharton conference, a young man who was enthusiastic about his religious experience at Seton Hall indicated his concern about where to find a parish to replicate that experience. The college chaplain suggested he interview the pastor and ask him why he ought to worship in his congregation. That would be a challenging dialogue!

University to parish connection has broader implications. Theological learning and discussion needs to be an ongoing task within the Church. Pursuing that task becomes difficult if one does not allow theological investigations to proceed within their own time frame and structure. Insofar as theology is a scholarly pursuit, the official assumption should be that the best correction of misdirection will come from within scholarly debate. The CDF pounced on Roger Haight for his book *Jesus: Symbol of God*.[10] The book has many valuable insights and raises important questions, but serious reservations were expressed in scholarly reviews. As indicated earlier in my discussion of the Eucharist, I, myself, am wary of "symbol" when talking about the presence of Christ. I believe that Fr. Haight would be delighted to debate his position with fellow scholars and then let the course of continued reflection prove or disprove the value of his interpretation. Nothing much is accomplished by the CDF's intervention. The fear that some innocent at the local parish will be led into heresy by the learned discourse of the professional theologians is a fantasy. Having personally led a discussion group on one of Cardinal Ratzinger's more accessible writings, the problem posed by professional theology to the faithful is not unbelief but bafflement.

If one can get over the barrier of haste and intellectual scrupulosity, I would suggest that a good dose of tough theology would be useful in shoring up the pastoral priesthood. It might cure the split between the Church in the university and the Church on Main Street. Official Church talk about the priesthood continually stresses "vocation." The priesthood is a vocation, but one hopes that everyone has a "vocation" in the sense of a life in which one can find a direction toward God. Before there is vocation, there is profession. We differentiate and offer a first evaluation of life tasks in terms of skills or professions: lawyer, doctor, engineer. There are specific skills and moral commitments that define each profession. One may not, however, have a *vocation* for a profession, even a profession that one practices. Vocation notes that one finds deep life-meaning in the profession, it is not just a "job." If there can be profession without vocation, in the case of the priesthood we seem to have vocation without a clear sense of profession. Yet there are "skills" normally expected from priests: preaching, personal counseling, presiding at liturgy, for example. One would suppose that there is a training for those skills. There are seminaries, of course, though one must judge from the almost universal complaint about sermonizing in the Catholic church that those skills are not acquired in that training. Putting the adequacy of seminary training aside, the greatest defect in the *profession* of priest is the lack of *ongoing*, professional study. Doctors and lawyers, either because of personal ethics or licensing, continue to update and perfect their skills. There is very little that is done on a systematic basis for the continued professional development of pastors. Not the least of the professional obligations should be close study of theological trends. While I have my reservations about some of the documents flowing from Rome, it would be a considerable advance for the Church if the local pastor were conversant with them and would convey their messages to the community of worshipers. Papal encyclicals are more likely to be reported in the *New York Times* than in the local pulpit.

These comments on practice and structure are only bare bones suggestions. If the hierarchy were to accept the responsibility of actual listening in depth to their own body of believers, I am certain that one could flesh out these suggestions and add many more. If, however, one maintains a picture of Truth cascading down from Rome, listening is at best a distraction, at worst destructive. I am not at all sanguine that the lesson of listening is likely to be learned by the present members of the hierarchy—particularly the American bishops who seem to have accepted the notion that the local Church is a franchise of the Vatican. If I have any hope for a listening Church it would be in applying the lesson of John Paul II's mission to the world outside the Church to the internal workings of Catholic life and thought.

## World Church

There is no question but that John Paul II was a great and transformative pope. The question is in what aspect of his long tenure does his greatness reside. I believe it was in his *presence* to the world. The high points of his papacy were not his voluminous writings and addresses but in his prayer at the Western Wall in Jerusalem, his visit to the synagogue in Rome, meeting the Archbishop of Canterbury, gathering leaders of the world religions for prayer at Assisi. If I were to single out one gesture to sum up these moments it would be when, on arriving on one of his visits to a country, he would fall on his knees and kiss the ground. I want to emphasize presence over proclamation. As was frequently remarked about the enthusiasm shown for John Paul at the World Youth Congresses: they loved the messenger, not the message. While this can be taken as a failure of the papal visits, it is at least worth recalling the argument made in this book about

Jesus. He is savior not in his message but in his presence. It is was not the message that was resurrected, it was the "messenger."

Not everyone would agree with locating John Paul's greatness in his worldwide journeys. There are many critics of John Paul both on the left and the right of Catholic opinion who would hold that he spent entirely too much time with the world, being a "media star," to the neglect of the internal world of the Church. He failed to manage the Vatican and reform the curia. Conservative critics thought that meeting with *imams* and the Dalai Lama blurred the lines of orthodoxy. Given my own emphasis on *voice,* it may also seem paradoxical that I locate John Paul's most effective *speaking* to the world in a silent gesture. But the burden of my argument is that the Church is better expressed in the listening voice, in silence, in being a loving presence than in the elaborations of the catechism or the elegances of encyclicals.

Praising John Paul for presence to the world—silent presence as he kissed the ground—is the proper moment to return to the issue of whether the pope should ever speak out loud and clear to the world. Pius XII has been severely criticized for his "silence" about the Holocaust. There may be political reasons for Pius' failure to issue a clear condemnation of racism in the manner of *Mit Brennender Sorge* (*With Burning Concern*), Pius XI's stinging 1937 letter condemning Nazism, but in the long run the pope's silence remains troubling. The example of Pius XII and the Holocaust may seem a serious counter to my argument for a listening voice of the Church. There are atrocities committed daily on every scale from domestic abuse to systematic genocide where the very audible voice of the pope should be heard. True, and I would not wish to discourage the most forceful denunciation of manifest evil. But it is not words that do the job. Effective speech must attain its own moment and style of "presence." The spoken word must come at the right time and in the right voice. A lover's kiss means more than protestations, but saying "I love you" at the proper moment in a voice of genuine affection is not to be discounted. The pope should take on the prophet's voice, convict the world of sin, but attaining the tone and content of that voice is not easy both inherently and because of the likely mode of reception.

As already discussed, the problem with papal protests is that they are likely to be received as some sort of moral argument rather than prophetic warning. Paul VI on "a contraceptive mentality" and John Paul II on "the culture of death" were prophetic on sin but were constricted in their message because they were interpreted by the public—and to a certain extent by the popes—to the limited moral issues of artificial contraception and abortion. Any specific action may be both immoral and sinful. The Church has a rich tradition of moral discussion and may denounce a practice on moral grounds alone. Moral denunciation may be well grounded and as definitive as moral discussion allows. Sin, however, is deeper and more deadly. The treatment of the Jews was profoundly immoral, but beyond that it exposed the sinful soul of a world that always demands an enemy. For Nazis it was the Jews; for Americans in World War II, "the Japs" were our "Jews." We only had "concentration camps" not "extermination camps," but the need for an enemy was at work. When the Church reaches for the prophetic voice to convict the world of sin, it is a message that the world is deeply reluctant to accept. The reluctance is similar to the resistance of patients as the psychotherapist approaches the core of the neurotic personality. Nor is the prophetic voice easy for the prophet to bear; he must confess his own weakness along with the failure of "the other." Had Pius XII condemned the Nazis, he should also have confessed the deep guilt of the Church in its treatment of the Jews. When one denounces *sin,* one is likely to have no allies. The Archbishop of Canterbury during World War II, William Temple, refused to pray for a British victory. God was not definitively on "our" side. Temple understood sin.

By all means, Pius XII should have spoken out loud and clear on Nazism. Better, instead of seeing himself as a "prisoner of the Vatican," the pope could have insisted that he be allowed to visit the camps. Surely he could have claimed the right to visit Dachau where during the war some four thousand Catholic priests were interned. When the Nazis issued an edict that all Danish Jews would be required to wear the yellow Star of David, the King of Denmark said that in that case he too would wear the star. The Nazi edict was never enforced. Imagine if Pius XII had agreed to wear the Star of David on his pontifical robes. I applaud Benedict XVI's clear rejection of the Nazi atrocities, but it does not add to his credit that during the four years that he was Archbishop of Munich there is no record that he ever visited Dachau, which is ten miles from Munich.[11] His visit to Auschwitz when he visited Poland in 2006 was a step in the right direction. His remarks, however, seemed to enclose the persecution of the Jews within a more generalized resistance to God thus blunting the direct anti-Semitism which is the looming *presence* at Auschwitz.

## Face to Face

If being present, silently kissing the ground, was a summative high point of John Paul II's pontificate, let me offer an example of failure of the papal voice. I choose for my example the publication *Crossing the Threshold of Hope*.[12] It may seem unfair to select only one document from the many thoughtful, earnest, and sophisticated works of the pope, but the document seems to me to signal something of a systemic failure. The nature of the failure can be seen by contrasting it with the triumphs of his papal visits and with the very doctrine espoused in the text itself.

*Crossing the Threshold of Hope* is a unique document from John Paul's papacy. It originated in 1993 when the pope accepted an invitation from Italian Radio and Television for a live interview on the occasion of the fifteenth anniversary of his election. A live interview with a pope would clearly be "a first." The interviewer, Vittorio Messori, submitted a list of questions for the interview. Because of time pressure or whatever, there were postponements and eventually the project was abandoned. Then, much to Messori's surprise, in 1994 Dr. Navarro-Valls presented him with a manuscript. John Paul had managed replies to Messori's questions in writing. Those remarks and some additional questions and answers constitute the text.

What are the problems with the voice of the text? There are minor annoyances. The human is universally referred to as "man." The dignity of man, the rights of man, man's destiny and so on. (Italian has no universal word like the Greek *anthropos* or Latin *homo* for human being, so the original would be "uomo," man as male, opposed to "donna," female.) I am not paranoid about gender neutrality in formal discourse. Among other things it is messy to keep saying he/she or alternating gender pronouns, but the incessant beat of man-man-man in the pope's answers is finally off-putting. Surely some remark could have been made to indicate the limitations of using "man" to mean "human being."

The substantial problem is the level and content of John Paul's presentation. There is an impressive display of philosophical and theological learning in the answers. In one paragraph alone he refers to Kantianism, Hegelianism, Husserl, Heidegger, Descartes, and St. Thomas' notion of God as *Ipsum esse subsistens*.[13] There are references to the writings of earlier popes: Paul VI, John XXIII, Benedict XII (d. 1342). Obviously there are copious quotations from Scripture and extensive inclusions from the documents of Vatican II. It is a remarkable text, but what will the world, the ordinary or even moderately literate man on the street, make of refutations of Descartes, the sayings of a fourteenth-century pope, and long quotations from the documents of Vatican II? As a philosopher, I am impressed, but I doubt that philosophical sophistication speaks to the soul.

The underlying problem may be that the original plan failed. In a *live* interview, I do not believe that even a person as erudite as John Paul would have been able to quote with such facility and length from a host of learned authorities and extended texts. Toward the end of the book, the pope notes with great approval the distinguished modern Jewish philosopher Emmanuel Levinas. John Paul saw his own philosophical writings about "personalism" paralleled in the work of Levinas. He sums up Levinas correctly as offering a "philosophy of the face." The philosophy of the face is similar to my argument that the heart of religious reality is presence, seeing the other present before me beyond any category of approbation or condemnation. Face-to-face is founded in forgiveness. Unhappily, "face" is just what is lacking in *The Threshold of Hope*. Instead of face-to-face as would have been the case with a live interview, there is an assemblage of learning. As they say about academic writings: "It smells of the lamp."

No doubt it is unfair to single out one document from the cornucopia of speeches, encyclicals, books, and all that marked this extended papacy. Nevertheless, the failure of face-to-face in this instance can be taken as a fundamental failure in how the papacy turns toward the world. John Paul notes repeatedly in *Threshold* how important face-to-face contact had meant to him as a youth in Poland, in his travels, in his meetings with other religious leaders, and with youth. He does not draw the lesson of his own experiences.

## Listening to the World

I want to turn from this account of the triumph and failure of "voice" in the papacy of John Paul II to make a final practical suggestion on how the Church could speak to the world *face-to-face*. Toward the end of *Crossing the Threshold of Hope*, Messori comments,

As you have recalled during our conversation, it certainly was no accident that your papacy began with a cry that had and still has profound echoes throughout the world: "Be not afraid!"

John Paul agreed that "Be not afraid" could be taken as a virtual *leit-motif*
of his papacy.

The exhortation "Be not afraid!" should be interpreted as having
a very broad meaning. In a sense *it was an exhortation addressed to all
people,* an exhortation to conquer fear for the present world situation,
as much in the East as in the West, as much in the North as in the
South.[14]

"Be not afraid" is the proper message on which to finish this investigation of the voice of faith. It is a message not only to the world, it is a
message that needs to be heard within the Church. At least from the time
of the Reformation, the Catholic Church has fallen into the temptation of
speaking with the voice of fear. As the tides of secularism have swept across
the traditional Christian heartland, the voice of the Church has often been
shrill and defensive. Whatever else one might say about Pius IX's *Syllabus
of Errors,* one would have to say that it is a defensive and denunciatory
document. The strength of Vatican II and the pope who called the council was lack of fear. The *world* was not seen as the enemy to be attacked with
ringing denunciation and anathema. Ormond Rush notes the change in
voice. "[Vatican II's] openness (not outright acceptance) to modernity
and to the world ended 150 years of suspicion, constituting a definitive
'micro-rupture' with the official stance of the Pian era (from Pius IX to
Pius XII)."[15]

The question that remains about interpreting Vatican II is whether
"Be not afraid" has remained as the fundamental voice of the Church to
itself and to the world. If one adopts the title and theme of conservative
George Weigel's book, *The Courage to Be Catholic,*[16] one would conclude that
being courageous is asserting Catholicism as a counter-culture. Catholicism should be known by its enemies in secular liberalism and moral relativism. True enough, the Church preaches a counter-culture to sin, but its
task is soul-therapy, not denunciation and defensive retreat. As a "soul-
therapist" the Church is obligated to practices and assumptions that

defensive Catholicism fails to encompass. First is the obligation for what I have been calling deep listening. The second is the assumption that guides listening: beneath the wayward ways of the world is the deep desire for God, the desire to be loved enough. The Church is not afraid, then, to listen to the neurosis, nonsense, and sin of the world because it believes that *au fond* it can discover a thirst for God. In any conversation with the world, the Church need not be afraid of *fundamental* contradiction. Because the basic desire below all the deviancies of sin is healthy. The good physician knows that the direction of the body is always toward health; his task is to let that natural bent assert itself. All Christian dialogue/therapy stands on "the threshold of hope."

How should the Church dialogue with the world? All the principles suggested above for the right practice for internal discussion apply. Dialogue with the world, the non-Christian religions, with secularism, and even "enemies" of religion, should be public, participatory, and patient. Most importantly, it should occur! Such dialogue does, in fact, occur but not in any obvious public way. The dialogue goes on in two forums: in academic discussion and through offices within the Vatican or national Church offices. In the academic arena, discussions cover almost every topic conceivable. Michael Buckley, S.J., has written a brilliant study of atheism and what it means for Christianity.[17] Catholic scholars like David Tracy have been engaged in long-term, in-depth discussions with thinkers from other religious traditions. The Vatican has offices for interreligious dialogue, which carry forward serious work. Sometimes these discussions result in public reconciliation, as in the agreement between Catholics and Lutherans on the vexed issue of "salvation by faith." My modest suggestion is that these discussions should be elevated to formal papal dialogue as the issue merits or the course of the discussion makes fruitful.

Conceive of the pope as the patriarch, the ideal parent hoping to shape the soul of humanity toward fulfillment; the Church as the therapist seeking to reshape the sinful soul of a beleaguered humanity. To accomplish the patriarchal task, the pope must listen as closely to the children of the world as a father must listen with love and care to his children—often wayward and distressed children. The good father does not rush to lecture and censure, he listens in love, seeking in this manifestation of patience to affirm the loving bond that will in turn become the instrument of healing. Given the model of the pope as parent, he should invite discussion with the world. In particular he should invite those most opposed to the Church, rebellious children let us say, to present their arguments, angers, and frustrations to the Church.

Let us imagine on some periodic time schedule, say every five years, a session of "The Papal Dialogue With the World." The subject matter would address those points of special contention between the Church and the world. One could imagine a number of topics. The Church has decided views on world poverty, but there are significant critics who believe that it neglects the realities of free-market economy. There are the obvious contentions about sexual behavior, marriage, and the family. One can be certain that there would be no lack of controversy between the Church and the world. The Pope should issue formal invitations to leading spokespersons on various sides of the issue selected. I assume that leading figures would attend. The pope may no longer command like Boniface VIII, but his power to summon would seem to be beyond that of almost any other world figure. Included, of course, would be leading Catholic theologians and moralists. Gather the invitees in the Sistine Chapel before Michelangelo's great fresco of the Last Judgment. My sense is that even the most determined opponent of Christianity or religion, the most bitter critic of some specific Catholic claim, would reach for a solemnity of argument that the flack of op-ed argument or academic squabbling misses. By his presence, the pope would signify in the clearest manner "be not afraid." The Church is a wise old institution; its deepest conviction is that God has rescued humanity and is still at work in the world and his Church. Why should the Church be afraid? The very act of listening shows confidence as well as a concerned attention even to what the Church may regard as the most mistaken of claims.

Given the setting and the participants, I would imagine something quite formal. There would be position papers carefully prepared and shared in advance. Central contentions and arguments for and against would be presented orally. Question and counter-questions would be formal and succinct. No assumption would be made that a "verdict" would be forthcoming. Again: this would be a time for the Church to listen. After the conclusion of the sessions, which I would not imagine to be very lengthy, there would a published document with the prepared statements and the discussions. The pope would append an official comment. One would not expect the Church comment to agree with the critics — not at all!

However, it would be an opportunity to offer Christian comment on the best statements of those who would dispute Church teaching. At a minimum, those who frame the Church reply should seek as much as possible not only to address the formal arguments but also the passions which compel the controversy.

Is a "Papal Dialogue" sheer fantasy? Perhaps, but it approximates the *disputatio de quodlibet* of the medieval university. Here is a description of that event:

> [O]nce or twice a year the *disputatio de quodlibet* was held, a public demonstration of the scholastic method as applied to any question whatsoever, freely chosen. The form of the disputation . . . in the early period of the university—say, in the Paris of the thirteenth century—could freely tackle difficult issues of the moment, even delicate religious and political problems.[18]

The "scholastic method" of the *disputatio* was modeled on legal argument: statement and counter-statement ending with a balancing of arguments and a verdict. Anyone familiar with St. Thomas' *Summa* will recognize the pattern. The power of the method was the strong statement of contradictory positions. Resolution had to address the rejected claim. The principle difference between the medieval exercise of scholastic *questiones* and my imaginary "Papal Dialogue," would be the absence of a demand for resolution. To be sure, there should be an official Catholic position stated that will, in many cases, contravene that of other presenters. If properly "voiced," the Church statement would, as suggested, deal not only with argument but with the human concerns that drive the opponents' argument.

### Pou meneis: Where Are You Living?

In the Gospel of Mark, Jesus comes upon Simon and Andrew. He says, "Follow me!" and "they immediately left their nets and followed him" (Mk 1:18). The disciples do not appear to have been "recruited" through some knowledge of Jesus' teachings. If they have any belief about Jesus, it turns out to be the wrong belief, the hope for a triumphal Messiah. It is the presence and person of Jesus that causes them to lay down their nets and follow. In the Gospel of John, the Baptist and two of his disciples catch sight of Jesus passing by. John says, "Look, here is the Lamb of God!" The two disciples catch up with Jesus. He turns and asks them "What are you looking for?" They answer with a question: "Where are you staying?" Jesus replies "Come and see" (Jn 1: 35–39).

The question that the two disciples ask as recorded in the Greek of the New Testament, *pou meneis,* is subject to many associated translations—all of which have resonance for the Church. John Vanier in his commentary on John translates the phrase, "Where do you live?"[19] Other translations might read: "Where are you taking a stand?" "Where do you remain?" In other uses the verb indicates something awaited or expected. All of these translations have been attached to the Church. The Church is where Jesus is staying, where he remains, continues, and takes a stand. The Church is the continuity of the *persona Christi,* where Jesus lives and is awaited and expected.

If we take the calling of the disciples as the basic lesson for the Church, one does not follow Jesus because of Creed but because of his presence. Jesus says, "Follow me!" and they "immediately left their nets and followed." The Baptist's disciples do not ask what program Jesus is advocating, they ask "Where are you living?" Jesus invites them to "come and see." I have tried to justify the Church as teacher and preacher. But what is taught and what is preached is a presence, Jesus, the one who says that *he* is the Truth. To teach the presence of Jesus, the Church must be a presence, face-to-face with the world. If there is preaching or prophecy, if there are teachings and codes, they can only emerge within presence. When Mother Theresa rescued the dying from the streets of Calcutta, she did not preach or seek to convert. Her presence to the dying "spoke" the Christian message.

The French priest novelist, Jean Sullivan, in his novel *Eternity, My Beloved,*[20] sketches out the career of a fictional priest whom he calls Strozzi. The protagonist was modeled on an actual person, Fr. Auguste Rossi, a long time acquaintance of Sullivan's. Rossi had an unofficial "parish" "among the prostitutes, thieves, and con men of the notorious Pigalle quarter of Paris."[21] Strozzi in the novel is an always present figure for the derelicts of the streets. He does not preach or judge, he does not condemn or reform, he is simply there, helping when he can, but being present when he cannot.

Strozzi's loose attitude toward professed beliefs and right conduct raises serious questions in the minds of his religious superiors and in the mind of the narrator of the novel who maintains a running dialogue with the priest. Finally, in exasperation the narrator confronts Strozzi.

> One day I tackled him head on. "Strozzi, where do you stand? What do you think about God?"
>
> "What do I think, Sullivan? What the Bible and the church tell us. But you have to understand: we're dealing with concepts. All these ideas—they're only a kind of insurance, like a mountain-climbing rope, or a parachute. Most of the time, you don't think about the rope or the parachute; if you did you wouldn't make it. I haven't yet begun to understand the things they say about God. Besides, there is a danger in understanding too fast, in thinking that you know all about it. Of course, it is useful in bringing about a superficial unity among believers. It isn't God who is difficult; it's men and women who are varied and complex. . . . God is the impossible, the immensity of the possible, the love beyond life which is at the heart of life, *that* to which life aspires.
>
> ". . . As I have often told you, I instinctively see Jesus, Son of God, in every human being. God has no other image except the face of a person, every person."[22]

# Notes

Preface

1. Jack Miles, "Three Differences between an Academic and an Intellectual: What Happens to the Liberal Arts When They Are Kicked off Campus?" *Cross Currents* 49, no. 3 (Fall 1999): 303–18.

2. Karl Rahner, *The Trinity* (New York: Crossroad Publishing, 1997), 47.

3. I discuss this tension in *The Idea of a Catholic University* (Chicago: University of Chicago Press, 2002). I am certain that Kierkegaard would have been delighted that a book on *Catholic* universities was written by someone who had never been at one. Talk about "indirection"!

4. Quoted in Dick Howard, *The Specter of Democracy* (New York: Columbia University Press, 2002), 248.

Chapter One. Is There a Voice for the Church?

1. Timothy Radcliffe, O.P., *What is the Point of Being a Christian?* (London: Burns & Oates, 2005).

2. David Gibson, *The Coming Catholic Church: How the Faithful Are Shaping a New American Catholicism* (San Francisco: HarperSanFrancisco, 2003), 312.

3. "Performing the faith" is the title of a book by Stanley Hauerwas: *Performing the Faith: Bonhoeffer and the Practice of Nonviolence* (Grand Rapids, MI: Brazos Press, 2004). The chapter in that book with the specific title "performing the faith" is richly suggestive, and I have benefitted and borrowed from his analysis.

4. Some of the material in the rest of this chapter appeared in a different form in *Commonweal,* September 10, 2004. It appears here with permission.

5. *America,* February 24, 2003.

6. Joseph Cardinal Ratzinger, *Principles of Catholic Theology: Building Stones for a Fundamental Theology,* trans. Sister Mary Frances McCarthy, S. N. D. (San Francisco: Ignatius Press, 1987), 390.

7. Ibid., 368.

8. In a recent interview, Fr. Camilo Maccisse, the former president of the Union of Superiors General which represents 240 male religious orders criticized the lack of contact between his group and the pope. Neither his union nor the counterpart union of female religious orders have been able to establish direct dialogue. The most recent meeting was held in 1990. *National Catholic Reporter,* Nov. 21, 2003, 8.

9. Nicholas Lash, "We Need More than Mitres," *The Tablet,* December 13, 2003, 32; italics in original.

10. Germaine Grizez, "Are There Exceptionless Moral Norms?" in *The Twenty-Fifth Anniversary of Vatican II: A Look Back and a Look Ahead; Proceedings of the Ninth Bishop's Workshop,* Dallas, Texas, ed. Russell E. Smith (Braintree, MA: The Pope John Center, 1990), 157.

11. Ibid., 159.

12. Raymond E. Brown, *Priest and Bishop: Biblical Reflections* (Paramus, NJ: Paulist Press, 1970), 77.

13. Ibid., 77–78.

14. Ibid.

## Chapter Two. *Extra ecclesiam nullus*

1. Gordon W. Lathrop, *Holy Things: A Liturgical Theology* (Minneapolis: Fortress Press, 1998). Lathrop uses the second-century *Apology* of Justin Martyr. Justin is defending the sobriety of Christian gatherings to the Emperor Antoninus Pius. The *ordo* of the Christian meetings involves ritual washing, teaching about Jesus Christ as conveyed from the apostles, and a meal.

2. The term "Holocaust" is somewhat controversial. Does it point to something absolutely unique, or are other genocidal events comparable? If I had a choice, I would prefer the Hebrew *Shoah* to categorize the Nazi destruction of European Jewry. I stick with "Holocaust" because of its common usage — in particular the implication (right or wrong) that the events gathered under the label were radically unique.

3. "Twice born" is William James' term, but I am not using it in James' sense. James divides humans into the once born and the twice born. My argument is that *everyone* is twice born, though not everyone may *recognize* that they are twice born and some may recognize that fact and *reject* that new status — often by elaborate ritual or simple self-delusion. The Christian call eventually comes down to recognizing with unblinking clarity the fact of being twice born: born again into history.

4. Ludwig Wittgenstein, *Culture and Value* (Oxford: Blackwell, 1980), 33; italics and capital letters in original.

5. N. T. Wright, *The Contemporary Quest for Jesus* (Minneapolis: Fortress Press, 2002), 1.

6. I am well aware that many distinguished theologians regard the Eucharist as a "symbol." Roger Haight has even written a whole book under the title *Jesus Symbol of*

*God* (Maryknoll, NY: Orbis, 1999). Many of these writers who use the notion of "symbol" have sophisticated definitions of the term. For theologians like Paul Tillich and Karl Rahner, "symbol" participates in the reality that it symbolizes. In that sense, one might regard Eucharist as symbol. Like good philosophers and theologians, these thinkers are attempting to give a precise meaning to a term by stipulating a meaning. Unfortunately, stipulative definitions tend to drag their ordinary, broader meanings in their wake. McCarthy and certainly O'Connor are using the broader common meaning of "symbol"—this is why we understand exactly the problem that O'Connor alludes to in resisting the notion that the Eucharist is *only* a symbol. In another context (my *The Idea of a Catholic University* [Chicago: University of Chicago Press, 1997], chap. 4), I have used the notion of "icon" as more appropriate. Traditional holy icons in the Orthodox tradition were regarded as participating in a reality beyond the depiction. True icons were made by holy monks and shared in the holiness of the maker.

7. David Ford, *Self and Salvation: Being Transformed* (Cambridge: Cambridge University Press, 1999), 144.

## Chapter Three.  Author! Author!

1. See, for example, Thomas Aquinas, *The Basic Writings of Saint Thomas Aquinas*, ed. and annotated by Anton C. Pegis (New York: Random House, 1945).

2. This topic and many of the arguments were first presented in my *The Idea of a Catholic University* (Chicago: University of Chicago Press, 1997, all rights reserved) chaps. 4 and 7. I have not hesitated to quote from myself because I haven't yet been able to construct a better expression of the argument. These passages appear with permission of the University of Chicago Press.

3. Harold Bloom, *Shakespeare: The Invention of the Human* (New York: Riverhead, 1966).

4. Henry James, *The Spoils of Poynton* (New York: Scribners, 1908), v–vi.

5. Richard Kalina, *Art in America* (December, 1999): 55.

6. Quoted in Lawrence L. Langer, *Admitting the Holocaust: Collected Essays* (New York: Oxford University Press, 1995). Langer notes in his preface that this quote from Améry is used so often in the book that it is a virtual "epiphany."

7. From *The Letters of Oscar Wilde*, ed. Rupert Hart-Davis (New York: Harcourt Brace & World, 1962), 487; as quoted in Anthony Bartlett, *Cross Purposes: The Violent Grammar of Christian Atonement* (Harrisburg, PA: Trinity Press International, 2001), 177.

8. The notion of God as supreme playwright has obvious connections to Hans Urs von Balthasar's notion that Christianity is best understood as a "theo-drama." Balthasar writes as a theologian for theologians while my purpose is to exploit *dramatic* structures as fully as possible with only a sideways glance at a specific theology and its special vocabularies. Balthasar's theodramatic analysis forms the

basis for Nicholas Healy's valuable exposition of ecclesiology, *Church, World and the Christian Life: Practical-Prophetic Ecclesiology* (Cambridge: Cambridge University Press, 2000). See chap. 3 "A Theodramatic Horizon." I am in broad agreement with Healy's analysis and views on ecclesiology. For a splendid and comprehensible discussion of God as "author," see Dorothy Sayers, *The Mind of the Maker* (San Francisco: HarperSanFrancisco, 1979; orig. 1941). Sayers is interested in developing Trinitarian theology on the model of Author-Work-Reception. I will concentrate on the "drama" as played. A particularly insightful work that relies on "drama" as the prime Christian category is Samuel Wells, *Improvisation: The Drama of Christian Ethics* (Grand Rapids, MI: Brazos Press, 2004). Wells' analysis of the five acts of the Biblical theodrama is excellent. My own work concentrates on Wells' Act III, "The Redeemer." I would like to think that I have spelled out the drama of Act III in greater detail than Wells' overall account allows.

9. A classic statement of the king-in-rags-as-king: Søren Kierkegaard, *Philosophical Fragments or a Fragment of Philosophy* (Princeton: Princeton University Press, 1946).

10. Etienne Gilson, *Being and Some Philosophers* (Toronto: Pontifical Institute of Medieval Studies, 1949), 15.

11. Flannery O'Connor, "A Good Man is Hard to Find," in *Three by Flannery O'Connor* (New York: New American Library, 1962).

12. Ron Mueck's "Dead Dad" at the Brooklyn Museum's 1999 *Sensation* show is a case in point.

## Chapter Four.  *La Divina Commedia*

1. Quoted in Robert Ellsberg, *All Saints* (New York: Crossroad, 1997), 257.

2. Reinhart Koselleck, *Future's Past: On the Semantics of Historical Time* (Cambridge: MIT Press, 1985).

3. Mircea Eliade, *Cosmos and History: The Myth of the Eternal Return* (New York: Harper Torchbooks, 1959).

4 . Quoted from Bonhoeffer's *Letters and Papers from Prison* (London: SCM Press, 1971), 229, in David Ford, *Self and Salvation: Being Transformed* (Cambridge: Cambridge University Press, 1999), 258–59.

## Chapter Five.  Exorcising the Subjective Voice

1. Quoted from Murdoch in Fergus Kerr, *Immortal Longings: Versions of Transcending Humanity* (Notre Dame, IN: University of Notre Dame Press, 1997), 76-77.

2. Franz Rosenzweig, *Understanding the Sick and the Healthy: A View of the World, Man, and God,* trans. Nahum N. Glatzer and T. Luckman, ed. Nahum N. Glatzer. (New

York: Noonday Press, 1954); this book is a translation of *Von gesunden und kranken Menschenverstand.*

3. Quoted in Fergus Kerr, *Theology After Wittgenstein* (London: SPCK, 1997), 60.

4. Jacob Vining, *The Song Sparrow and the Child: Claims of Science and Humanity* (Notre Dame, IN: University of Notre Dame Press, 2004), 53.

5. Quoted from Karl Popper, *The Open Society and its Enemies,* in Hans Meyerhoff, *Philosophy of History in Our Time* (Garden City, NY: Doubleday, 1959), 308.

6. Paul Ricouer, *Oneself as Another,* trans. Kathleen Blamey (Chicago: University of Chicago Press, 1992).

7. Isaiah Berlin, *The Hedgehog and the Fox: An Essay on Tolstoy's View of History* (New York: Simon & Schuster, 1966).

8. J. L. Austin, *Philosophical Papers,* ed. J. O. Urmson and G. J. Warnock (Oxford: Clarendon Press, 1961); see chap. 10, "Performative Utterances."

## Chapter Six. Pope: Professor, Judge, or Patriarch

1. Richard Bernstein, "Faith and Reason," *Books and Culture* 5 (July/August 1999), 32; italics in original.

2. N. T. Wright, *The New Testament and the People of God* (Minneapolis: Fortress Press, 1992), xvii–xviii.

3. See, for example, John Noonan, *A Church that Can and Cannot Change: The Development of Catholic Moral Teaching* (Notre Dame, IN: University of Notre Dame Press, 2005), a book to which I shall return in a later chapter.

4. An earlier version of the Pope as patriarch entitled "Thou Art Peter" appeared in *Cross Currents* 46, no. 3 (1996): 379–87. It appears here with permission.

5. Quoted in Peter Hebblethwaite, *Paul VI: The First Modern Pope* (New York: Paulist Press, 1993), 9.

6. Franz Rosenzweig, *The Star of Redemption* (Notre Dame, IN: University of Notre Dame Press, 1970), 342.

7. Elizabeth A. Johnson, *She Who Is: The Mystery of God in Feminist Theological Discourse* (New York: Crossroad, 1992).

8. Deborah Tannen, *Gender and Discourse* (New York: Oxford University Press, 1994).

## Chapter Seven. The Voice of the *Persona Christi*

1. Søren Kierkegaard, *Concluding Unscientific Postscript,* trans. Walter Lowrie (Princeton: Princeton University Press, 1941), 178.

2. Rowan Williams makes this point emphatically in discussing the development of Christological titles in the first centuries of the Church. The aim was not to

achieve some philosophically precise description, it was to describe Jesus in a manner that justified the way of life practiced by Christians. Rowan Williams, *Why Study the Past: The Quest for the Historical Church* (Grand Rapids, MI: Eerdmans, 2005), 42 et seq.

3. "[I]f there is a Doctor of Philosophical truth in the complex personality of St. Thomas Aquinas, it is only with the theologian that we can hope to find him." Etienne Gilson, *The Christian Philosophy of St. Thomas Aquinas,* trans. L. K. Shook, C.S.B. (New York: Random House, 1956), 6.

4. Ludwig Wittgenstein, *Culture and Value* (Oxford: Blackwell, 1980), 83e.

## Chapter Eight.   Saving Morality

1. John Noonan, *A Church that Can and Cannot Change: The Development of Catholic Moral Teaching* (Notre Dame, IN: University of Notre Dame Press, 2005).

2. Alisdair MacIntrye, *Whose Justice, Which Rationality* (Notre Dame, IN: University of Notre Dame Press, 1988).

3. Alistair McFayden, *Bound to Sin: Abuse, Holocaust and the Christian Doctrine of Sin* (Cambridge: Cambridge University Press, 2000).

4. "Seminary Leaders Foresee Tightening up of Moral Issues," *The National Catholic Reporter,* January 6, 2006, 5.

5. Sigmund Freud, *Civilization and its Discontents,* trans. James Strachey (New York: W.W. Norton, 1962), 556-58.

6. Joseph Conrad, *Lord Jim* (New York: Signet Classic), 159–60.

## Chapter Nine.   The Forgiving Voice

1. Our contemporary sense contrasts propaganda with fact and truth. An older and nonpejorative sense of propaganda is used when we talk about the *propaganda fidei:* the propagation of the faith.

2. I note the presumed exception of Socrates who is generally held to be the model "teacher" because he professes his own ignorance and engages in open-ended dialogue. This is a truncated Socrates—and not Plato's. Socrates no less than Kant holds that there are eternal forms to be known. In fact, he believes that his interlocutor *already* knows the truth. The pedagogical problem is dragging recognition out of the other as in the *Meno.* To hold that there is a rational truth above which we can know is not to say that getting to that truth is easy. It takes some ten books of the *Republic* to shape up the philosophic mind!

3. John Dominic Crosson, *The Historical Jesus:The Life of a Mediterranean Jewish Peasant* (San Francisco: Harper, 1991). "Cynic" did not have the wholly negative cast that attaches to its modern usage. Essentially, the Cynics were simply those who re-

jected the self-assured morality of the establishment. Up to a point it seems to fit Jesus' preaching.

4. There is a classic story about the early practice of psychoanalysis. Both Freud and Breuer were evidently pursuing similar talking therapy. Both came to the realization that the patient was developing strong affective ties to themselves. Breuer was so agitated that he broke off the therapy and took a vacation with his wife. Freud persevered and the rest is history!

5. For a disastrous experiment to prove that schizophrenics recognize their own aberrancy see Milton Rokeach, *The Three Christs of Ypsilanti: A Psychological Study* (New York: Columbia University Press, 1964).

6. Jean-Paul Sartre, *Being and Nothing,* trans. Hazel E. Barnes (New York: Philosophical Library, 1956), 50–54.

7. Ludwig Wittgenstein, *Lectures and Conversations on Aesthetics, Psychology and Religious Belief,* compiled from notes taken by Yorick Smythies, Rush Rhees, and James Taylor, ed. Cyril Barrett (Berkeley: Univ. of California Press, 1967), 44; italics in original.

8. For the purposes of this discussion it would have been too much of a diversion to consider the specific character of *Gestalt* therapy. It is worth noting, however, that *Gestalt* approximates the notion of "interpretation." *Gestalt* means "form." One may see many facts and details but lack the *Gestalt,* the form of the facts, that sums the meaning of the various parts. Interpretation of assorted behaviors into a *Gestalt* resembles poetic interpretation.

9. Ibid., 41.

10. I have written on Freud's Enlightenment transcendence of history. See George Dennis O'Brien, "*Psyche* and *Geist* in History," in *Substance and Form in History: A Collection of Essays in Philosophy of History,* ed. L. Pompa and W. H. Dray (Edinburgh: University of Edinburgh Press, 1981), 58–76.

11. Philip Larkin, "Faith Healing," in *Collected Press,* ed. Anthony Thwaite (Boston: The Marvell Press, 1988), 126.

## Chapter Ten.   Practice and Structure

1. Sigmund Freud, *Civilization and its Discontents,* trans. James Strachey (New York: W. W. Norton, 1962), 23.

2. Ibid., 24.

3. Garry Wills, *Papal Sins* (New York: Doubleday, 2000).

4. David Gibson, *The Coming Catholic Church: How the Faithful are Shaping a New American Catholicism* (San Francisco: HarperSanFrancisco, 2003), 152.

5. "The Church in America: The Way Forward in the 21st Century," a conference at the Wharton School, University of Pennsylvania, July 7, 2003.

6. John Allen, "Report from Rome #19," *National Catholic Reporter,* October 22, 2005.

7. For a discussion of Weigel's view and a comment see "Wanted: Manly Men" in *Commonweal*, February 10, 2006.

8. The distinguished Church historian, Francis Oakley, offers a devastating critique of the papal intrigues and theological manipulations that submerged conciliarism in the Catholic Church; see his *The Conciliarist Tradition: Constitutionalism in the Catholic Church 1300–1870* (Oxford: Oxford University Press, 2003).

9. The eleventh General Assembly of the Synod of Bishops, Rome, Oct. 2–23, 2006. The discussions touched on such problems as irregular Mass attendance and the shortage of priests, but no concrete suggestions emerged for remedying the situation beyond exhortation and better catechesis.

10. Roger Haight, *Jesus: Symbol of God* (New York: Orbis, 1999).

11. Timothy Ryback, "Forgiveness," *The New Yorker*, February 6, 2006, 66–73.

12. John Paul II, *Crossing the Threshold of Hope* (New York: Alfred A. Knopf, 2005).

13. Ibid., 51.

14. Ibid., 218–19, italics in original.

15. Ormond Rush, *Still Interpreting Vatican II: Some Hermeneutical Principles* (New York: Paulist Press, 2004), 17.

16. George Weigel, *The Courage to Be Catholic: Crisis, Reform, and the Future of the Church* (New York: Basic Books, 2002).

17. Michael J. Buckley, *At the Origins of Modern Atheism* (New Haven: Yale University Press, 1987).

18. Rainer Christoph Schwinges, "Student Education, Student Life," chap. 7 in *Universities in the Middle Ages*, ed. H. De Ridder-Symoens, vol. 1 of *A History of the University in Europe* (Cambridge: Cambridge University Press, 1992), 232.

19. Jean Vanier, *Drawn into the Mystery of Jesus through the Gospel of John* (New York: Paulist Press, 2004), 39.

20. Jean Sullivan, *Eternity, My Beloved* (St. Paul, MN: River Boat Books, 1999).

21. Ibid., from the introduction by Joseph Cuneen, iii.

22. Ibid., 124–25.

# Index

**George Dennis O'Brien**

is President Emeritus of the University of Rochester.

He is the author of a number of books,

including *The Idea of a Catholic University*.